Digital Tools for Qualitative Research

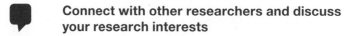

Digital Tools for Qualitative Research

Trena M. Paulus / Jessica N. Lester / Paul G. Dempster >

Los Angeles | London | New Delhi
Singapore | Washington DC

SAGE

Los Angeles | London | New Delhi
Singapore | Washington DC

SAGE Publications Ltd
1 Oliver's Yard
55 City Road
London EC1Y 1SP

SAGE Publications Inc.
2455 Teller Road
Thousand Oaks, California 91320

SAGE Publications India Pvt Ltd
B 1/I 1 Mohan Cooperative Industrial Area
Mathura Road
New Delhi 110 044

SAGE Publications Asia-Pacific Pte Ltd
3 Church Street
#10-04 Samsung Hub
Singapore 049483

Editor: Katie Metzler
Production editor: Ian Antcliff
Copyeditor: Richard Hutchinson
Proofreader: Kate Harrison
Indexer: Avril Ehrlich
Marketing manager: Ben Griffin-Sherwood
Cover design: Francis Kenney
Typeset by: C&M Digitals (P) Ltd, Chennai, India
Printed in Great Britain by Henry Ling Limited at
The Dorset Press, Dorchester, DT1 1HD

Library of Congress Control Number: 2013940584

British Library Cataloguing in Publication data

A catalogue record for this book is available from
the British Library

ISBN 978-1-4462-5606-0
ISBN 978-1-4462-5607-7 (pbk)

MIX
Paper from
responsible sources
FSC
www.fsc.org   FSC™ C013985

Table of Contents

Acknowledgements

We would like to thank the following friends, colleagues and students. Without their support, feedback, technical assistance and hard work writing this book would have been a much less enjoyable experience: Ginny Britt, Doug Canfield, Kathy Evans, Richard Lehrer, Debby Lee, Jennifer Lubke, Lisa Scherff, Mary Alice Varga, Alan Wallace and a very special thank you to Jaewoo Do for supporting us throughout the writing process.

Thanks to Susanne Friese, Anne Kuckartz, Marcus Ogden, Julia Schehl and David Woods who contributed vignettes and reviewed sections of the book around the CAQDAS tools.

Thank you to the many vignette writers for sharing their experiences: Carlos Anguiano, Tim Barko, Ron Bridges, Ginny Britt, Christopher Brkich, James Dorough, Hannah Dostal, Kathy Evans, Rachael Gabriel, Carlos Galan-Diaz, Ron Hallett, Art Herbig, Aaron Hess, Teri Holbrook, Craig Howard, Melanie Hundley, Joshua Johnston, Derya Kulavuz-Onal, Chad Lochmiller, Jennifer Lubke, Ray Maietta, Lisa McNeal, Emily Miller, Monique Mitchell, Everett Painter, Jonathan Pettigrew, Anton Reece, Prisca Rodriguez, Lisa Scherff, Rebecca Williams, Lisa Yamagata-Lynch and Fanny Yeung.

Thank you to Katie Metzler and Anna Horvai at SAGE for all their support, guidance and encouragement.

Thanks to the various software companies who have provided support and expertise throughout the book-writing process.

Trena would especially like to thank all of the students in the Digital Tools course at the University of Tennessee for inspiring this book, and David for his understanding and support throughout the process.

Jessica would especially like to thank Chad for his support and encouragement.

Paul would like to thank Jonathon Whitmore at Nuance, Roger Tucker at Audio Notetaker and Lunis at Knowbrainer. Paul is grateful to Tracy, Calvin, John and Joseph for their patience and encouragement.

Companion Website

Book Home | Student Resources

About the Book

Welcome to the companion website for the first edition of *Digital Tools for Qualitative Research*.

Digital Tools for Qualitative Research shows how the research process in its entirety can be supported by technology tools in ways that can save time and add robustness and depth to qualitative work. It addresses the use of a variety of tools (many of which may already be familiar to you) to support every phase of the research process, providing practical case studies taken from real world research.

The text shows you how to select and use technology tools to:

Authors: Trena Paulus, Jessica Lester and Paul Dempster

Pub Date: December 2013

Pages: 224

Learn more about this book

* engage in reflexivity
* collaborate with other researchers and stakeholders
* manage your project
* do your literature review
* generate and manage your data
* transcribe and analyse textual, audio and visual data
* represent and share your findings.

The book also considers important ethical issues surrounding the use of various technologies in each chapter.

Whether you're a novice or expert social researcher, this book will inspire you to think creatively about how to approach your research project and get the most out of the huge range of tools available to you.

On this companion website to the textbook, you'll find...

§SAGE researchmethods

Find out more ⊙

Methodspace

Connecting the Research Community

Student Resources

This section of the site is freely accessible to any student who is using *Digital Tools for Qualitative Research* by Trena Paulus, Jessica Lester and Paul Dempster.
Student resources are organised by chapter, and offer a range of content including:

* **Web links:** access relevant web links to supplement your study of the book, from leading technology blogs, forums and archives to recommended software and handy tools to aid your research
* **SAGE Journal articles:** additional reading recommended by the authors, with free access to complete journal articles from SAGE
* **Video links:** carefully selected, web-based video resources including lectures, presentations and other content to help you explore key discussion topics
* **Audio links:** including audio diaries and soundscapes
* **Activities:** practice your research skills using our online activities

About the Authors

Trena M. Paulus holds a Ph.D. in Education/Instructional Systems Technology and currently teaches qualitative research methods, discourse analysis and instructional technology courses at the University of Tennessee, USA, where she is an associate professor. She has published articles in the areas of qualitative research methods, instructional technology and computer-mediated communication. She teaches a doctoral level course on Digital Tools for Qualitative Research which provided the motivation for this text.

Jessica N. Lester is an assistant professor in Inquiry Methodology at Indiana University and holds a Ph.D. in Educational Psychology and Research. She teaches research methods courses, including a course focused on the uses of digital tools in qualitative research. She has published journal articles in the areas of qualitative methodologies, disability studies, discourse studies, and refugee studies. She recently co-edited a book focused on performance ethnography and schooling practices.

Paul Dempster is an applied health researcher who specialises in qualitative research. He is particularly interested in caqdas methods and has taught internationally on their use. He is a consultant methodologist for Transana at the university of Wisconsin and works for the NHS in Newcastle.

All figures are available to view on the companion website:

www.uk.sagepub.com/paulus

ONE
Why Digital Tools?

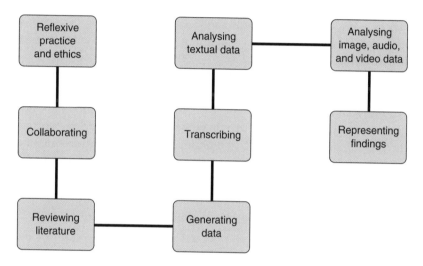

Companion website materials available here:

www.uk.sagepub.com/paulus

Learning Objectives

- Highlight the historical perspectives around the use of digital tools within the qualitative research process.
- Consider how the diffusion of innovation theory might serve to explain technology adoption by the qualitative research community.
- Examine the concepts of affordances and constraints as related to digital tools.
- Identify the crosscutting themes of the book, including reflexive practice, collaboration, transparency and ethics.

Introduction

From paper and pen for taking notes in the field to tape recorders and video cameras for capturing interviews and social interactions, qualitative research has always been shaped by the tools we choose to use. We now live in a digital age, where cloud computing, mobile devices and social media are constantly changing the nature of our relationships with technology and with each other. We acknowledge that the use of digital tools for qualitative research is not a new idea, nor has it been without controversy. Davidson and Di Gregorio (2011) provided a comprehensive overview of the history of technology in qualitative research, highlighting the uneasiness between the two. Of particular concern has been the use of data analysis software. Paulus, Lester and Britt (2013) noted in their discourse analysis of introductory qualitative research textbooks that most authors limited their discussion of digital tool use to devices such as audio recorders, transcribing machines and data analysis software. Further, many of the texts framed the use of digital tools (especially data analysis software) as something to be done with caution. We feel that this overriding focus on data analysis software, while important, has resulted in the exclusion of a broader discussion regarding the potential affordances and constraints of digital tools *across the qualitative research process*. Twenty years ago, Miles and Huberman outlined 14 uses for 'computer software' for qualitative research: see Table 1.1.

These uses for digital tools are still relevant to qualitative practice today, but few such applications are discussed with much regularity in our qualitative research community. While the CIBER (2010) report published by University College in London found that researchers are using social media for increased communication, access to research communities and greater dissemination of findings, the study also noted that most researchers were not yet using the full

Table 1.1   Uses of computer software in qualitative studies (from Miles and Huberman, 1994)

1. Making notes in the field

2. Writing up or transcribing field notes

3. Editing: correcting, extending, or revising field notes

4. Coding: attaching keywords or tags to segments of text and making them available for inspection

5. Storage: keeping text in an organized database

6. Search and retrieval: locating relevant segments of text and making them available for inspection

7. Data 'linking': connecting relevant data segments to each other, forming categories, clusters or networks of information

8. Memoing: writing reflective commentaries on some aspect of the data as a basis for deeper analysis

9. Content analysis: counting frequencies, sequences or locations of words and phrases

10. Data display: placing selected or reduced data in a condensed organized format, such as a matrix or network, for inspection

11. Conclusion drawing and verification: aiding the analyst to interpret displayed data and to test or confirm findings

12. Theory-building: developing systematic, conceptually coherent explanations of findings; testing hypotheses

13. Graphic mapping: creating diagrams that depict findings or theories

14. Preparing interim and final reports

range of tools available. There seems to be a large gap between *awareness* of new tools and the actual *use* of them, attributed to a lack of clarity around the benefits of the tools and/or lack of time to learn them. This matches our own experiences as researchers, and, we suspect, the experiences of many others.

While lack of knowledge may be one reason for lack of use, digital tools also challenge the way things have traditionally been done. Rogers' (2003) diffusion of innovations theory notes that the moment an innovation is introduced, communication begins between the 'early adopters' – those who quickly accept and begin to use the innovation – and the 'late' or even 'non-adopting' resisters – those who delay acceptance and/or may reject the innovation altogether. Those who do adopt the innovations learn about the benefits the tools can bring and eventually incorporate them into their daily work. Rogers argued that *how* the new innovation is communicated to people is important and suggested that it is the early adopters and the resisters who can be highly influential to those who remain undecided. In the case of qualitative research, it is possible that the way that the established scholars in the field (methods instructors, book authors, leaders in the field) talk about the importance (or lack thereof) of digital tools across the qualitative research process may shape how new researchers (students) adopt the tools in their own practice.

Digital tools for qualitative research can mean much more than the use of specialized software packages for data analysis. Whenever we have discussed this book with audiences, no matter what the venue, their assumption has been that by digital tools we must be referring only to data analysis tools. While specialized software packages certainly have an important role to play, there are many more tools available and many more phases of the research process in which to explore their role. Our students, for example, often want to know how to use the digital tools they use in their everyday lives for their fieldwork. Prensky (2011), a game designer, has written extensively about how university students today represent the first generation to grow up with new technologies as part of their everyday lives. Prensky referred to these individuals as *digital natives*. In contrast, those of us who did not grow up with, but have adopted the new technologies, are referred to as *digital immigrants*. While many of us who teach qualitative research methods are digital immigrants, our students are digital natives, and they understandably expect to learn about how they can use the tools they grew up with in their research practice.

Our intent with this book is to reframe how we talk about digital tools for qualitative research. We argue that just as they are an essential, inescapable part of our daily lives, digital tools can be an essential part of our research lives. We hope this book will help researchers conceptualize how the qualitative inquiry process *in its entirety* can be supported by digital tools in ways that can add robustness and depth to qualitative work. More specifically, we have written this book not only for those who are learning about qualitative research, but also for those who teach qualitative research, and those who have been doing qualitative research for some time and who wish to learn more about how digital tools can support, if not transform, their process.

About the Authors

Our own paths to qualitative research and to the exploration of digital tools to support the process have varied. I (Trena) have a background in applied linguistics, teaching English as a second/foreign language and, more recently, in instructional technology and online learning environments. I teach qualitative research methods at the graduate level but came to the use of digital tools somewhat reluctantly. I consider myself a relatively late adopter of digital tools, needing to first be convinced that a new tool's added value will be worth my investment of time and effort in learning it. Computer-mediated communication is one of my research areas, and I have had my students keep reflective blogs for many years. So, the use of social media tools for collaboration and engaging in researcher reflexivity was one of the first ways I explored using digital tools in my research practice. It was not until after I was tenured and promoted that I felt I could take the time to learn a data analysis tool (ATLAS.ti), but doing so transformed my entire research practice in ways that I could not have envisioned. I have since become an advocate for increasing access to and support for computer-assisted qualitative data analysis software (CAQDAS) at my university, and, through the process of writing this book (and teaching a course on the same topic), I have learned a great deal myself.

I (Jessica) was first introduced to digital tools to support research practices as a PhD student. Early on in my training, my adviser (Trena) encouraged me to begin blogging about my research experiences, chronicling my questions, concerns and musings. I maintained this private blog throughout my thesis work, with only my adviser and two colleagues being given permission to read and respond to my posts. Further, I have been trained in several CAQDAS packages (ATLAS.ti, MAXQDA, NVivo and Transana), eventually incorporating these tools into my research practice. Yet, as graduate school ended and I moved into a full-time faculty position, I quickly became aware of my lack of experience and understanding of how new forms of social media might shape my everyday research practices, from data collection to the dissemination of research findings. For instance, despite being engaged in the ongoing collection of naturally occurring classroom conversations, I was somewhat late to consider the potential uses of mobile devices for data collection. Just recently, I have begun to use my smartphone, iPad and a variety of 'apps' to support my research process. Of course, these new tools bring with them ethical dilemmas, something that we have attended to throughout this book.

I (Paul) was an early adopter of CAQDAS software, being the first person at my university to pioneer its use. Indeed, throughout my whole research career I have always used a variety of digital tools. I became involved almost 13 years ago in the debates being held with software developers as they tried to incorporate useful features for researchers. As a natural progression, this led to work as a freelance trainer, mainly teaching NVivo, and latterly as a methodological consultant for Transana. I have a long-standing interest in developing functionality within software and continue to work as a beta tester on a number of software packages. My work as an applied health researcher has allowed me to interact with a range of technologies, applying them in novel ways to research problems, and also to explore large-scale implementation of digital tools in the National Health Service. I also work as a methodological troubleshooter and trainer, finding digital solutions to research problems at a university level.

As you read the book, we encourage you to reflect upon your own use of digital tools. Do you consider yourself an early adopter, late adopter and/or resister? What has influenced your views of technology? How do you orient to the use of digital tools for particular aspects of the qualitative research process (e.g. collecting data, transcribing, representing findings)? As you consider these questions, we invite you to examine how the tools you take up bring with them particular affordances and constraints.

Affordances and Constraints of Digital Tool Use

Throughout the book, we draw upon the theory of affordances. This theory originated with J.J. Gibson in the late 1970s and was popularized in the 1980s by Donald Norman, a pioneer in the field of human-centred design. Norman (1999) suggested that new inventions come with 1) conceptual models, 2) possible and actual uses of a device as perceived by the user (affordances) and 3) constraints. Any innovation presents the user with both affordances and constraints. For example, a simple audio recorder affords you the ability to listen to an interview numerous times. On the other hand, it does not capture non-verbal interaction, and recording people's voices presents new ethical challenges that simply taking notes during an interview did not – both of which can be considered constraints of the tool.

We have provided a number of opportunities within each chapter for you to consider the affordances and constraints of the tools we introduce. This, we suggest, is part of engaging in reflexive practice. As such, the concept of affordances frames how we discuss digital tools in both explicit and implicit ways.

Visit Web Resource 1.1 to read more about affordances.

Our goal for this book is to provide you with practical guidance on selecting and using digital tools *across the research process*. We hope to provide a foundation for you to think about the affordances and constraints of such tools in a meaningful way. Throughout the chapters, we develop several themes that we describe next.

Crosscutting Themes

We suggest that new tools have the potential to enable greater *researcher reflexivity*, *transparency of research decisions* and *collaboration*. New tools also bring into focus *ethical dilemmas* that need to be kept at the forefront of our practice. Thus, across the book, we give particular attention to the ways in which digital tools impact these four areas.

Reflexive Practice

Within each chapter, we incorporate *reflexive practice* activities in which we ask you to engage with the topics being discussed, as you try out new tools and reflect on their affordances and constraints. Many of these activities provide an opportunity to situate your reflections in the context of a research study that you would like to design. Thus, we encourage you now, before continuing on to Chapter 2, to think of a particular research study you would like to design, or are currently engaged in, that can serve as a context for your explorations in this book. In Chapter 2, you will create a reflexive practice blog, and throughout the book you will be encouraged to make regular posts to this blog in conjunction with the reflexive practice activities. In preparation for this, consider Reflexive Practice 1.1.

REFLEXIVE PRACTICE 1.1

Think of a research study that you would like to design, or are currently engaged in. Briefly describe the project, its features and key points. Don't worry if your ideas are vague at this point. This study idea will serve as a context for the tools that you will explore in this book. Hold on to these notes and you will enter them into your reflexivity blog, which will be introduced in Chapter 2.

Collaboration

Social media, cloud computing and mobile devices have made it much easier to connect not only with other researchers, but with participants, their communities and the public at large. Chapter 3 is specifically dedicated to the topic of collaboration, but the theme is revisited throughout the book. We encourage you to be reflexive about how digital tools expand how we stay connected with others in our communities, refine how we make sense of our data, and shape who has the power to participate in our study and how.

Transparency

From data analysis software packages resulting in a more visible analysis process to websites which open up your work to public critique, we argue that many digital tools serve to increase the transparency and thereby trustworthiness of your study. The ability to use mobile devices to document what is happening in the field and immediately share your work with collaborators can create an immediate audit trail and afford transparencies in ways that have not been possible before. Throughout the book, we discuss how digital tools can contribute in various ways to this transparency.

Visit Web Resource 1.2 for a link to Tracy's (2010) article on eight criteria for evaluating the quality of qualitative work.

Ethics

Not only do digital tools present opportunities to support and even transform our research, but at times they may threaten our ability to engage in ethical practices. Within each chapter, we give particular attention to the ways in which digital tools present ethical challenges and dilemmas. We ask you to consider these dilemmas in the context of the reflexive practice activities. Ethical qualitative researchers are reflexive researchers; thus, we seek to maintain a close connection between the two.

Organization of the Book

We made a choice to situate our discussion of digital tools in the broader context of the qualitative research process. In other words, we start with good qualitative research practice and then turn to how tools can support that practice. We highlight the ways in which digital tools can even *transform* aspects of the research process, while also considering times at which digital tools may limit our ability to practise ethical research. We have organized the book around the following qualitative research activities: engaging in reflexive practice, collaborating, reviewing the literature, generating data, transcribing, analysing textual data, analysing audio, image and video data, and writing and representing findings. Each chapter begins with a graphic (Figure 1.1) to remind you of where we are in the process.

We acknowledge that research is never a linear process, and that there is no such thing as *one* qualitative research process. Your process may look quite different depending on what type of qualitative work you are engaged in (e.g. ethnography, grounded theory or discourse analysis). However, we feel that most, if not all, research traditions attend to these phases at some point during an inquiry cycle. Thus, while the distinction of the phases is somewhat artificial, our hope is that it serves as a useful organizing tool. In the same vein, while we discuss the phases of the research process in individual chapters, we acknowledge that the process is iterative, emergent and dynamic. You may well be engaged in multiple phases of the process simultaneously. However, we do suggest that it is useful to think about how specific tools impact various aspects of the research process, with researcher reflexivity and ethical practices being foundational to your work.

Within each chapter, we first discuss some foundational issues to that particular phase of the process and some of the decisions that must be made as you design your study. We follow with an introduction of tools that we have found useful during that phase of the process, including **figures** to help illustrate our

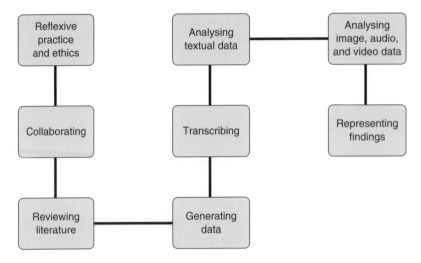

Figure 1.1 The qualitative research process

discussion. We provide **case studies** that illustrate issues introduced in the chapter. **Vignettes** – stories authored by qualitative researchers in the field – provide real-world examples of how the tools have been used in a variety of contexts. As noted earlier, **reflexive practice activities** are incorporated throughout each chapter to encourage you to apply what you are reading to a study of your own design. We conclude each chapter with **suggestions for further reading** as well as **chapter discussion questions**.

What this book cannot do is provide you with step-by-step guidance for learning particular tools. It is not a 'how to' manual, because the tools change too quickly for such instructions to remain accurate for long. We do, however, have a **companion website** for the book, where we provide extended coverage of the topics introduced in each chapter. Each chapter's **web resources** direct you to our companion website.

Visit Web Resource 1.3 for a link to Jane Hart's Best of Breed Tools.

Visit Web Resource 1.4 for a link to Bamboo Digital Research Tools (DiRT).

The companion website is designed to extend what is discussed in the book, while also providing additional examples and ideas for further consideration. Finally, we have strived to introduce not only proprietary, commercial tools but also freely available tools.

Overview of the Chapters

As a qualitative researcher, *you* are the instrument, and at the centre of the research process. Chapter 2 examines how the choices and decisions you will make, consciously and unconsciously, will impact all aspects of your study, making reflexive practice critical. Reflexive practice is very much linked to ethical practice. From online journals (blogs) to audio and video recorders to cloud-based note-taking systems, there are a variety of digital tools that you can use to keep a reflective journal. Each of these tools comes with affordances and constraints, as well as ethical questions. We introduce some of these ethical dilemmas in Chapter 2 as well.

Chapter 3 explores how digital tools can support what we see as *creative conversations* between collaborators. Digital tools can support networking, meeting, resource sharing and collaborative writing. New tools can present ethical dilemmas such as the security of data stored in the cloud and how to properly credit collaborators for their contributions to a project.

Literature reviews for qualitative research studies, discussed in Chapter 4, involve understanding the current state of the field in order to join the scholarly conversation. Locating, organizing, reading, analysing and synthesizing the literature can be supported by a variety of tools beyond the database searches most researchers are familiar with. Search alerts and social bookmarking tools can make the process of locating sources more systematic and transparent. Citation management tools function as comprehensive document management systems for electronic resources. Mobile computing devices combined with e-reader applications are making 'going paperless' for academic reading a possibility.

Generating data, discussed in Chapter 5, is a central aspect of the research process. Historically, there has been a greater focus on collecting researcher-generated data, such as interview and focus group data. Digital tools now afford researchers opportunities to collect other forms of data, including naturally occurring data, such as everyday conversations. Field notes can be synchronized with mapping tools. Recording audio and video data can now be done with mobile devices and new tools such as Smartpens. Online communities provide an additional site for qualitative exploration, but entering these sites in an ethical manner requires careful forethought. Digital tools also support innovative methods such as walk-alongs, soundscapes and photovoice studies.

Transcribing recordings into written texts is typically a central part of the qualitative research process, and the first layer of analysis. Chapter 6 introduces several ways of transcribing that can be supported by transcription software or voice recognition software. With Transana, multiple transcripts can be used to represent different layers of the audio and video data. It is also possible for researchers to bypass the transcription process entirely by directly coding audio and video files.

Chapter 7 discusses how effective use of computer-assisted qualitative data analysis software (CAQDAS) packages entails selecting the features that will best support your analytic approach. A software package can serve as the organizational container for your study, as well as allowing you to annotate, link, search, code and visualize your data. Understanding the affordances and constraints of the software packages can help you decide when and how to use them in your work.

Chapter 8 explores the use of image, audio, and video data to support our understandings of everyday life. New digital tools provide features such as synchronized transcripts, waveform representations, time stamping, direct coding and geolinking. Further, Transana, designed specifically for the analysis of video data, provides a variety of features that support in-depth analysis and manipulation of video files.

Writing and representing the findings, discussed in Chapter 9, is fundamental to the research process. Qualitative researchers have typically relied upon the written word to represent their research. Yet digital tools afford researchers opportunities to write about, represent and disseminate their research in new ways. Further, many qualitative researchers have become interested in how digital tools can be used to reach a greater audience. From digital ethnographies to digital storytelling to websites to online soundscapes to documentary films, there are a variety of tools that can support qualitative researchers in representing their research.

In the final chapter of the book we look to the future of digital tools and qualitative research, as well as propose new innovations that would be useful for the qualitative research community.

Final Thoughts

We hope that our introduction of a variety of digital tools, along with vignettes, case studies and reflexive practice activities will inspire you to carefully consider how new technologies might impact your research practice. We encourage you to consider each tool in relation to its affordances and constraints, recognizing that there are indeed tools beyond those mentioned in the book that may be useful in your work. We would also love to hear about the ways in which you are using digital tools in your work, and invite you to share your experiences with us.

Chapter Discussion Questions

1. What tools have you used in your own research practice? Are you an early adopter or a resister of new technologies, or somewhere in between?
2. What is the most recent technology you have started to use in your daily life? How might this tool afford particular uses for qualitative research? What constraints might it present?
3. Describe the research study that you will be designing in conjunction with this book. In what phases of the study might digital tools be particularly useful?

Suggestions for Further Reading

Though not focused solely on qualitative research, Anderson and Kanuka (2003) is one of the only texts that attends to the use of digital tools across the research process. The chapters on literature reviews, ethics, collaboration, interviews, focus groups and dissemination of findings are particularly helpful. Davidson and Di Gregorio (2011) is a valuable resource for understanding the history of the relationship between the qualitative research community and technological innovations. Paulus et al. (2013) present findings from a discourse analysis study of introductory qualitative research textbooks in which a discourse of 'caution' was found to be contrasted with a discourse of 'opportunity' around the use of digital tools.

References

Anderson, T., and Kanuka, H. (2003) *E-Research: Methods, Strategies and Issues*. Boston, MA: Allyn & Bacon.

CIBER (Centre for Information Behaviour and the Evaluation of Research), University College London (2010) *Social Media and Research Workflow*. London, UK: Emerald Group Publishing Ltd.

Davidson, J. and Di Gregorio, S. (2011) 'Qualitative Research and Technology: In the Midst of a Revolution', in N.K. Denzin and Y.S. Lincoln (eds) *The SAGE Handbook of Qualitative Research* (4th edition). London, UK: SAGE.

Miles, M.B. and Huberman, A.M. (1994) *Qualitative Data Analysis: An Expanded Sourcebook*. London, UK: SAGE.

Norman, D.A. (1999) 'Affordance, conventions and design'. *Interactions*, 6(3), 38–42.

Paulus, T., Lester, J. and Britt, V. (2013) 'Constructing hopes and fears: A discourse analysis of introductory qualitative research texts'. *Qualitative Inquiry*, 19(9).

Prensky, M. (2011) 'Digital native, digital immigrants'. *On the Horizon*, 9(5), 1–6.

Rogers, E.M. (2003) *Diffusion of Innovations* (3th edition). New York, NY: The Free Press.

TWO
Engaging in Reflexive Practice and Making Ethical Choices

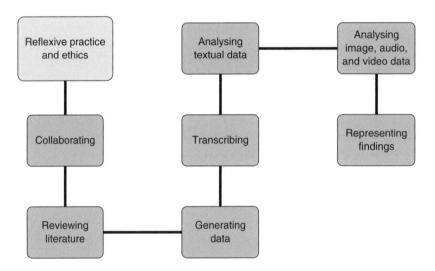

Companion website materials available here:

www.uk.sagepub.com/paulus

Introduction

In Chapter 1, we presented the phases of the research process that are common across most approaches to qualitative inquiry. We discussed the ways in which the use of technology to support qualitative research has frequently been limited to data collection, transcription and data analysis. We also suggested that new tools, particularly social media and Web 2.0 tools, can enable greater researcher reflexivity, transparency of research decisions and collaboration among researchers, participants and the community. By the end of Chapter 1, we asked you to identify a hypothetical or actual research topic as a context for the activities included through the remainder of this book.

In this chapter, we first define reflexive practice. We then illustrate the use of blogs, audio and video recorders, and cloud-based note-taking and archiving systems to support reflexive practice. We conclude by introducing some of the ethical issues raised by the various digital tools that will be discussed throughout the book. By the end of this chapter, you will have set up your own reflexive practice blog and have made several posts.

What is Reflexivity?

Whether it is labelled reflexivity (Hertz, 1997; Pillow, 2003), bracketing (Dowling, 2005; Giorgi, 1985), positionality (Glesne, 2011) or some other related concept, understanding the relationship between the researcher, context and participants is central to nearly all qualitative traditions (Watt, 2007). A fundamental assumption is that the researcher is the instrument of the study. As such, a researcher's choices, assumptions and biases impact all aspects of the study. Reflexivity is the process of intentionally attending to the perspectives, attitudes and beliefs that shape how you design a research study and make sense of your data. As a reflexive researcher, you should continually examine your choices, while taking note of how your positionality limits and privileges what you come to know and understand. See Case Study 2.1 to explore these ideas further.

CASE STUDY 2.1 ┤ **Who I Am Matters**

Estella conducted an ethnographic study examining the everyday experiences of Latina/o youth who recently immigrated to a new country. She was particularly interested in the ways in which her participants navigated and made sense of their schooling experiences. Throughout her four-year project, she reflected often upon her own identity as a Chicana scholar, former schoolteacher and immigrant. As she collected and analysed data, she wrote frequently about the ways in which her own experiences learning English and resettling in a new country shaped how she made sense of the participants' interview data. Throughout the project, she remained aware of her tendency to see what she already knew. At the same time, she recognized that who she was allowed her to make sense of and align with the experiences of the participants in unique and meaningful ways.

Engaging in reflexive practice adds transparency to the research process, allowing outside readers to better evaluate how interpretations were made. As we practise reflexivity, we seek to acknowledge and work through the realities of *always* being a part of the research process. As Atkinson and Delamont (2005) stated, 'the process of analysis stretches far beyond the mere manipulation of data ... All scholars recognize that this process is not innocent' (p. 834). We must always be asking how we participate in the making and remaking of social science. How, though, do we go about practising reflexivity in an ongoing fashion?

Engaging in Reflexive Practice

By maintaining a research journal, you can keep track of your 'experiences, ideas, fears, mistakes, confusions, breakthroughs, and problems that arise during fieldwork' (Spradley, 1980, p. 71). This then becomes a key location for you to openly reflect on what transpires during the research process, while leaving an audit trail for outsiders to become familiar with your decision-making process (Creswell and Miller, 2000). Case Study 2.2 illustrates how Paul made explicit how he shaped his research project.

CASE STUDY 2.2 ─ **Paul's Reflexivity Statement**

When I was considering a PhD, I was exploring topics around death and dying. It did not make sense completely (to others) why I would gravitate toward this field of research. Along with natural curiosity, a couple of moments in my history influenced the decision. One of these was when I worked as an undertaker. The second was when I was profoundly influenced by the death of a person whom I had looked after for two years. One day she simply vanished. I came in for my shift to find another elderly resident in her room. No one had said anything about her death to me. Years later, those experiences helped shape my curiosity about what to study for my PhD. I wondered whether there were other caregivers with similar experiences. Were there other males, working in a predominately female environment, that had experienced death in these settings? How did they deal with it? How about cooks and cleaners; what was their experience? It became clear that I needed to write some of this down, work out what influences were energizing my thinking. Also, was there anything that I was avoiding? This is the reflexive self.

Visit Web Resource 2.1 to read a reflexivity statement written by Kathy Evans while engaged in her thesis work focused on the experiences of youth sent to in-school suspension.

Keeping an ongoing record of experiences, reactions and emerging awareness during a study does not need to be done in isolation. In fact, it is often quite useful to share your reflections with others. In this way, alternative perspectives and understandings can emerge. Turn now to Reflexive Practice 2.1.

─────────── **REFLEXIVE PRACTICE 2.1** ───────────

Before we go on to look at blogs, think about the ways in which various identities (race, ethnicity, gender, sexual orientation, dis/ability, etc.) shape how you make sense of the world? How might your previous experiences influence how you enter the context of your proposed study?

There are a variety of tools you can use to maintain a research journal. Web logs, or blogs, provide a space in which being reflexive does not have to be a solitary process (LaBanca, 2011), but can instead allow you to share your reflections with your mentors and/or collaborators. You might also decide to use an audio or video recorder to chronicle your experiences. Finally, cloud-based note-taking and archiving systems can be accessed from multiple locations.

Visit Web Resource 2.2 to view a video about the meaning, purpose and function of 'the cloud' and 'cloud computing'.

Blogs as a Tool for Reflexive Practice

Blogs are defined as 'easy-to-update websites characterized by dated entries displayed in reverse chronological order' (Stefanac, 2006, p. 230) and have become increasingly popular since the late 1990s. Blogs can be used as an online journal to chronologically record your thoughts and ideas, while providing a place for others to respond. Though the privacy settings can be changed, by default the blog space is open for anyone to read. Posts can include text, links to websites or even audio or video clips. Once a post is made, readers can respond to the post and to one another's comments. Compared to traditional forms of journalling, the commenting feature of blogs supports reflection in relationship to others. LaBanca (2011) shared the ways in which he used blogging as a tool for reflexivity in his own research practice, suggesting that it functioned to increase trustworthiness. This, he argued, is particularly true because outsiders can audit the researcher's unfolding process by reading the blog. The asynchronous nature of blogs makes it possible for people to participate in a conversation at their convenience. Further, creating a blog requires relatively little technological expertise.

Visit Web Resource 2.3 to view a video introduction to the purpose and function of a blog.

Blogs are examples of 'persistent conversations' and can be referenced months or years later. They can be updated remotely via mobile phones, making it possible for researchers in the field to be consistently engaged in reflexive practice.

Blogger is one of many free platforms that support private and/or multi-user blogs, with each entry (posts and comments) being time stamped. Blogger is integrated with Google's email service, Gmail, and can be easily accessed while using other Google tools (see Figure 2.1).

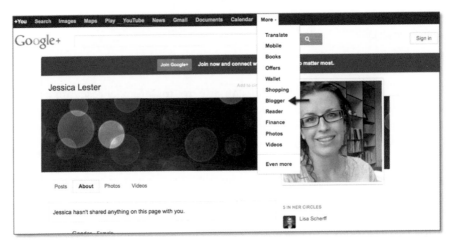

Figure 2.1 Blogger and Google tools

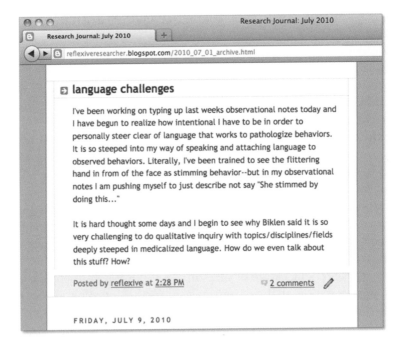

Figure 2.2 A post in Blogger

After you set up your account, you must choose a name and web address for your blog. It is often useful to give the blog a title related to a given project, or more generically refer to it as your 'Reflexivity Journal'. There are also several template options for personalizing the layout of your blog.

Figure 2.2 displays a post that Jessica made during her study of the discursive construction of autism. Notice that the post was made by 'reflexive', a blog identity Jessica chose to use rather than her real name.

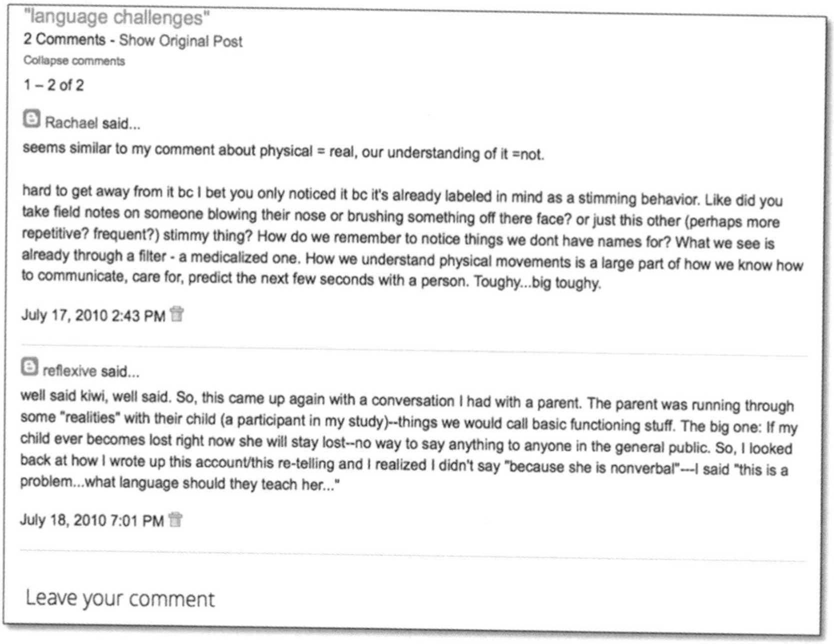

"language challenges"

2 Comments - Show Original Post

Collapse comments

1 – 2 of 2

Rachael said...

seems similar to my comment about physical = real, our understanding of it =not.

hard to get away from it bc I bet you only noticed it bc it's already labeled in mind as a stimming behavior. Like did you take field notes on someone blowing their nose or brushing something off there face? or just this other (perhaps more repetitive? frequent?) stimmy thing? How do we remember to notice things we dont have names for? What we see is already through a filter - a medicalized one. How we understand physical movements is a large part of how we know how to communicate, care for, predict the next few seconds with a person. Toughy...big toughy.

July 17, 2010 2:43 PM

reflexive said...

well said kiwi, well said. So, this came up again with a conversation I had with a parent. The parent was running through some "realities" with their child (a participant in my study)--things we would call basic functioning stuff. The big one: If my child ever becomes lost right now she will stay lost--no way to say anything to anyone in the general public. So, I looked back at how I wrote up this account/this re-telling and I realized I didn't say "because she is nonverbal"---I said "this is a problem...what language should they teach her..."

July 18, 2010 7:01 PM

Leave your comment

Figure 2.3   Comments in Blogger

During the course of this particular study, Jessica invited only two people to read her blog – a mentor and a colleague. They commented often on her posts, resulting in a conversation that pushed her thinking and ultimately shaped how she engaged in the data collection and analysis. Figure 2.3 illustrates how the commenting features make reflexivity a dialogical process.

Using a pseudonym and password-protecting access to your blog adds a layer of protection for your research site and participants. Figure 2.4 shows the various access levels Blogger provides: making the blog open to the public at large, adding other authors with full administrator rights, or inviting only a select few to read the blog.

Password-protecting your blog and only inviting select readers may be the best choice when keeping a research journal in this way. Next, turn to Reflexive Practice 2.2.

REFLEXIVE PRACTICE 2.2

Engaging in reflexivity is a major part of being a qualitative researcher. We suggest that you take some time now to create your own blog. Your first entries can be your notes from Reflexive Practice 1.1 and 2.1. Within each of the upcoming chapters, we will pose reflexive practice questions that you can respond to on your blog. If you are reading this textbook as part of a class, consider commenting on each other's posts throughout the semester.

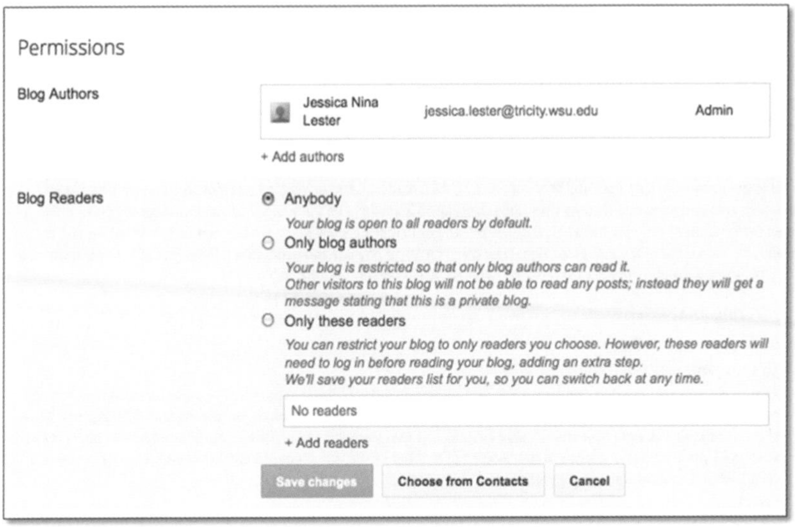

Permissions

Blog Authors

Jessica Nina
Lester   jessica.lester@tricity.wsu.edu   Admin

+ Add authors

Blog Readers

⊙ Anybody
  Your blog is open to all readers by default.
○ Only blog authors
  Your blog is restricted so that only blog authors can read it.
  Other visitors to this blog will not be able to read any posts; instead they will get a
  message stating that this is a private blog.
○ Only these readers
  You can restrict your blog to only readers you choose. However, these readers will
  need to log in before reading your blog, adding an extra step.
  We'll save your readers list for you, so you can switch back at any time.

No readers

+ Add readers

Save changes   Choose from Contacts   Cancel

Figure 2.4   Selecting a blog's level of privacy

Audio and Video Recording Devices as Tools for Reflexive Practice

Using an audio or video recorder to engage in reflexive practice might be particularly appealing for those researchers who are already using such a device for data collection. Chapter 5 provides detailed guidance in selecting audio and video recording devices. In Vignette 2.1, Kathy Evans describes the way in which she used her audio recorder in this way.

Vignette 2.1 | **Recording for Reflexivity**

Kathy Evans, Eastern Mennonite University

I would love to say that I began using my digital recorder out of a commitment to researcher reflexivity; but honestly, it started out as a convenient tool for remembering my 'to-do' list. While I was driving, I could remind myself to send in a student assent letter or to contact the principal of a school where I hoped to interview a student. I knew others who kept online reflexivity journals and I had been encouraged by my professor to do so as well; but typing my thoughts didn't always work and sometimes I couldn't wait until I returned to my computer to begin reflecting on my research. The digital recorder was great as a tool for more immediate reflection – a digital journal of sorts.

For my thesis research, I conducted interviews with students about their experiences with in-school suspension. My initial plan was to meet with the student, explain the study, have them sign the letter of assent, and then

---

schedule another meeting for the interview. After the first meeting with a student, I sat in the car, recording my reflections on how complicated the process seemed to be. Later, I was able to listen to that self-reflection and devise a much more fluid way of meeting and interviewing the students. A couple of days later, after conducting the first interview, I went immediately to my car and recorded the following: 'I think I must be doing something wrong; how do you get middle school students to open up and talk to a complete stranger?' That first interview had lasted just under seven minutes and, as I sat in the parking lot of the middle school, I thought out loud with my recorder about what my expectations had been. I was able to immediately record pertinent information about the interview, context, disposition of the student and other details that would not necessarily have shown up in the interview recording.

There are things that I have learned since then that I would do differently. For example, had I transcribed these recorded reflections I might have been able to more thoroughly see and analyse my own positionality and incorporated those reflections into the data analysis. I still carry my digital recorder around with me, using it to reflect in the moment on all sorts of things – including future research projects.

Researchers engaged in some forms of phenomenology might already be engaged in audio-recording their reflexive practice. For example, prior to conducting interviews, phenomenological researchers typically complete a bracketing interview in which another researcher asks the primary researcher to talk about the phenomenon of focus (Valle, King and Halling, 1989). The interview is often audio-recorded and transcribed and can be positioned as part of the data set. Case Study 2.3 provides an example.

CASE STUDY 2.3 | A Bracketing Interview

Amy was planning to conduct a phenomenological study of primary school teachers using a scripted reading programme in which teachers are told exactly what to say and do throughout a reading lesson. She had strong feelings about scripted curricula, and knew it would be important to be reflexive about her own biases. Amy asked another researcher, Jenny, to conduct a bracketing interview prior to data collection. The following excerpt illustrates how the interview began.

Jenny: Amy, tell me about your experiences with reading instruction like the scripted programme.

Amy: I have never taught using a scripted programme. I was able to teach using whatever methods I wanted to. So my original thoughts on the scripted programme were that I disagree with it because I don't think a scripted programme can provide the kinds of

(Continued)

(Continued)

experiences necessary for kids to use it. But what I've read about it, it has had some limited success, typically short term.

Within this short excerpt, Amy's own experiences and biases against the scripted pro-gramme are displayed. As the interview continued, Jenny encouraged Amy to expand upon her perspectives. Amy audio-recorded her bracketing interview and eventually transcribed it, including it in her overall data set, helping her to consider her assumptions as she ana-lysed the data.

Video recording devices can also be used to support reflexive practice. For instance, in the 'Living Text' project, media scholars Art Herbig and Aaron Hess chronicled their experiences (via the social media sites Twitter, YouTube and Facebook), collecting images, interviews and various events commemorating the tenth anniversary of the terrorist attacks on the World Trade Center in New York City. Through videos, they documented their experience of data collection, opening up their process to public response and critique. Displayed in Figure 2.5 are some of the images, videos, and reflexive musings posted on their publically available Facebook page.

Figure 2.5   Art Herbig's and Aaron Hess' audio and video posts

Visit Web Resource 2.4 to see the Herbig and Hess *Living Text* project.

Today's mobile phones and web cameras can support the use of video for reflexive practice. Jessica recently began recording video reflections every time

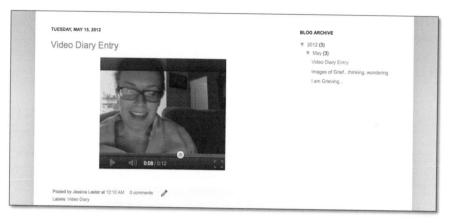

Figure 2.6 Reflexivity video journal

she transcribed an interview from a study focused on graduate students' experiences of grief. After transcribing an interview, Jessica often felt the need to talk through her own emotions. She would turn on her computer's video camera and talk through her reactions to the data collection event. She then uploaded the videos to a password-protected blog that she shared with her collaborators (see Figure 2.6).

Other researchers involved in the project uploaded their own video diary entries. These recordings were useful when they began analysing the interview data, reminding them of the raw emotions they felt after conducting and transcribing interviews. The videos, then, served to capture aspects of the research experience that were part of and shaped their understanding of the data. Now consider Reflexive Practice 2.3.

REFLEXIVE PRACTICE 2.3

How might you use audio or video recorders to engage in reflexive practice? If you post your reflections for others to listen to or watch, what are some of the ethical concerns you should consider? Make a post in your reflexivity blog.

Cloud-Based Note-taking and Archiving Systems as Tools for Reflexive Practice

A third way to engage in reflexive practice is through a cloud-based note-taking system, such as Evernote. Many of us have different computing devices and/or notebooks that we may use throughout the day and it can be easy to lose track of notes, journal entries or other research documentation. Cloud-based note-taking tools enable you to engage in multiple tasks that can be synchronized across computing devices. For instance, perhaps you want to be able to write field notes, record audio files, make to-do lists and archive emails while in the

Figure 2.7   Evernote's notebooks and tags

field but not have to transfer them to your home computer later. Evernote uses the cloud to synchronize these items across all of your computing devices immediately. Even when working in a location with no Internet access, you can create a new 'note' that will later be synchronized once you are back online.

Your notes can be organized into 'notebooks' and tagged with descriptors to help organize them. For instance, Jennifer, a PhD student, created a notebook for a discourse analysis project entitled 'DA Project'. Within this one notebook, she wrote and tagged her notes as observational notes (ON), theoretical memos (TM), analytical memos (AM) and reflexive memos (RM) (see Figure 2.7). When she had overlap within her notes, she would simply tag the note more than once, for example, AM and RM. She developed other tags that were specific to her unfolding interpretations. As she engaged in deeper levels of data analysis, she was able to easily retrieve these tags using Evernote's filter feature. If she wanted to only review those notes that were 'reflexive memos', she simply searched for 'RM'. This helped her create an audit trail, increasing the transparency of her research.

Evernote's notebooks can be shared with others. Just as with blog posts, you need to be sure to protect any confidential information. Indeed, whether typed and saved on a personal computer or archived on a cloud-based system, it is important to consider all potential risks in relation to information being unintentionally disclosed.

Visit Web Resource 2.5 to learn about Moleskine's 'smart notebook', that integrates with Evernote.

Take a moment to reflect upon the ethical dilemmas inherent in using cloud-based computing in Reflexive Practice 2.4.

REFLEXIVE PRACTICE 2.4

Cloud computing takes electronic files out of your direct control. What ethical considerations does cloud computing raise? What might be the risks of storing a reflexive journal in
the cloud? What can you do to limit the risks?

Reflexive Practice 2.5 gives you a chance to explore features of Evernote, and to
reflect on your experience.

REFLEXIVE PRACTICE 2.5

Take a moment to sign up for and download Evernote on your computing device(s). Create
a note and some tags. What worked well? What was difficult?

Ethical Considerations of Digital Tools for Qualitative Research

From contemplating how best to navigate entry to a research site to concerns
around unfair and even damaging representations of people, places and spaces
(Knight, 2000; Wax, 1995), qualitative research requires you to remain reflexive
about the ethical dilemmas that will inevitably arise. While the meaning of ethics is complex and open to debate (Hammersley and Traianou, 2012), there are
guidelines that serve to shape how you can and even should carry out your
research studies.

Emerging from the concerns surrounding the atrocities associated with medical research conducted by the Nazis during World War II, the Nuremburg Code
of 1947 put ethical principles specific to medical experiments in place. This code
was eventually more broadly applied within the field of psychology. In 1964, the
World Medical Association released the Helsinki Declaration, which outlined
principles for conducting fair and humane medical research with human subjects. Further, the Belmont Report, released in the United States in 1979, outlined basic research practices for biomedical and behavioural research scientists.
This report presented three primary ethical principles, to: 1) protect the auton-
omy of research participants by engaging in an informed consent process;
2) minimize harm and maximize benefits to participants; and 3) engage in non-
exploitative research procedures.

Hammersley and Traianou (2012) noted that, regardless of your research
pursuit, there are at least three primary 'values' to consider when engaging in
qualitative research (p. 56). These include a commitment to: 1) minimize harm
done to participants; 2) respect and acknowledge the rights of participants to
decide whether to participate or withdraw from a study; and 3) protect the
identity of the participants and/or community within which you engage in
research.

Visit Web Resource 2.6 to review ethical guidelines and statements from a variety of professional organizations.

Using digital tools for qualitative research presents new ethical considerations, as well as exciting possibilities. In McKee and Porter's (2009) text on Internet research ethics, for example, they reminded us that the first guiding principle for researchers is to do no harm – not only to potential research participants, but also to their communities. Failure to approach research in an ethical manner could threaten not only future research access to a community, but could endanger the community itself, as members may begin to feel unsafe. McKee and Porter (2009) acknowledged that many ethics boards are unfamiliar with Internet research or the best way to protect everyone involved. They argued that ethics should be seen as an ongoing *process of reflection, analysis* and *action* and, since every community is unique, the use of heuristics, rather than hard and fast rules, should guide ethical decisions.

Throughout this book, we will discuss some of the ethical dilemmas raised by the use of digital tools. For instance, Chapter 5 will explore how the Internet has muddied what researchers and participants consider to be public versus private information. Markham (2006) wrote of how Internet texts are often defined by institutional review boards as public texts rather than data generated by human subjects. In such cases, then, the very notion of informed consent shifts. Ongoing reflexive practice is inherently linked to practising ethical research. Markham (2006) aptly noted that regardless of whether a researcher is working 'online or off, an ethical researcher is one who is prepared, reflexive, flexible, adaptive, and honest' (p. 39). Consider, for instance, Vignette 2.2.

Vignette 2.2	**Online Communities as Research Contexts**

Trena Paulus, University of Tennessee

As avid hikers, my colleagues and I were interested in exploring an online hiking community for how it could be seen as a site of informal learning. The community we were interested in had user profiles, photos and discussion forums. The online discussions are open to the public – anyone can read them without logging in or being a member of the community. Members of the community use screen names and do not share their real identities. After talking with the institutional review board at our university, we found out that we were not required to obtain informed consent in order to treat these publicly visible discussions as data. To be on the safe side, we checked to be sure that there was nothing in the site's user agreement specifically prohibiting research use of the discussions. We also considered McKee and Porter's (2009) heuristic of variables for guidance as to whether seeking informed consent was advisable. In this case, since the conversations were public, the topics were not sensitive, the participants were not especially vulnerable, and we did not intend to interact with them in any way, we were comfortable proceeding with our study.

REFLEXIVE PRACTICE 2.6

Reflect on Vignette 2.2 above. Would you have made the same decision? What ethical dilemmas might you encounter in the study that you are designing?

Each chapter of this book provides an opportunity for you to reflect upon the ethical implications that come with digital tool use. Table 2.1 provides an overview of some of the ethical questions and concerns that we address in the upcoming chapters.

Table 2.1 Ethical questions considered across the book

Chapter	Topic	Ethical Questions Raised
3	Collaborating and Managing Projects	• How might collaboration impact the ownership of ideas? • What are the benefits and risks of storing material in the cloud?
4	Reviewing the Literature	• What are some ways to transparently share your literature review process to ensure that sources are properly credited? • What are the ways in which you might avoid unintentional plagiarism?
5	Generating Data	• When is it necessary to acquire informed consent before studying a publicly visible online community? • How might collecting data in the form of images present new ethical dilemmas?
6	Transcribing Audio and Video Data	• Should you anonymize data prior to, during, or after transcription? • When a transcript is synchronized with media files and then shared with others, how might this compromise confidentiality?
7	Analysing Textual Data	• Computer-assisted qualitative data analysis packages make it easier to share analysis as it is occurring. How can we ensure confidentiality at the same time?
8	Analysing Image, Audio and Video Data	• How can you protect the identity of participants when their voices and faces are part of the data set? • How might linking your data to your research location compromise the anonymity of your participants?
9	Writing and Representing Findings	• How might popularizing research findings compromise your ability to protect your participants?

Visit Web Resource 2.7 to read a *Qualitative Research* article (Iphofen, 2011) discussing ethical decision-making.

Final Thoughts

Engaging in reflexive practice is a key component of qualitative research and can add trustworthiness and transparency to your work. This process can be supported by a variety of tools, some of which you may already be using in your non-academic life. If you have never engaged in reflexive practice while conducting a research study, we encourage you to begin your practice by experimenting with and finding a tool that feels comfortable to you. Each tool comes with its own affordances and constraints – blogs make it easier to participate in collaborative reflexivity through dialogue; audio recorders allow you to reflect when on the go; and tools such as Evernote enable you to use any computing device at any time for reflection. Reflexive practice requires you to keep ethical concerns at the forefront of your research process, providing a space and a process for documenting decisions along the way. Ensuring that the identities of research participants and contexts are protected is one such consideration to keep in mind.

Chapter Discussion Questions

1. Have you kept a journal before? Was your journal handwritten, typed, written online or recorded in some other way?
2. How might digital tools afford a more transparent and collaborative approach to reflexive and ethical practices?
3. What other tools, besides those mentioned in this chapter, could be used for reflexive practice?
4. What ethical dilemmas have you encountered in your research practice, and how did you resolve them?

Suggestions for Further Reading

Watt (2007) chronicles her reflexive journey and provides a rationale for engaging in regular reflexive practice. LaBanca (2011) highlights the ways in which reflexive blogs increase trustworthiness. Hertz's (1997) edited volume explores the various ways in which reflexivity plays a role in various methodological traditions. McKee and Porter (2009) provide heuristic guidance for making ethical decisions when researching a variety of online groups. Buchanan and Ess (2009) also explore issues around Internet research specifically, as do the 2012 recommendations by the Association of Internet Researchers.

Visit Web Resource 2.8 to review the recommendations from the Association of Internet Researchers Ethics Working Committee.

References

Atkinson, P. and Delamont, S. (2005) 'Analytic Perspectives', in N.K. Denzin and Y.S. Lincoln (eds) *The SAGE Handbook of Qualitative Research* (3rd edition), pp. 821–40. Thousand Oaks, CA: SAGE, Inc.

Buchanan, E. and Ess, C. (2009) 'Internet research ethics and the institutional review board: Current practices and issues'. *Computers & Society*, 39(3), 43–9.

Creswell, J.W. and Miller, D.L. (2000) 'Determining validity in qualitative inquiry'. *Theory into Practice*, 39, 124–30.

Dowling, M. (2005) 'From Husserl to van Manen: A review of different phenomenological approaches'. *International Journal of Nursing Studies*, 44(1), 131–42.

Giorgi, A. (1985) *Phenomenology and Psychological Research*. Pittsburg, PA: Duquesne University Press.

Glesne, C. (2011) *Becoming Qualitative Researchers: An Introduction* (4th edition). New York, NY: Addison Wesley Longman.

Hammersley, M. and Traianou, A. (2012) *Ethics in Qualitative Research: Controversies and Contexts*. London, UK: SAGE.

Hertz, R. (1997) *Reflexivity and Voice*. Thousand Oaks, CA: SAGE.

Iphofen, R. (2011) 'Ethical decision making in qualitative research'. *Qualitative Research*, 11, 443–6.

Knight, M. (2000) 'Ethics in qualitative research: Multicultural feminist activist research'. *Theory into Practice*, 39(3), 170–6.

LaBanca, F. (2011) 'Online dynamic asynchronous audit strategy for reflexivity in the qualitative paradigm'. *The Qualitative Report*, 16(4), 1160–71.

McKee, H.A. and Porter, J.E. (2009) *Internet Research: A Rhetorical, Case-Based Process*. New York, NY: Peter Lang Publishers.

Markham, A. (2006) 'Method as ethic, ethic as method'. *Journal of Information Ethics*, 15(2), 37–55.

Pillow, W. (2003) 'Confession, catharsis, or cure? Rethinking the uses of reflexivity as methodological power in qualitative research'. *International Journal of Qualitative Studies in Education*, 16(2), 175–96.

Spradley, J. (1980) *Participant Observation*. Montreal, Quebec, Canada: Holt, Rinehart & Winston.

Stefanac, S. (2006) *Dispatches from Blogistan: A Travel Guide for the Modern Blogger*. Berkeley, CA: New Riders.

Valle, R.S., King, M. and Halling, S. (1989) 'An Introduction to Existential-Phenomenological Thought in Psychology', in R.S. Valle and S. Halling (eds) *Existential-Phenomenological Perspectives in Psychology*, pp. 3–16. New York: Plenum Press.

Watt, D. (2007) 'On becoming a qualitative researcher: The value of reflexivity'. *The Qualitative Report*, 12(1), 82–101.

Wax, M.L. (1995) 'Knowledge, power, and ethics in qualitative social research'. *American Sociologist*, 26, 22–34.

THREE
Collaborating and Managing Projects

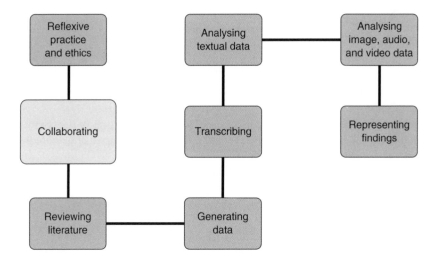

Companion website materials available here:

www.uk.sagepub.com/paulus

Introduction

In Chapter 2, we illustrated the use of digital tools to engage in reflexive practice, asked you to create your own reflexive practice blog and introduced ethical concerns that may arise with the use of such tools. In this chapter, we focus specifically on how digital tools can be used to support collaboration among researchers, participants and even the broader community. We start this chapter with a brief discussion of the role of collaboration in qualitative research, and conceptualize collaboration as a *creative conversational process*. We discuss how new tools can help us network with others, hold meetings, share resources and write collaboratively.

Collaboration and Qualitative Research

Collaboration can occur in nearly every aspect of the research process, and digital tools are playing an increasingly important role. The 2010 CIBER report on social media and research workflow noted that new tools are 'helping fulfill the demand for cheap, instant communication between researchers fueled by the growth of collaborative and interdisciplinary research' (p. 2). The authors of the report noted, however, that there is 'a large gap between awareness and actual use for the majority of the tools' (p. 2). As we described in Chapter 1, we too have been somewhat reluctant to adopt new tools until presented with compelling evidence (or convincing arguments by our colleagues and students) to do so.

Qualitative research has long been considered a solitary endeavour, domi-nated by the image of a 'lone ethnographer' (Lee and Gregory, 2008) travelling to foreign cultures. In actuality, collaborative teams are becoming more prevalent in the qualitative arena, particularly in work funded by agencies such as the Economic and Social Research Council in the UK, the Social Sciences and Humanities Research Council in Canada and the National Science Foundation in the USA. Working in teams can have many benefits, such as improved research quality, richer interpretations and higher levels of conceptual thinking (Barry et al., 1999). Well-functioning teams increase overall satisfaction with the research process.

Challenges to teamwork include working across time zones, relationship breakdowns, too much disagreement or, conversely, too much 'group think' (Anderson and Kanuka, 2003). Intercultural teams may have very different norms, values and assumptions, all of which must be navigated with care. Further, writing collaboratively can pose problems in terms of ownership of ideas. Lee and Gregory (2008) suggested that obtaining ethics approval for all collaborators, clarifying workflow processes and setting project outcome expec-tations can all increase the chances of success.

Researchers are not only collaborating more often with each other, but increasingly with participants as well. As participatory and collaborative action research methodologies become more prevalent (e.g. Kemmis and McTaggert, 2005), researchers are seeking better ways to stay connected with participants, procure feedback on data interpretations and represent their findings in useful ways. Patient and public involvement has become a key part in health research funding, especially in the UK. Digital tools can support this methodological commitment to invite the participation of the community members. Fitzgerald and Findlay (2011) argued that 'we live in a highly participatory world of blogs and wikis where users want to share their opinion and co-create', warning that 'researchers that do not engage participants as co-creators may find it increasingly difficult to recruit participants and are ultimately at risk of producing low-quality research findings' (p. 306). Case Study 3.1 illustrates the use of a blog (see Chapter 2) to invite ongoing community participation.

CASE STUDY 3.1 — Inviting Ongoing Participation

Esther is engaged in an ethnographic study of physiotherapists at a paediatric centre for children with multiple disabilities. After interviewing the physiotherapists, Esther wanted to invite them to engage in ongoing dialogue in order to more actively shape the direction of her research. To do so, Esther set up a collaborative blog (password protected) in which they all began posting questions, ideas and challenges related to the process of informing parents of a treatment plan. Eventually, the blog became the site in which the physiotherapists and Esther began outlining future research questions and practical implications, while also serving to refine her unfolding interpretations.

At its core, successful collaboration is a *creative conversational process*. These conversations are eventually reified through final products such as journal articles, books and performances (see Chapter 9), which themselves become part of the research conversation. Creative conversations depend on good relationships (Paulus, Woodside and Ziegler, 2008; 2010); establishing common ground helps build these relationships (Barry et al., 1999). As Olesen et al. (1994) pointed out, teamwork requires even more reflexive practice than 'non-collaborative' qualitative research. Take a moment to consider Reflexive Practice 3.1.

=== **REFLEXIVE PRACTICE 3.1** ===

What experiences with teamwork have you had in your professional life? In what ways might the study that you are designing in conjunction with this book be a collaborative one?

Digital Tools to Support Collaborative Research

Fostering effective collaboration is no small task. As the three of us were writing this book, we were living in two different countries and across three time zones. We were only able to meet face-to-face once, so we relied on a combination of digital tools. In Table 3.1 we describe the ways we used tools for our creative conversations.

In addition to relying on these tools out of necessity, we have found that digital tools have the added advantage of documenting team processes and

Table 3.1 Communication preferences

Trena	Jessica	Paul
The time differences eventually became quite useful in our collaboration. I could write in the morning and leave materials for Jessica to pick up when her morning came around. By the time Paul got up, the materials were ready for him. We were careful to make sure that we copied our emails to all of us to keep everyone in the loop. Creating the Google site in which we stored all of our materials fell to me, but it was quickly populated by all of us with ideas for chapter structures and other resources. Everyone could comment on items as they were uploaded, which was useful (when we remembered to read the comments)!	Regular conversations – that was the secret. Skype's video and text chat features were useful as I could not always interpret Paul's thick Scottish accent. While we had an eight-hour time difference, Paul and I used Skype's text chat to talk about questions and ideas. Dropbox also became a place to store files, while the Google site gave me a structure from which to write. We developed effective ways of letting each other know when we had added new materials for each other to comment on, through email or text chats.	The time difference for me meant using Skype in the evenings, which could be tiring after a day at the office. I used the text chat feature in Skype a lot to communicate as I could see when Jessica and Trena were online. This meant that emails did not have to sit around waiting for an answer. It was a good social and motivational tool as well. Skype's audio alerts let me know when a message had arrived while I was working on other things. I preferred the instant nature of messaging rather than leaving notes on the Google site.

decisions. This made our process more visible than it may otherwise have been. We have identified several key areas in which digital tools can be useful in collaboration: networking, meeting, resource sharing and writing.

Networking

There are many ways that people connect with potential research collaborators. Graduate students and their research mentors may continue to collaborate even after the student has moved on, multiple primary investigators may be working on funded research, or community members may be working alongside social scientists toward common goals. Opportunities for collaboration often occur spontaneously in the normal course of our professional lives. Face-to-face attendance at professional meetings has long been associated with the networking that can lead to a new project.

While opportunities for face-to-face interaction are still valued and play an important role in professional growth, they can be expensive in terms of both money and time. Digital tools make it possible to attend professional events remotely. Paul, for example, has presented at conferences by recording a video of his talk to be 'presented' by collaborators in the United States on his behalf. Others have given talks through virtual conferencing software such as Google Hangouts or Skype (described later in this chapter), which allow participants to see and hear the presenter in real time and also ask questions.

For many years now, conversations with colleagues have been occurring on discipline specific email lists hosted by management software such as jiscmail and listserv. The Linguist List, H-Net (Humanities and Social Science Online) and the University of Georgia's QUALRS-L (Qualitative Research for the Human Sciences) are examples of email lists launched in the early 1990s. Email as a 'push' technology results in messages coming directly to you, rather than requiring you to 'pull' the messages from a website, but it also means that inboxes fill up fast.

Web 2.0 and social media, defined as the 'practice of sharing and connecting of both people and information in a peer-to-peer collaborative spirit via the Internet' (Chenail, 2011, p. 250), came on the scene in the 2000s. Blogs, Twitter (a micro-blogging site) and Facebook are all examples of Web 2.0 social media platforms which may eventually replace the email list. boyd and Ellison (2007) defined social networking sites as those which allow users to: '(1) construct a public or semi-public profile within a bounded system, (2) articulate a list of other users with whom they share a connection, and (3) view and traverse their list of connections and those made by others within the system' (p. 211).

Visit Web Resource 3.1 for more on social networking sites.

The CIBER (2010) report found that social media tools are indeed being used by scholars to identify research opportunities, communicate internationally, connect with people outside the academy and target research communities.

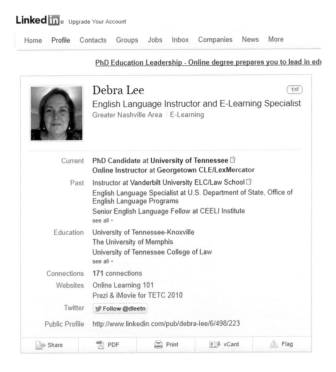

Figure 3.1   LinkedIn profile

LinkedIn and Academia.edu are two examples of professional social networking sites. LinkedIn, launched in 2003, bills itself as the world's largest professional network on the Internet with over 200 million users. Geared toward the corporate and non-profit audience, members create résumé-style profile pages (see Figure 3.1), which can be public or private. Instead of 'friends', you make 'connections' which are then visible from your profile page.

Individuals, professional groups and organizations can all have a presence in LinkedIn, and the site provides a running feed of status updates and other activities occurring in the site. Becoming part of LinkedIn is one way to stay up to date with where colleagues are working and what kinds of projects they are engaged in.

Academia.edu, a social networking site launched in 2008, has over 2.5 million users. It is geared directly toward academic audiences with the banner tag line 'share research'. Complete with profile pages and status updates, users on this site 'follow' each other's work and publications rather than becoming 'friends' or 'connections' (see Figure 3.2). Users can also follow the activities of research groups organized around particular topics.

Google Scholar citations profile pages have been launched more recently (see Figure 3.3) and must be activated by the researchers themselves, with Google pulling all published citations into the site.

The Scholar citations page shows all of the publications and the number of times they have been cited. The 'follow' feature allows you to be alerted when a new article is published.

Figure 3.2   Academia.edu activity feed

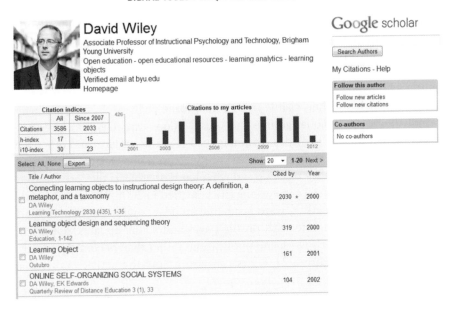

Figure 3.3   Google Scholar citations page

Twitter, launched in 2006, is a micro-blogging platform that limits its status updates, called 'tweets', to 140 characters. Twitter encourages you to 'follow' other tweets and gain 'followers' for your tweets. In Vignette 3.1, Prisca Rodriguez describes her use of Twitter to connect with other researchers.

Vignette 3.1 — **Qualitative Research and Social Media**

Prisca M. Rodríguez, University of Florida

One of my most meaningful networking experiences via social media happened at the 2012 American Educational Research Association (AERA) meeting. Several colleagues and I presented an interactive symposium focusing on the virtual in qualitative research. For months in advance, @AERA_EdResearch and others tweeted updates and announced the sessions being presented. Anyone interested in following the conversation would simply type the conference's hashtag: #AERA2012.

A 'hashtag' is a keyword made and used by any participant of the Twitter community to highlight and identify specific updates. A hashtag makes specific tweets accessible to a particular audience. For example, to highlight a session at the conference, presenters using Twitter assigned a hashtag to their session (e.g. #QRVIR) and included the year's conference hashtag (e.g. #AERA2012).

Twitter in particular has helped me connect with other researchers I may not have had the opportunity to converse with otherwise. At this

Prisca MRC
@pm_rodriguez

Follow

#AERA2012 #QRVIR would like to invite people tweeting the conference to join usSun Apr 15-8:15AM via Twitter or at the session...

← Reply ⇄ Retweet ★ Favorite

7:15 AM - 12 Apr 12 via web · Embed this Tweet

year's AERA presentation, it also afforded additional opportunities to extend the conversations that took place, exchange resources and connect with others interested in collaborating outside of the conference.

Lovejoy and Saxton (2012) noted that non-profit organizations are using Twitter to share information (e.g. current events), build community (e.g. soliciting responses from stakeholders) and promote action (e.g. encouraging attendance at events). Beyond just non-profits, many organizations, companies and groups have Twitter feeds. Some of these organizations have real-time events and meetings, such as #edchat, where everyone gathers at a specified time and chats for an hour on a topic related to education.

Visit Web Resource 3.2 for videos, news articles and ideas about how Twitter can be used in research.

Social media affords a means to stay up to date with what colleagues are doing in their professional (and sometimes personal) lives, engage in conversations and share resources without leaving your office. One of the constraints of social media is that it is easy to reach 'information overload' from following too many status updates and news feeds. We recommend finding out from leaders in your field where 'the action' is and concentrating your efforts there. Start your exploration of social media by answering the questions in Reflexive Practice 3.2.

=== **REFLEXIVE PRACTICE 3.2** ===

Set up your Google Scholar profile and/or create a profile on Academia.edu. How might social media be useful in your research collaborations?

Meeting

While it's no longer necessary for team members to be located in the same place to work together, it's still important to find effective ways to communicate. Finding the right balance of asynchronous (such as email) and synchronous communication (such as telephone calls) will be necessary for each collaborative project. Calendaring tools, collaboration spaces, video conferencing and desktop sharing tools may all be useful. We will explore each in turn.

Visit Web Resource 3.3 to read more about synchronous and asynchronous communication tools.

Calendaring Tools

For those times when you need to meet synchronously (face-to-face or virtually), online calendaring tools such as Doodle can be useful. It is free and does not even require creating an account, though doing so allows you to connect Doodle with your calendar and save all of your polls. The person organizing a meeting can identify a range of potential times based on her own availability and then share a polling link with the group. Each member opens the link and indicates with a check mark whether or not they are available during that time. When everyone has indicated their availability, the organizer can tell at a glance which times will work for most people (see Figure 3.4).

Online calendaring tools such as Doodle can save the huge amount of time and energy previously spent on keeping track of emails sent by numerous people (or making many phone calls) to identify a common meeting time.

Visit Web Resource 3.4 for guidance on managing research projects and selecting communications technologies.

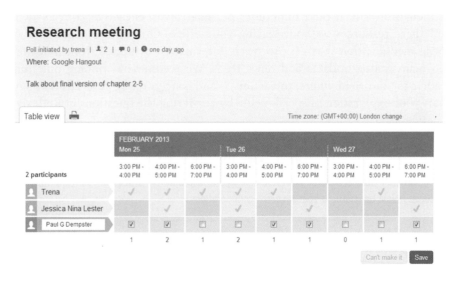

Figure 3.4 Doodle poll

Collaboration Spaces

There are an increasing number of group collaboration spaces available online, some of which are open source or free (e.g. Google communities, Wiggio, Zoho, Trello), and some of which are commercial, proprietary and/or more expensive (e.g. Microsoft Sharepoint, Moodle). Such spaces provide a variety of tools for communication (e.g. discussion forums, email systems and video conferencing) and project management (e.g. whiteboards, calendaring systems, to-do lists). Commercial tools may afford greater stability, security of information and customer support, but are likely to be more expensive and only available through institutional subscriptions. If your institution already subscribes to a digital work environment or course management system, such as Sharepoint or Moodle, it may be easiest to learn and use that particular system since you will be likely to use it regularly. However, you will want to see whether your institution will allow collaborators from outside your institution to access the system.

Open source or free spaces may be on the cutting edge, with new features added regularly to meet user demand. However, the free versions of these spaces may have limited functionality and/or little to no user support. Additional features and support may be available with fee-based 'premium' versions. Another constraint of the free tools is that these environments may eventually be bought out by a commercial interest or disappear over time. It is also important to know who owns and has access to the information and data stored there. For example, the University of York entered into extensive negotiations with Google about who owned data, where it would be stored and what security precautions would be in place before they migrated staff and students to the products.

Any digital meeting space is going to require somewhat of a learning curve, but if you are going to be collaborating on a long-term project it may be worth the investment. See Vignette 3.2 for a description of how Lisa McNeal used Moodle in her collaborative work with Emily Miller.

| Vignette 3.2 | Using Moodle as a Collaboration Space |

Lisa McNeal, Appalachian State University

After attending my first International Congress for Qualitative Inquiry, I began to see myself as a qualitative researcher and not just a part-time doctoral student. I made a crazy vow: to return as a presenter. I asked Emily Miller, another doctoral student, to write with me (see the Companion Website for Emily's take on their team process).

Emily and I used an autoethnographic approach for our work, and I proposed that we use Moodle (see Figure 3.5), our university's course management system, as our digital workspace because it was convenient, free of charge and familiar to both of us. The system was already integrated with our university accounts and passwords, so we knew that our work would be secure.

(Continued)

(Continued)

After creating our private Moodle course, I uploaded our key articles and created three discussion forums, one for each round of writing. During each round, we read a few articles, wrote a reflection, pasted it directly into a forum, and then responded to each other. The threaded nature of the forums allowed us to trace our online conversations and respond quickly. Overall, Moodle worked nicely as a repository for articles and links, and provided a home for our initial writing. However, we unearthed a few limitations.

After writing together for several months, we realized that we needed a more robust tool to weave our writing together. I copied our posts from the forums and pasted them into a Google document. Another limitation is that some universities limit access to students, faculty and staff; guest access may not be an option for collaborators outside your institution.

I recommend using a private Moodle course as an initial workspace for collaborative writing because it is an easy-to-use, cost-effective way to manage files and write back and forth. Knowing the project was in a secure, password-protected environment gave me peace of mind. Furthermore, I could access the project from anywhere, at any time, as long as I had an Internet connection. Moodle allowed me to focus my creative energy on writing rather than learning new software or frantically searching my computer or USB drive for the latest version of the paper.

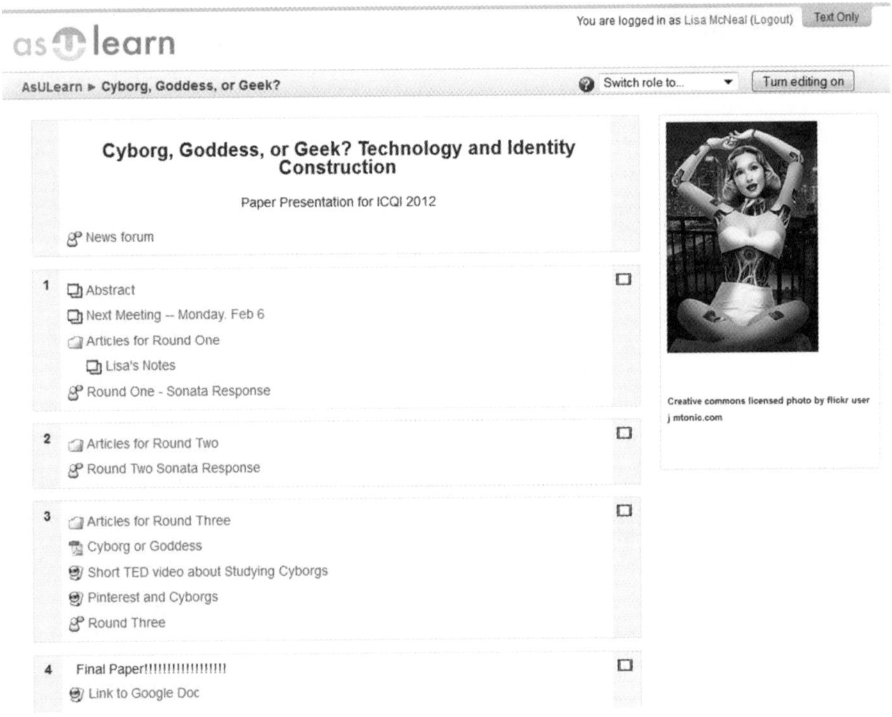

Figure 3.5 Moodle main page

Videoconferencing Tools

As we wrote this book, we relied heavily on the desktop videoconferencing tool Skype for synchronous meetings. For Google users, Hangouts are another option for meeting in real time. While the basic version of Skype is free, we paid to upgrade to the group version so that all three of us could participate in the calls. Even on days when we did not have calls scheduled, we often left Skype running in the background so that we could chat through its messenger feature when needed (see Figure 3.6). In this way, we recreated the informal daily *creative conversations* that colleagues who are in the same office can have. Skype also includes a status setting where users can indicate whether they are 'online', 'away', or ask that others 'do not disturb'. We used this as necessary to indicate our availability to chat. One constraint we encountered was that at times we had to turn off Skype's video feed and rely solely on the audio due to slow Internet connections.

Visit Web Resource 3.5 to learn about tools for recording Skype calls.

Figure 3.6 Skype screenshot

Desktop Sharing Applications

Desktop sharing applications allow collaborators to share what is on their computer screen and remotely control each other's computer. TeamViewer, which is free for non-commercial use, supports meetings with up to 25 people. The remote control feature is a great way for teams to demonstrate work or troubleshoot problems for each other. TeamViewer also includes text chat, a shared whiteboard and file sharing features. One of the challenges with the remote control feature, though, is figuring out who is controlling the computer at a given time. If both users are trying to do something at once it can interrupt the flow of the interaction. See Case Study 3.2 to consider how TeamViewer might be used to collaborate.

| CASE STUDY 3.2 | **TeamViewer to Support Learning and Writing** |

Maria and Nina conducted a discourse analysis of how Russian newspapers constructed the identities and educational possibilities of youth with disability labels. They wanted to have weekly data analysis sessions, but living 1,600 miles apart made face-to-face meetings impossible. They also wanted to use the qualitative data analysis package ATLAS.ti, something that Maria had never used previously. By using TeamViewer, Maria could give Nina remote control of her computer, allowing both of them to manipulate files stored on Maria's computer. Prior to beginning the analysis process, Nina taught Maria how to use ATLAS.ti via TeamViewer. With Maria's ATLAS.ti program open, and remote control granted to Nina, they were both able to talk through the useful features of ATLAS.ti. While Maria 'tested things out', Nina was there to support, intervene and/or model where appropriate. While TeamViewer supports video or audio chats, they found that the system became a bit slow when adding this additional feature. Instead, they used TeamViewer to share screens while simultaneously using Skype to chat.

Through a combination of tools (e.g. Doodle, Moodle, Skype, TeamViewer), your team can stay connected throughout your collaborative work together. Consider Reflexive Practice 3.3.

REFLEXIVE PRACTICE 3.3

Practise using one of the meeting tools introduced in this section with a colleague. What was the experience like? How might you use this tool in your research work?

Resource Sharing

While emails and attachments can be misplaced or lost, cloud computing technologies store resources in central locations for access by all team members. Dropbox is a free application that stores two gigabytes of data per user at no charge on a remote server (in the cloud). All of the files saved to the Dropbox folder are automatically synchronized across computing devices, as well as on the Dropbox website. Not only does this allow you to easily access all of your files from wherever you are, but it also allows you to share these files with others on your research team. Dropbox eliminates the need to rely on external hard

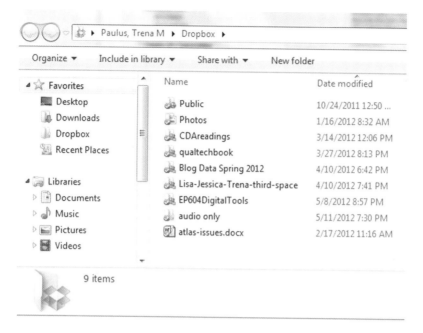

Figure 3.7 Dropbox folders

drives, flash drives or other devices to ensure that materials are backed up. In Figure 3.7, various Dropbox folders, being used to store work on a variety of projects, are displayed.

Dropbox shows up as an additional storage space on your computer (see the icon under Favorites in Figure 3.7) and the green checkmark in front of each file indicates that the documents have been synchronized across computers.

Visit Web Resource 3.6 for links to a number of cloud storage sites.

REFLEXIVE PRACTICE 3.4

Choose a cloud storage program and install it on your computer. Practise sharing files with a colleague or collaborator. What challenges did you encounter?

Google Sites is just one of a plethora of free Google products, many of which are useful for collaborative work, such as Google Docs, Hangouts and Communities. A Google Site is, in essence, a website that can be edited by any or all members of a group. Figure 3.8 shows one of the pages of the Google Site that we used while writing this book. The 'file cabinet' template allowed us to store and share web links, attachments and notes about our project as it was evolving. The name of the person posting the resource and when it was posted is also included on the page.

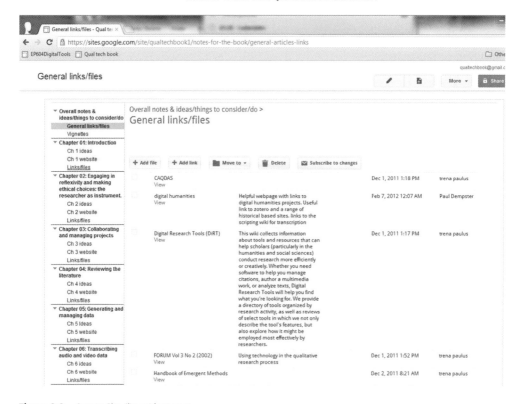

Figure 3.8 Google Site file cabinet page

Google Sites can be public, private or shared with select collaborators. Users can comment on what has been posted. A site can be configured so that an email is sent to members to let them know when something has been changed. While there are many benefits to storing resources in the cloud, there are constraints as well. One is the security risk of storing information on servers outside of your direct control. While the Dropbox website dedicates several pages to addressing security concerns, there is no way to guarantee complete privacy for information that is stored on someone else's server. Similar security concerns exist around the use of Google Sites. Depending on your country of residence, copyright laws may regulate where and how proprietary resources can be stored. Encryption software (introduced in Chapter 4) is one possibility for keeping your files secure.

Writing

In collaborative work, one team member may take primary responsibility for writing up the findings, or multiple members may be involved in the process. While a variety of tools are available to support collaborative writing, Noel and Robert (2004) reported that most co-authors rely on email and individual word processing programs rather than specialized groupware. They also noted that co-authors want the ability to visibly track changes. Birnholtz and Ibara (2012), however, noted that tracking changes may incite group conflict and so must be handled with care. Noel and Robert found that most participants used an asynchronous writing strategy, working individually and then integrating the work near the end of the process.

Our own experiences with collaborative writing have been similar. We relied on email, word processing and Dropbox. Other writers we know collaborate through wikis, websites that were created specifically to support collaborative writing. The main advantage of a wiki is that previous versions are available, and the changes that have been made are visible. Fitzgerald and Findlay (2011) described the four views of a wiki document: article view (the current version of the document), discussion view (where creators can engage in conversation around the document), edit view (where the page is changed by the creators) and history view (where the previous versions of the documents can be reviewed). Together, Fitzgerald and Findlay argued, these features make wikis well suited for engaging in knowledge creation as a group, as evidenced by Wikipedia, the world's most popular wiki.

Young and Perez (2011) described their use of a wiki in an international collaborative project and suggested that a 'wiki uploaded with multi-media data can become a site for researchers to engage in "serious play"' (p. 10). However, wiki programs can be difficult to learn and people may be reluctant to change each other's work directly, instead preferring to use tools such as Microsoft Word's commenting feature. Conversely, one member of the team may dominate the process or reject changes made by other members. ReStore recommends that teams have conversations early on in the process about how editing and revisions will take place. They note, too, that eventually the document must be exported from the wiki into a word processing or other product for final dissemination.

Visit Web Resource 3.7 for tips on using wikis for collaborative writing.

In Vignette 3.3, Debra Lee shares her experience of using a wiki for collaborative writing.

| **Vignette 3.3** | **Collaborative Wiki Use** |

Debra S. Lee, Vanderbilt University

Since 2008 I have used wikis to create courses and work on projects, such as grant proposals, collaboratively. Although I have tried other methods of collaboration, creating a wiki is still my first choice. For a multi-million dollar grant submission with multiple subcontractors, I created a wiki that was used by all participants to upload needed information, such as course

(Continued)

(Continued)

syllabi, budgets, résumés and project summaries. Instead of having to organize multiple emails from subcontractors and co-authors, all of the information was in one place that could be easily updated by all parties. The final project was copied and pasted into a Word document that was used for the final grant submission. As the wiki administrator, I could tell when pages had been updated and who needed to be contacted to provide more information just by checking the Users tab on the wiki. Additionally, as the grant submission deadline drew near, I changed my email notification status for updates, so that I received a new message each time the wiki was updated.

Wikis, of course, have both positive and negative sides. To use all aspects of a wiki, such as tracking changes with page history (see the image below), does require some training and it is helpful if one collaborator is familiar with HTML. However, for me, the ability to keep all of my documents in one location and make changes that are easily visible makes it worth the investment of time.

Comparing versions of Peer Editing with Wikis
Showing changes between November 22, 2011 at 8:48:15 pm (crossed out) and November 22, 2011 at 10:46:40 pm (underlined)

Have the students copy and paste their essay from a Word document to the wiki page (or if you are working with them in a computer lab, they can type their papers directly into the wiki).
Once the students have pasted their papers onto the wiki, their partners (assigned by you) can edit the page and make comments on the content and organization.
The original author will be able to review the changes and decide to accept them or not. The final product will belong to the original writer. Plus the editing changes made by the partners can also be reviewed and noted by the instructor.
Knowing what your peer editors are doing can help you train your students to be better peer editors.
Student Access to the Wiki
With the classroom edition of PBWorks, These pages tell you have two choices when setting up your wiki and inviting users.
You can use student emails and invite them more about using their email addresses. The students then have wikis for peer editing.
Click the links to find the invitation email, which sometimes goes into spam folders, and accept the invitation detailed descriptions of how to the workspace.
You can create set up student access to "invite only" wikis, set up a classroom accounts account for the students.
You begin by clicking the USERS tab on your wiki (see the image below).
Then you click the ADD USERS button course, and to add your students.
If you have your students email addresses, type them in find the box that opens when you click the "add users" button.
Type in the email addresses.
Select what type of access you want to give them (For students to be able to revert to prior versions of the wiki, you rubric we will have use to make them Editors. (Writer is peer edit the default choice. As a writer, you can compare versions, but not change back to an earlier version of the page.).
If you don't have their email addresses or don't want to use them, then click the CREATE ACCOUNTS FOR YOUR STUDENTS LINK. (More on sample student essays in this later.)
Remember course.
Student Access to click on the ADD USERS button on the box that opens (Finish – Add Users on the image in the Word document). Wikis
Setting up Classroom Accounts
Setting up Classroom Accounts may be easiest for you if you also see your students face-to-face. See the images below for what happens when you set up Classroom Accounts. It is really very easy to do:

Collaborative research and writing requires honest and open conversations around who will get authorship credit and how. Young and Perez (2011) noted that authorship attribution can become complicated – at what point in the idea-sharing process do contributors deserve official recognition as authors? See Figure 3.9 for two answers to this question.

The American Psychological Association states that: *Authorship credit should reflect the individual's contribution to the study. An author is considered anyone involved with initial research design, data collection and analysis, manuscript drafting, and final approval. However, the following do not necessarily qualify for authorship: providing funding or resources, mentorship, or contributing research but not helping with the publication itself. The primary author assumes responsibility for the publication, making sure that the data is accurate, that all deserving authors have been credited, that all authors have given their approval to the final draft, and handles responses to inquiries after the manuscript is published.*

ReStore's Authorship and Recognition of Contribution policy: *How many published outputs, how will they be authored, how authorship and contribution to the project, particularly of research assistants and more junior staff, should be recognised should be agreed early in the project. If this is not done, it can be embarrassing to discuss and problematic to agree which authors will be recognised, and for what percentage contribution, at a later stage.*

See the Companion Website for links to the full texts of each statement.

Figure 3.9   Guidelines for authorship

Consider your own experiences with collaborative writing by pondering the questions in Reflexive Practice 3.5.

—————————————— **REFLEXIVE PRACTICE 3.5** ——————————————

What experiences with collaborative writing have you had? What digital tools, if any, did you use to support the process? How did you determine authorship credit for the final product?

Final Thoughts

Collaboration is becoming more common in qualitative inquiry, not only among researchers, but also between researchers and participants, and researchers and the community. While there are both benefits and challenges to working with others, successful collaborations are those that have at their core a commitment to a *creative conversational* process. This process can be supported by digital tools that facilitate networking, meeting, resource sharing and collaborative writing. It is also important to consider ethical practices in sharing resources in the cloud and writing with others, ensuring that any proprietary information is protected and that everyone is given proper credit for their contributions.

Chapter Discussion Questions

1. What are some inherent risks in collaboration? How might digital tools play a role in aggravating or alleviating these risks?

2. What are some ways that you can engage in professional networking beyond attending conferences?

3. What kinds of meetings do you prefer? What is gained and lost as you move meetings from in person, to the telephone, to online platforms?

4. How can you ensure ethical practices in sharing resources and writing collaboratively with colleagues?

Suggestions for Further Reading

For a more in-depth look at how qualitative research can be conceptualized as a creative, conversational process, read Paulus, Woodside and Ziegler (2008). Fitzgerald and Findlay (2011) provide a fascinating look into how wikis and other online spaces can support collaborative research. Finally, the CIBER (2010) report provides useful insights into trends in the use of social media amongst researchers.

References

Anderson, T. and Kanuka, H. (2003) 'Collaborative E-Research', Chapter 6 in *E-Research: Methods, Strategies and Issues*. Boston, MA: Allyn & Bacon.

Barry, C.A., Britten, N., Barber, N., Bradley, C. and Stevenson, F. (1999) 'Using reflexivity to optimize teamwork in qualitative research'. *Qualitative Health Research*, 9(1), 26–44.

Birnholtz, J. and Ibara, S. (2012) 'Tracking changes in collaborative writing: Edits, visibility and group maintenance'. *Proceedings of the Computer-Supported Cooperative Work Conference* (CSCW 2012), 809–18.

boyd, d.m. and Ellison, N.B. (2007) 'Social network sites: Definition, history, and scholarship'. *Journal of Computer-Mediated Communication*, 13(1), Article 11. Available at: http://jcmc.indiana.edu/vol13/issue1/boyd.ellison.html (last accessed 16 July 2013).

Chenail, R. (2011) 'Qualitative researchers in the blogosphere: Using blogs as diaries and data'. *The Qualitative Report*, 16(1), 249–54.

CIBER, University College London (2010) *Social Media and Research Workflow*. London, UK: Emerald Group Publishing Ltd.

Fitzgerald, R. and Findlay, J. (2011) 'Collaborative Research Tools: Using Wikis and Team Learning Systems to Collectively Create New Knowledge', in S. Hesse-Biber (ed.) *The Handbook of Emergent Technologies in Social Research*. Oxford: Oxford University Press, pp. 300–19.

Kemmis, S. and McTaggert, R. (2005) 'Participatory Action Research', in N. Denzin and Y.S. Lincoln (eds), *The SAGE Handbook of Qualitative Research* (3rd edition), pp. 559–603. Thousand Oaks, CA: SAGE.

Lee, B.K. and Gregory, D. (2008) 'Not alone in the field: Distance collaboration via the Internet in a focused ethnography'. *International Journal of Qualitative Methods*, 7(3), 30–46.

Lovejoy, K. and Saxton, G.D. (2012) 'Information, community and action: How nonprofit organizations use social media'. *Journal of Computer-Mediated Communication*, 17, 337–53.

Noel, S. and Robert, J.M. (2004) 'Empirical study on collaborative writing: What do co-authors do, use and like?' *Computer Supported Cooperative Work*, 13, 63–89.

Oleson, V., Droes, N., Hatton, D., Chico, N. and Schatzman, L. (1994) 'Analyzing Together: Reflections of a Team Approach', in A. Bryman and R.G. Burgess (eds) *Analyzing Qualitative Data*. London, UK: Routledge.

Paulus, T., Woodside, M. and Ziegler, M. (2008) 'Extending the conversation: Qualitative research as dialogic, collaborative process'. *The Qualitative Report*, 13(2), 226–43.

Paulus, T., Woodside, M. and Ziegler, M. (2010) '"I tell you it's a journey, isn't it?" Understanding collaborative meaning making in qualitative research'. *Qualitative Inquiry*, 16(10), 852–62.

Young, S. and Perez, J. (2011) '"We-research": Adopting a wiki to support the processes of collaborative research among a team of international researchers'. *International Journal of Music Education*, Online First, 1–15.

FOUR
Reviewing the Literature

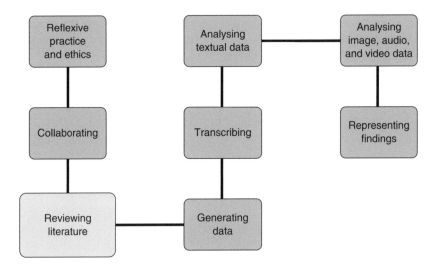

Companion website materials available here:

www.uk.sagepub.com/paulus

Learning Objectives

- Articulate the purpose of a literature review.
- Develop strategies for locating and evaluating relevant sources for the literature review.
- Select and critique appropriate digital tools for locating and retrieving, storing and organizing, reading and annotating, and analysing and synthesizing literature sources.
- Consider the pros and cons of 'going paperless' during the literature review process.
- Have strategies to ensure ethical practices in reviewing the literature.

Introduction

In Chapter 3, we discussed ways that digital tools are changing how we network, meet, share resources and write collaboratively. We described collaboration as *creative conversations* among members of a research team. In this chapter, we extend the conversational metaphor as we turn to the literature review, which can be viewed as engaging in the larger scholarly conversation of a field. We first discuss the purpose and the nature of the literature review in qualitative work. We then illustrate how the four main phases of the process can be supported by digital tools: 1) to locate and retrieve; 2) to store and organize; 3) to read and annotate; and 4) to analyse, synthesize and critique literature sources.

Literature Review as Joining the Conversation

When we have problems to be solved or questions to be answered in our daily lives, we have a variety of places to turn, such as friends, libraries or the Internet. In our professional lives, ideas for research often emerge from problems that arise in our practice as health-care workers, educators, or in other areas of the social sciences. There, too, we have resources to turn to – colleagues, professional journals and, increasingly, the Internet. Before we conclude that a research study is needed to solve a problem or answer a question, it makes sense to be sure that solutions and answers haven't already been identified by others. Reviewing the literature is in part a search for any existing answers and solutions. Having a thorough understanding of what a field knows or does not know around a particular topic is essential to be able to fully justify the need for additional research.

Reviewing the literature is the process of becoming and remaining familiar with what others have done before us to make sense of the world – be it through generating theories, synthesizing the findings of others or conducting original research. Because the nature of qualitative inquiry is often emergent (starting with a context of interest rather than with a predetermined hypothesis) there is flexibility in the direction a study could take. Thus, the literature is used in ways that may differ from quantitative work. Still, it is important to demonstrate that you have taken the time to understand previous work and to situate your ideas in a discipline's larger context – to identify the conversation that you intend to join through your work.

Research is, in essence, participation in an ongoing conversation amongst a community of scholars, and the only way to become part of that conversation is by immersing yourself in what has been said before. In most qualitative work the literature review provides the overall conceptual framework for the study, defines key terms and situates the study both methodologically and epistemologically. When the literature review is conducted and where it appears in the research report can vary. While some traditions, such as grounded theory (Glaser, 1978; Strauss and Corbin, 1998), suggest waiting until after initial data analysis so as not to be unduly influenced by previous work, most researchers acknowledge that the literature should be reviewed early and often. Realistically, thesis committees, funding organizations and research councils will look to a literature review for justification that the proposed work will make a worthwhile contribution. Reviewing the literature can help guide you in the design of your study as well as the analysis and interpretation of your data (Anfara and Mertz, 2006). Thus, the literature review may appear in the introduction, in a separate literature review section and/or in the discussion of the findings.

Visit Web Resource 4.1 for examples of published literature reviews.

Figure 4.1 is an excerpt from a literature review summary that establishes the need for a study on engaging faculty in reflective practices through online professional development.

Dr Ron Bridges, Pellissippi State Technical Community College

In summary, this section of the literature review has demonstrated that faculty do engage in reflection as part of their teaching (McAlpine & Weston, 2000) and that faculty members engage in different levels of reflection that can potentially lead to transformative learning (Kreber, 2005b; Kreber & Castleden, 2009). It is also clear that levels of reflection can be identified and distinguished within written work (Kember et al., 1999; 2008) and within the online environment (Boyer et al., 2006; Lord & Lomicka, 2007; Whipp, 2003). What remains to be studied is whether Mezirow's (1991) levels of reflection as delineated by Kreber and Cranton (2000) and Kember et al. (1999) can be identified and distinguished within online reflective postings of college professors within a collaborative inquiry professional development experience.

Figure 4.1   Excerpt of a literature review summary

Literature Review as a Critical and Creative Process

Literature reviews demonstrate your ability to critique and synthesize the previous research in such a way that a new perspective is gained (Boote and Beile, 2005). Rather than a simple summary, a literature review should, through critical analysis, articulate a new interpretation of previous work to be shared with the research community. Contrary to how the literature review is often understood, it is a *creative* process 'in which the knower is an active participant constructing an interpretation of the community and its discourse' (Montuori, 2005, p. 375). It is a *construction*, through critical analysis, rather than a mere *reproduction*, through summary, of what has been said before.

Developing the ability to be selective about the sources that you review is critical in this information age. Like qualitative inquiry as a whole, reviewing the literature is an interpretive process, without one 'right' answer. As Charmaz (2006) pointed out, 'Although scholars may don a cloak of objectivity, research and writing are inherently ideological activities. The literature review and theoretical frameworks are ideological sites in which you claim, locate, evaluate, and defend your position' (p. 163). Thus, it is important to consciously reflect on the process. See Reflexive Practice 4.1.

Literature reviews can have a variety of functions, to:

- distinguish what has been done from what needs to be done
- synthesize and gain a new perspective
- identify relationships between ideas and practice
- establish the context of a topic or problem
- identify the main methodologies that have been used (Hart, 1998, p. 27)

For what reasons and at what point during your study will you review the research literature?

Literature reviews should be considered 'situated, partial, perspectival' rather than comprehensive (Lather, 1999, p. 3). Thus, locating yourself in the review will be important. By continuing to engage in reflexive practice you can take responsibility for the critique you are making of the work you review.

Evaluating Source Quality

Locating relevant literature involves amassing articles and books from a variety of sources that can provide a meaningful contribution to the story you will be telling about the 'state of the topic'. These sources (especially those that are online) must be screened for practical value and methodological quality (Fink, 2010). Major and Savin-Baden (2010) recommended establishing inclusion and exclusion criteria for sources, such as including only studies published after a particular date, with a particular population or using a particular methodology.

First and foremost, sources need to be reputable (e.g. peer-reviewed journals or books from high-quality publishers), recent (unless they represent seminal thinking in the field) and accurate, that is, not highly biased or flawed in their research design. Internet sources must be screened even more carefully, as there is no inherent quality control over materials published online. Fink (2010) recommended noting who funds the online site, who stands to profit from it and the qualifications of the authors.

Cultivating a reference list that presents a variety of positions on the topic is essential so as not to present a distorted view of the state of the field. Along the same lines, relevant sources will not only be found inside your own discipline, but also in related disciplines. Often, several disciplines are working on related problems, so analysing and critiquing those intersections can be valuable to your field.

Visit Web Resource 4.2 to learn about Rachael Gabriel's and Carlos Anguiano's use of a free online tool, Survey Monkey, to do an initial screening of the literature.

Digital Tools to Support the Literature Review Process

Digital tools can assist you in four phases of the literature review process: 1) locating and retrieving; 2) storing and organizing; 3) reading and annotating; and 4) analysing and synthesizing literature sources.

Locating and Retrieving Sources

The types of literature that you may need to review will vary by topic and field, and should be agreed upon in conjunction with those familiar with your topic area. The timeliness and authoritativeness of your sources will factor into how thorough and useful your final literature review will be. Figure 4.2 provides an overview of resource types organized by recency, authority and the type of information that can be found in each.

Recency:	Years	Months	Weeks	Days	Current
Authority:	More authority				Less authority
Resource Type	Books, monographs and reference works	Conference presentations and proceedings, journals and periodicals	Popular and trade magazines	Newspapers	Websites and blogs
Content Type	Theoretical foundations, definitions, research, key concepts and constructs	Recent research, theoretical discussion and debate	Current issues, debates, applications, practices and field problems	Current issues, debates and field problems	Up-to-date issues, debates, practices and applications

Figure 4.2 Types of literature sources (adapted from Machi and McEvoy, 2009, p. 40)

While books and journals are often considered the most authoritative sources, there is often a long delay between when the work was done and when it is published – in part because the quality of the information is being vetted by experts in the field. Websites, on the other hand, can make information available instantly, but often the information has not yet been checked for accuracy by anyone other than the creator of the site.

Visit Web Resource 4.3 for a tutorial on the Journal Citation Index.

Once you have identified the types of publication you are looking for, you can conduct keyword searches in academic databases such as those outlined in Table 4.1.

Subject librarians should be consulted early on and often throughout your review process, particularly in terms of identifying relevant databases and accurate keyword or thesaurus search terms. They can assist you in locating hard-to-find materials through services such as interlibrary loan.

Table 4.1 Examples of databases by discipline (adapted from Phelps, Fisher and Ellis, 2007)

Discipline	Database
Natural sciences	ScienceResearch, Wiley Interscience, Web of Science
Engineering	Engineering and Applied Science Online, Web of Science
Health Sciences	PubMed, Medline
Education	ERIC, Education Full Text, Psych Info
Business and Management	LexisNexis International, Business Source Premier
Social sciences and Humanities	Academic Search Premier, JSTOR, ASSIA
Law	Lawbook Online, LexisNexis, WestLaw
Arts	Art Abstracts, Art Index
General coverage	Proquest, Ingenta Connect, Academic Search Premier

REFLEXIVE PRACTICE 4.2

Select a database in your field and do some initial searching on your research topic. What search strategies did you use? Did it turn up the types of articles that you expected?

Searching for literature should be embraced as an ongoing process throughout the course of your study (and your career as a researcher), rather than viewed as an activity to be completed once. Beyond keyword searching, there are additional strategies you can use to keep up with the literature. One strategy is what Banudra, Miskon and Fielt (2011) called 'backward' and 'forward' searching. Backward searching entails reviewing the references page of a useful article to identify important articles. Forward searching entails using a tool like Google Scholar to identify more recently published work that cites the article you have found useful. Databases such as Thomson Reuters Social Science Citations Index show who cites particular papers, allowing you to trace publication trajectories over the years.

Visit Web Resource 4.4 for a link to the Social Science Citation Index.

Another strategy is, with your mentor's help or through a citation index, to identify the top peer-reviewed journals in your field and review the tables of contents over a particular period of time (e.g. the past five years) to identify relevant articles that may have been missed in initial searches. This can provide a more holistic sense of the conversations underway in various journals, leading to ideas for where to publish your work. Table of contents alerts directly email you when a new journal issue is released. Similar alerts can be created in Google Scholar – see Reflexive Practice 4.3.

──────────────────────────── **REFLEXIVE PRACTICE 4.3** ────────────────────────────

Set up a Google or a journal search alert specific to your research study. Write an entry in your reflexivity journal about your experience setting it up.

If you have set up your Google Scholar Profile as described in Chapter 3, new recommendations related to your citations will automatically be displayed, as illustrated in Figure 4.3.

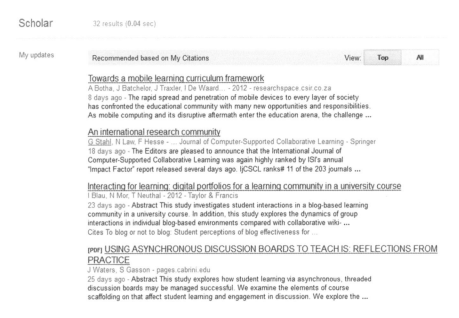

Figure 4.3   Example of 'My updates' provided by Google Scholar

In addition to following specific journals and setting up search alerts, you may want to directly follow the top scholars in your field, through citation indexes or by 'following' scholars through a social networking site like Academia.edu or Google Scholar (described in Chapter 3). Mendeley (described later in this chapter) can also be useful for this purpose. Keep in mind that you can conduct searches and create search alerts not only by topic area but also by author name.

Another potential source of relevant literature is known as 'grey literature'. Grey literature includes conference proceedings and reports produced by government agencies, research institutes or other organizations that are disseminated outside of traditional publication outlets, usually for a professional audience.

Visit Web Resource 4.5 for links to several databases of grey literature.

Now that more of the grey literature is being made available online, effective Internet searches are particularly important. Delicious, a free social bookmarking

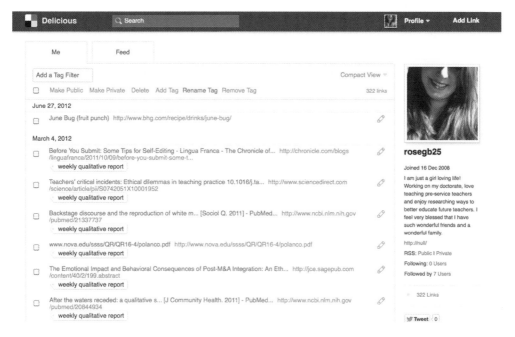

Figure 4.4   Main view of the Delicious website

site, can help you manage and organize the grey literature and other Internet resources. Figure 4.4 shows the main page of a Delicious account, with the links that have been saved listed in reverse chronological order. Clicking on the link takes you to the online resource.

Tags can be created for links to help organize them by topic, and the tags can be sorted alphabetically or by frequency of use. Clicking on one of the tags brings up all of the links for only that tag. In this way, Delicious can help you organize online resources (such as grey literature) in a way that is easy to retrieve for your review.

REFLEXIVE PRACTICE 4.4

Set up a Delicious site and explore the various features. How might you use Delicious for your literature review?

It is becoming increasingly important to include a description of your search process, as many choices and interpretations are made along the way. For example, including the keywords, databases and journals that you searched makes your process more transparent. Figure 4.5 is an example of such a description that was submitted as part of a thesis proposal.

Visit Web Resource 4.6 for a link to Readability, a free application that will strip extraneous content from a web page (e.g. advertisements) and download it for offline reading.

Anton Reece, University of Tennessee

My search strategy for this literature review on the relationship between faculty-student engagement and first year student retention was comprised of five phases, including conducting searches in Educational Resources Information Center (ERIC), Google Scholar, and Educational Full Text databases using the following keywords: *first year studies, first year seminars, dropout, retention, persistence, freshmen, attrition, first generation, faculty-student engagement, collaborative learning, student to student interaction,* and *college teaching.* I identified relevant studies in peer-reviewed journals and reviewed the seminal works on faculty-student engagement, teaching excellence, first-year courses, and first-year student retention. Phase one of my search strategy was to review first-year student dropout (Elkins et al., 2000; Freeman et al., 2007) and first-year courses (Barefoot, 2004; Gardner, 1986; Pascarella & Terenzini, 2005). In phase two, I focused on teaching and learning excellence (Bain, 2004; Barkley, 2010; Bruffee, 1999; Chickering & Gamson, 1987). In phase three, I explored in detail faculty-student engagement theories and studies that included contemporary scholars (Berger & Braxton, 1998; Chickering & Gamson, 1987; Kuh, 2003). In phase four, I concentrated on studies that supported and utilized related research on student dropout (Bean, 1985; Durkheim, 1951; Pascarella & Terinzini, 1983; Spady, 1970; Tinto, 1975) and studies that identified limitations of the seminal works (Tierney, 1992). In phase five, I reviewed and explored additional articles on faculty-student engagement in peer-reviewed journals on retention including the *Journal of Higher Education, New Directions for Higher Education, Research in Higher Education, About Campus, Journal of Experiential Education, Research of Higher Education, Journal of Higher Education, Journal of College Student Personnel, Journal of College Student Development,* and national resources such as the National Association of Student Personnel, National First-Year Experience Center, National Student Survey of Engagement, and National Center of Education Statistics. These various resources described the three leading best practices programs focused on retention: first-year studies, supplemental instruction, and learning communities (Barefoot, 2004; Gardner, 1986; Noel & Levitz, 2009).

Figure 4.5   Example of search strategy description from Anton Reece's thesis proposal

Visit Web Resource 4.7 for a link to Diigo, another social bookmarking site that lets you highlight, annotate and insert comments on the web content as you read.

Storing and Organizing Sources

It is likely that many of your resources will have been obtained in a digital format, such as PDF copies of journal articles accessed from an online database. Documents that have been scanned or created as images will need to be converted using optical character recognition (OCR) so that they are searchable and recognizable as text. For example, if you photocopy and digitize or scan a book chapter, it may not initially be recognizable as text. You can use a program such as Adobe Acrobat Professional, Abbyy FineReader or OmniPage Professional to convert documents to a searchable text format.

Once you have located your sources, always keep copies of your personal library system in multiple places in case of a hard drive failure or other technological catastrophe that may result in loss of data. For example, back up your files on a shared server, external hard drive, jump drive or perhaps in the cloud. Consider adopting a naming convention for your electronic documents – such as author last name and publication date (e.g. Edwards-2007). This allows you to sort your documents in alphabetical order and more easily track references.

Storing a copy of your literature sources in a cloud storage system such as Dropbox (described in Chapter 3) will allow you to integrate your sources with a citation management system, such as Mendeley, and e-reader annotation systems, such as GoodReader. Instead of lugging around paper copies, you can access your articles from computing devices at home, at the office or on a plane. Google Drive, launched in early 2012, is another option for a cloud-based storage system that can be synchronized with your other Google accounts. More secure options may be to encrypt your files or set up your own server, as described in Case Study 4.1.

CASE STUDY 4.1

Devlin backs up his files using the FreeFileSync synchronization tool which checks whether a file has been updated since the last save. He keeps an encrypted copy of the files (using Truecrypt) on his home server created by Polkast. Copies of really important files are kept on an external drive at work and a further set of DVDs are periodically updated at a third secure location.

Visit Web Resource 4.8 for links to several encryption software programs.

Citation management systems, such as Endnote, RefWorks and Zotero, can be used as comprehensive electronic document management systems. Most can be used to search academic databases and download relevant articles directly into the program, along with the metadata to assist with generating bibliographies and in-text citations. These systems can help you more efficiently store, organize and manage your literature. In a review of four citation management systems, Mendeley was described as 'the next generation of citation management software' (Hensley, 2011, p. 207). A relative newcomer on the scene, launched in 2008, Mendeley is a free program that includes features such as PDF annotation, teamwork support, social networking and synchronized access to your library across mobile devices. Similar to Academia.edu (discussed in Chapter 3), Mendeley members have profile pages as well as a 'contacts' feature for connecting with others.

Mendeley serves as its own cloud storage device and is accessible on the web, mobile devices and desktop computers. Increased storage space is provided with the fee-based version of Mendeley. Figure 4.6 illustrates the Mendeley desktop library interface, with folders and groups listed on the left, documents in the middle and metadata on the right.

References can be organized through folders, subfolders, tags and keywords. Tags and keywords allow organization across themes or areas of interest within multiple folders. One helpful feature of Mendeley is the 'watched folder'. Once you set up a watched folder on your computer, any article that you add to this folder will automatically be imported into Mendeley. Mendeley supports group resource sharing, and all members of the group can view the annotations made on the documents. Annotated files can then be exported, downloaded, printed and/or shared with others on the research team (see Figure 4.7).

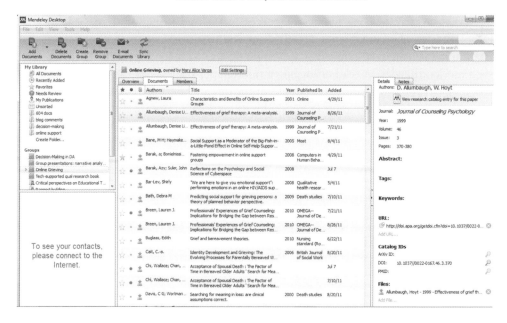

Figure 4.6   Mendeley library

The ability to automatically generate the reference list is often the citation management system feature that is initially appealing to researchers. It promises an alternative to the tedious task of formatting the reference information according to your discipline's citation style (e.g. APA, MLA, Chicago, etc.). However, the automatic formatting feature can require considerable time and effort 'tweaking' the system before the metadata is properly extracted and accurately formatted.

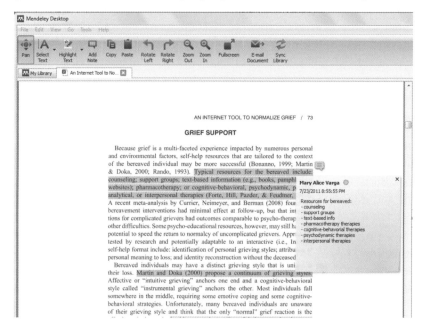

Figure 4.7   Mendeley's document annotation features

Visit Web Resource 4.9 to read about Jennifer Lubke's metadata extraction comparison.

Factors besides the reference generator should be considered when choosing a citation management system. These include cost, storage capacity, mobile access, social networking, collaboration support, annotation features and, of course, accuracy of metadata extraction. Take a look at Reflexive Practice 4.5.

─────────────── **REFLEXIVE PRACTICE 4.5** ───────────────

Citation management systems are changing rapidly, with features converging and new features being added. Do some investigating into two or more of the following programs: Endnote, RefWorks, Zotero, and Mendeley.

Find out how they compare on these key features:

- Price
- Storage capacity, location and associated costs
- Synchronization across mobile computing devices
- Social networking features
- Collaboration/team support
- Annotation/highlighting in PDFs
- Ability to customize settings to improve citation format
- Ability to print out annotations or extract them to other software.

Now, take a moment to explore Reflexive Practice 4.6.

─────────────── **REFLEXIVE PRACTICE 4.6** ───────────────

Download one of the citation management systems and explore its features in relation to your own literature review process. Make an entry in your journal about your experiences.

Visit Web Resource 4.10 for Lisa Yamagata-Lynch's description of Zotero, another citation management system.

Reading and Annotating Sources

It is often during the reading and annotation phase of the process that the question of whether to read and take notes on paper or on screen becomes particularly relevant. Advances in mobile technologies are encouraging more academics to 'go paperless' in their academic work. While reading on paper is more familiar, easier on the eyes and doesn't rely on battery or computer power, going paperless can be a more efficient way to do your academic work. Electronic articles and books are more portable and searchable, and afford the ability to copy and paste text elsewhere. Those with long commutes may find it helpful to be able to listen to their academic books and articles and speak their notes into a handheld recording device. The 'read out loud' command in Acrobat Reader does just that: turns a PDF into an audio file by reading it out loud.

Yet even researchers who have digital sources and electronic storage systems may end up printing out hard copies – either for safe keeping (in case of computer failure) and/or to be able to read and annotate the articles by hand. Often, the more important the document, the more likely it is to be printed out (Hillesund, 2011). Reading, annotating and writing are at the heart of our work as researchers, and changing these processes is akin to changing the essence of how we think. The desire to be comfortable, to curl up with an article or book, and to be able to mark up the text by hand is, not surprisingly, very important to academic readers (Rose, 2011).

Visit Web Resource 4.11 to read articles comparing onscreen and on-paper reading.

However, a variety of new tools is beginning to make going paperless for academic reading more feasible. Mobile computing devices such as tablet computers (e.g. iPads) and smartphones are more portable, lightweight and support new applications which are better suited to embodied habits of reading. Still, even mobile computing devices are limited in their ability to recreate the experience of having many articles open at once on your desk, enabling you to flip back and forth to compare passages. It can be difficult to overcome the 'screenness' that comes with reading on an electronic device (Rose, 2011). However, strategies like using multiple screens (e.g. dual monitors) can make the process more comfortable. One of the simplest ways to experiment with reading onscreen is by using the free software Adobe Reader X, which offers basic highlighting and annotation features. For a more robust tool, there are an increasing number of e-reader applications designed specifically for tablet computers, such as GoodReader (see Figure 4.8). Multiple articles can be open at once and a variety of annotation tools are available (highlighting, arrows, free-hand writing, etc.). Documents can also be zoomed in and out for easier reading.

In Vignette 4.1, Ginny Britt shares her journey to becoming entirely paperless in her academic work through the use of a tablet computer and the GoodReader application.

| Vignette 4.1 | The Paperless Literature Review |

Ginny Britt, University of Tennessee

In my early years as a graduate student, I found myself spending time each week downloading articles, printing them out, taking notes and highlighting in preparation for class. With the introduction of mobile devices, such as smartphones and tablets, I knew that there had to be a way to eliminate my need for printing and amassing piles of paper. After acquiring an iPad, I decided to test out the e-reader program GoodReader and create my own 'paperless literature review' process.

The 'paperless literature review' process started by locating articles through keyword searches of academic databases, after which I would download a PDF of the relevant article and store it in a Dropbox folder. I designated this folder as a 'watched folder' so that any time I added a new article it was automatically entered into Mendeley. I also synchronized the Dropbox folder with GoodReader so that I could access and read, highlight and take notes on the articles. I could then return the annotated articles to Dropbox where they could be accessed from my laptop and imported into ATLAS.ti for analysis.

The GoodReader application is easy to use and synchronizes well with other programs. Some of its weaknesses, however, include the inability to annotate Microsoft Word Documents or PDFs that have not been converted to text with an OCR converter.

One potential disadvantage of shifting to onscreen reading and annotation is the flip side of an advantage – the ease with which you can copy and paste text from original sources. This could lead to unintentional plagiarism. To avoid this, it's

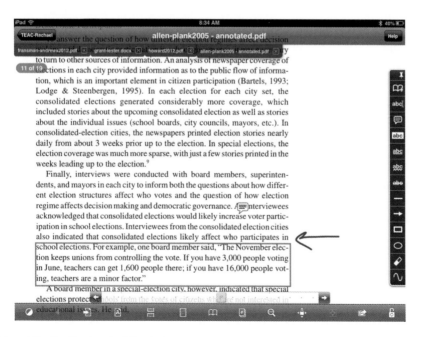

Figure 4.8 GoodReader annotation tools

even more important to include the author, year and page number citations alongside any direct quotes that you copy out of a source. Take time to consider the questions posed in Reflexive Practices 4.7 and 4.8.

============================ REFLEXIVE PRACTICE 4.7 ============================

Plagiarism can happen unintentionally. What are some of the ways that you can check to make sure you avoid plagiarizing within your literature review and broader research study? How might being transparent about how you conducted your literature review help you avoid plagiarism?

============================ REFLEXIVE PRACTICE 4.8 ============================

Select an annotation program (e.g. GoodReader, Adobe Acrobat or Mendeley) and annotate a document specific to your research study. Make an entry in your reflexivity journal chronicling your experiences.

Analysing and Synthesizing Sources

Beyond reading and annotating, a literature review requires being engaged in analysing, critiquing and ultimately synthesizing the sources to tell the story about your topic. Finding a way to systematically, rigorously, transparently and even collaboratively analyse and critique the literature can be challenging. The purpose of your literature review will inform how you approach analysing your sources, and there are several excellent resources that can guide you in this process (Fink, 2010; Hart, 1998; Machi and McEvoy, 2009; Major and Savin-Baden, 2010). We provide here some general guidance on how you might approach the analysis process with the support of digital tools.

Onwuegbuzie, Leech and Collins (2012) pointed out that in many ways an analysis of literature is similar to the analysis of qualitative data, so techniques such as constant comparative analysis, domain analysis or theme analysis could be used. Computer-assisted qualitative data analysis software (CAQDAS, described in more detail in Chapter 7) can be used to systematize the literature review process, much as they do the data analysis process. Learning a CAQDAS program during the literature review process can even give you a head start on being ready to use it later for data analysis.

The code and retrieve feature of CAQDAS tools can make the literature review process more efficient. In Vignette 4.2, Joshua Johnston describes his use of ATLAS.ti during the literature review process.

| Vignette 4.2 | Using ATLAS.ti for Literature Reviews |

Joshua Johnston, University of Tennessee

I have found ATLAS.ti to be a helpful tool for reviewing the literature around teacher identity as part of my dissertation work. While using software does not necessarily speed up the process, it does add a sense of order that can help as you move into the actual writing.

For any non-electronic literature sources, I typed up notes as a new text document in ATLAS.ti., and I imported electronic copies of articles that I already had as PDF or .doc files. I named each of these 'primary documents' (as ATLAS.ti calls them) using an author-and-publication-year convention (e.g. Richards and Curtis 1972) so that I could sort the sources alphabetically within ATLAS.ti.

I began my review by coding the bibliographic information at the top of each primary document by document name. Because all my notes include citations to the major studies and theorists cited in the source, these codes created a network of influences. In other words, not only do I have quick access to 'Richards and Curtis 1972' within ATLAS.ti, but I can also connect that source with all the other sources that cited it. Attaching a memo to this code with a brief description of the source and its major claims allowed me to refresh my memory any time I encountered a connection between sources. I also used document families to organize the sources by type of article (e.g. empirical study, concept piece, practitioner article), type of study (e.g. experimental design, discourse analysis, survey) and theories (e.g. communities of practice, cooperative learning, narrative identity). This allowed me to, for example, search for relationships between claims made in the studies and the type of studies they were.

I then broadly coded each source for what it claimed about teacher identity. I initially used descriptive codes to capture ideas with subtle distinctions. It is much easier to combine codes later if two codes are approximately equal than it is to separate a category that was too general to begin with. In this way I created nearly 80 unique codes following the format 'identity as X' (e.g. situated, contextual, social). Only after coding all of the sources did I merge these codes.

Once all the coding was completed, I could easily see which codes were most salient by sorting these codes by the ones that I had used most frequently. I then began with the code I used most often, retrieved all of the text I had coded in that way and began constructing my arguments about what the literature says about teacher identity.

Figure 4.9 is taken from our own literature review that we did using ATLAS.ti in preparation for writing Chapter 8 of this book. It illustrates some highlighted text from an article (called a 'quotation') that has been coded as 'advantages and limitations of visual methods'. The smaller box on the right shows the eight quotations that have been coded this way. By clicking on each, the quotation is pulled up in the context of the larger document for further analysis.

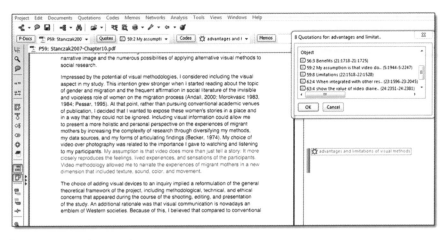

Figure 4.9 Codes in ATLAS.ti

Figure 4.10, again from our literature review for Chapter 8, shows the memoing feature that can be used for annotating literature. The memo makes note of a common theme across the literature, in this case about the advantages and limitations of visual methods, that should be considered in subsequent analysis. These memos can be directly linked to the quotations in the text for easy retrieval and review.

In addition to coding the literature during the review for themes or categories, you may also want to analyse the arguments present in or across the literature. Here, using *mapping techniques* can help you identify claims, evidence and warrants made in the arguments. There are a variety of mapping techniques to assist with this process, such as feature maps, tree constructions and concept maps (see Hart, 1998; Machi and McEvoy, 2009 for details on mapping types). ATLAS.ti can support mapping through its 'networks' feature. In Figure 4.11, all of the codes used in the initial review of the literature for Chapter 8 have been imported into a 'network view' to provide a graphical display. By visualizing the codes in this way, we could rearrange the images and draw connections between them as we worked to make sense of the overall structure of the arguments we were making about the use of audio and visual data.

Other CAQDAS packages offer similar features and you may find them just as helpful for the literature review.

Figure 4.10 Memoing feature of ATLAS.ti for literature reviews

Visit Web Resource 4.12 for articles and a webinar on using NVivo for literature reviews and how it integrates with the citation manager Endnote.

Final Thoughts

While literature reviews are an iterative and ongoing part of your research work, be careful not to get stuck in the reading phase. The only way to fully interpret what you are reading is by writing. You must not only read, but also critique and analyse through the writing process – telling the story of what is known about your research topic, what is not yet known, and how you plan to engage in the academic conversation around your topic. Understanding your audience and the expected format of your literature review is important – the final length may vary from a few references in a conference presentation to an entire chapter in your dissertation, grant application or final report. Remember, too, to ensure ethical practices by avoiding unintentional plagiarism when working with digital sources and to store sources in a secure location.

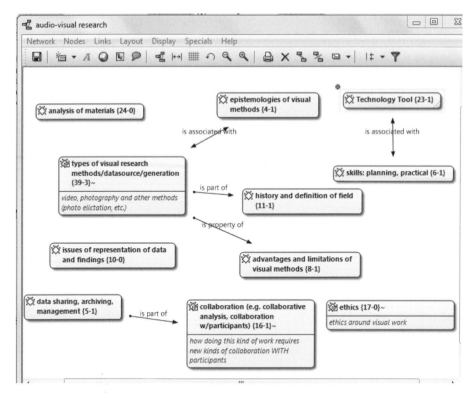

Figure 4.11   Network view in ATLAS.ti

Chapter Discussion Questions

1. What will be the purpose and goals of your literature review?
2. What are some strategies you can use for locating and evaluating relevant sources of literature for your review?
3. How could using digital tools promote a more systematic, transparent and collaborative literature review process?
4. What are some of the pros and cons of 'going paperless' in your academic reading endeavours?
5. How can you ensure ethical practices as you review the literature for your research study?

Suggestions for Further Reading

For an excellent overview of how to critique the quality of literature reviews, see Boote and Beile (2005). Hart (1998) provides thorough guidance on how to analyse arguments in published work, as well as a comprehensive treatment of how to conduct literature reviews at the graduate level. O'Dochartaigh (2012) is packed full of search strategies for identifying relevant resources, and Phelps, Fisher and Ellis (2007) provides many useful organizational tips for managing the overall research process, with several chapters dedicated specifically to the literature review process.

References

Anfara, V. and Mertz, N. (2006) *Theoretical Frameworks in Qualitative Research.* Thousand Oaks, CA: SAGE.

Banudra, W., Miskon, S. and Fielt, E. (2011) 'A Systematic, Tool-Supported Method for Conducting Literature Reviews in Information Systems', in V. Tuunainen, J. Nandhakumar, M. Rossi and W. Soliman (eds) *Proceedings of the 19th European Conference on Information Systems* (ECIS 2011), Helsinki, Finland.

Boote, D.N. and Beile, P. (2005) 'Scholars before researchers: On the centrality of the dissertation literature review in research preparation'. *Educational Researcher*, 34(6), 3–15.

Charmaz, K. (2006) *Constructing Grounded Theory: A Practical Guide Through Qualitative Analysis.* Thousand Oaks, CA: SAGE.

Fink, A. (2010) *Conducting Research Literature Reviews: From the Internet to Paper.* Thousand Oaks, CA: SAGE.

Glaser, B.G. (1978) *Theoretical Sensitivity.* Mill Valley, CA: The Sociology Press.

Hart, C. (1998) *Doing a Literature Review: Releasing the Social Science Research Imagination.* London: SAGE.

Hensley, M.K. (2011) 'Citation management software: Features and futures'. *Reference & User Services Quarterly*, 50(3), 204–8.

Hillesund, T. (2011) 'Digital Humanities: Why Worry about Reading?' in K. Grandin (ed.) *Going Digital: Evolutionary and Revolutionary Aspects of Digitization*, Nobel Symposium 147. Stockholm, Sweden: The Nobel Foundation, pp. 128–60.

Lather, P. (1999) 'To be of use: The work of reviewing'. *Review of Educational Research*, 69(1), 2–7.

Machi, L.A. and McEvoy, B.T. (2009) *The Literature Review: Six Steps to Success.* Thousand Oaks, CA: Corwin Press.

Major, C.H. and Savin-Baden, M. (2010) *An Introduction to Qualitative Research Synthesis: Managing the Information Explosion in Social Science Research.* New York, NY: Routledge.

Montuori, A. (2005) 'Literature review as creative inquiry: Reframing scholarship as a creative process'. *Journal of Transformative Education*, 3(4), 374–93.

O'Dochartaigh, N. (2012) *Internet Research Skills* (3rd edition). London, UK: SAGE.

Onwuegbuzie, A.J., Leech, N.L. and Collins, K.M. (2012) 'Qualitative analysis techniques for the review of the literature'. *The Qualitative Report*, 17(56), 1–28.

Phelps, R., Fisher, K. and Ellis, A. (2007) *Organizing and Managing your Research: A Practical Guide for Postgraduates.* London, UK: SAGE.

Rose, E. (2011) 'The phenomenology of on-screen reading: University students' lived experience of digitized text'. *British Journal of Educational Technology*, 42(3), 515–26.

Strauss, A. and Corbin, J. (1998) *Basics of Qualitative Research: Grounded Theory Procedures and Inquiry*. Newbury Park, CA: SAGE.

FIVE
Generating Data

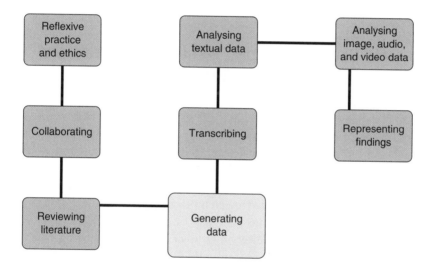

Companion website materials available here:

www.uk.sagepub.com/paulus

Learning Objectives

- Articulate the differences between naturally occurring and researcher-generated data.
- Select and critique appropriate digital tools for generating field notes, recording conversations or interview data, exploring online communities and archives, and generating images.
- Have strategies to ensure ethical practices in generating data.

Introduction

In Chapter 4, we considered the ways in which reviewing the literature can be supported with a variety of digital tools. In this chapter, we consider some of the digital tools that have shifted what can be considered qualitative data and the tools that support generating that data. With the emergence of the Internet and other types of computer-mediated communication, new sites of study and ways of engaging with participants have emerged (Hine, 2008). Further, various digital tools now afford new possibilities for gathering a variety of data types across great distances (Gratton and O'Donnell, 2011). We begin this chapter by differentiating between naturally occurring and researcher-generated data types. We then explore how digital tools can be used to generate both naturally occurring data such as field notes, conversational data, online communities and archives, and researcher-generated data such as interviews and focus groups, walk-alongs and images.

Data Generation Types: Naturally Occurring and Researcher-Generated Data

As you design your research study, you will be faced with a series of decisions about how to (1) define your research problem, (2) situate your work both methodologically and theoretically, and (3) decide what will count as data. Your methodological approach and research questions will shape the type of data collection techniques you choose. Qualitative researchers often use multiple data sources to warrant their claims. Historically, interviews and/or focus groups, observations and document collections have dominated qualitative research practices.

In the social sciences there has generally been more emphasis on collecting researcher-generated data, e.g. interviews, over naturally occurring data, e.g. a family dinner-time conversation (Attenborough and Stokoe, 2012). Digital tools, though, have made it easier to collect the naturally occurring data that can help us understand how people enact and perform their identities and experiences. Sacks (1992) suggested that:

> if we are to understand and analyze participants' own concepts and accounts, then we have to find and analyze them not in response to our research questions, but in the places they ordinarily and functionally occur in the activities in which they're employed. (p. 27)

For example, mobile devices make it easier to collect naturally occurring data, such as conversations between friends, in a less obtrusive manner, as more people are already documenting their lives by collecting voice, image and video data on a regular basis.

In contrast, interviews and focus groups are examples of data which would not exist apart from the researcher's involvement (Silverman, 2001). Interviews and focus groups, for instance, entail asking a series of questions and recording participant responses. This type of data in some cases can be collected more quickly and is under the researcher's control. These two categories, however, are not mutually exclusive, as no social interaction would be treated as 'data' without some human intervention. We select what to record in any context that we study.

Generating data involves producing a 'diverse collection of materials that enable you to engage with and think about the specific research problems or questions' (Rapley, 2007, p. 10). Practically, this entails managing and collecting a variety of data sources. Take a moment to respond to the questions posted in Reflexive Practice 5.1.

REFLEXIVE PRACTICE 5.1

What types of data will you collect for the study you are designing? Will they be primarily researcher-generated? Naturally occurring?

Digital Tools for Naturally Occurring Data

We discuss next the ways in which various digital tools can be used with naturally occurring data such as field observations, conversations, online communities and Internet archives of multimedia.

Recording Field Notes

Taking field notes is a well-established data collection method (Spradley, 1980). One of your first choices is how to position yourself: as a complete participant, a complete observer or somewhere in between. This decision will influence how you record your field notes. You may choose, for instance, to write them by hand, make an audio recording or type them on a laptop or mobile device.

To minimize your presence at the site, you will want to use a device that is not distracting to those around you. If you are recording observations in a social space in which mobile devices are an integral part of the environment, you could use one to take notes, perhaps using an application such as Evernote (as discussed in Chapter 2). In Vignette 5.1, Everett Painter describes his use of mobile devices.

Vignette 5.1	Utilizing Mobile Devices in the Field: Field Notes

Everett Painter, University of Tennessee

The current trend in technology convergence, particularly focused on mobile devices, presents many new options for data collection. During a recent qualitative study I took some of this technology into the field with

(Continued)

(Continued)

high expectations. I consider myself somewhat of an 'early adopter' of technology, always looking for ways to incorporate new advances in my work as a counsellor. I was confident these new tools would enhance my fieldwork and research efforts as well.

In an effort to better manage my data, I made the decision to use a tablet (iPad) for note taking and journalling. I quickly learned this was not going to be as smooth as I had imagined. My first attempts were awkward and clumsy. The device was difficult to hold and type on at the same time. I found my onscreen typing speed to be much slower than writing by hand. Frustrated, I returned to writing my field notes by hand in a notebook, but they turned out messy and difficult to read. I made the commitment to return to the iPad for subsequent observations. With practice and the use of shorthand, my speed increased. Having notes in a digital format was advantageous because they were easier to read and ready to be processed, cutting out the stage of note conversion and thereby saving me a good deal of time. Additionally, in my research setting (a church), the iPad was a more unobtrusive option than a laptop. In hindsight, I should have practised note taking in order to reach a proficient speed before attempting to collect notes in the field.

Thus, it is important to practise your data collection techniques prior to going into the field, and to tailor your use of technology to what will work best for each context.

As you take field notes, it may be useful to map your data set. A global positioning system (GPS) uses satellites to locate a particular position on Earth, and linking this geographical and spatial data to your field notes could allow you to, for example, examine how place and space might be linked to power (Creswell, 2004; Helfenbein and Taylor, 2009). Christensen et al. (2011) illustrated how GPS and mobile phone technologies can be used to generate a deeper understanding of children's everyday movements.

Visit Web Resource 5.1 to read Christensen et al. (2011) – a mixed methods study that used ethnographic fieldwork and global positioning technology.

GPSLogger is a mobile application that allows you to log or record your GPS location at specific time intervals. These time intervals can be displayed with the specific coordinates and/or in a map view. It supports the geotagging of images, which may be useful for building a visual map as part of the field notes.

Visit Web Resource 5.2 to review a list of applications that can support the collection of data using mobile devices.

Turn now to Reflexive Practice 5.2.

―――――――――――――――――― **REFLEXIVE PRACTICE 5.2** ――――――――――――――

Review Web Resource 5.2 and choose an application (such as GPSLogger) that may be useful for the study you are designing. Download it and begin to learn it. Reflect on your experiences.

Recording Conversations

For certain research approaches such as conversation analysis, you may find it particularly useful to audio- or video-record naturally occurring interactions, such as family mealtime conversations or institutional talk between doctors and patients. Having a recording of the interaction makes it possible for you to 're-experience' it for analytic purposes (Ashmore and Reed, 2000; Sacks, 1984). Audio or video recording allows you to attend more to the non-verbal interactions and/or interact with the participants during the observation. Nonetheless, as Ochs (1979) suggested, 'the problems of selective observation are not eliminated' (p. 44), as not even a recording device can capture everything that is happening in the environment. Choices must be made as to what, when and where to record.

Investing in quality recording equipment that is well suited for the research environment is an important first step. You must also decide where to place the recording device. When making decisions about the types of equipment to use, as well as where to locate the equipment, it is important to seek the advice of researchers who have conducted similar studies, as is illustrated in Case Study 5.1.

┌─ **CASE STUDY 5.1** ─┤ **Video-Recording Conversational Data** ├─────────┐

Angela was planning to conduct a discourse analysis of the classroom talk of primary students. Her participants included 33 children, one teacher and one classroom assistant. She decided to video-record the one-hour maths lessons over the course of three months. She talked with other researchers who had done similar studies and was advised to purchase a refurbished digital video camera with a memory card and a tabletop tripod. From previous observations, Angela knew that the teacher would be doing most of the talking while standing at the front of the room. Thus, she set up the camera on a desk directed towards the front of the room with a wide-angle lens to capture at least some of the children's movements. She also decided to purchase wireless microphones to place throughout the room, in order to capture the responses to the teacher's questions. While she worried about not capturing all of the non-verbal interaction taking place around the room, she felt that her observational notes would suffice. Her biggest challenge would be to match up her observational notes with the video recordings.

The lightweight Dictaphone-style audio recorders marketed by Olympus, Sony, Philips, Panasonic and others have seen constant development and change, making them an ideal technology for recording. Many of the newest audio and video recorders have a greater storage capacity than most researchers will ever need. These devices often have a USB port to transfer data directly onto a password-protected laptop. Some of the latest models have their own password protection and encryption, and some can be used for transcribing notes directly into Microsoft Word via Dragon Dictate (see Chapter 6).

While many of these devices have built-in microphones, external micro-phones may still be preferable. If there is important interaction occurring in a particular area (e.g. the front of a classroom or meeting room), a directional microphone would be appropriate. Boundary microphones are placed in one location and non-selectively capture a wide range of sounds; for soundscape research (discussed in Chapter 8), this type of microphone might be best. If there is a particular individual whose talk you are focused upon, such as a teacher or facilitator, a lavaliere microphone will likely meet your needs. Most microphones are battery powered, so always bring a spare set with you.

Computing devices such as laptops and mobile phones often have built-in video and audio recorders. This allows recording in a less obtrusive way. See Case Study 5.2.

CASE STUDY 5.2 — **Using a Computer to Record Video Data**

Kelli was collecting conversational data between adults with aphasia (a language impair-ment) and their speech-language therapists. Long before Kelli began her study, the thera-pists used the video cameras built into their computers to record their therapy sessions so that they could send a DVD of the session home with their client. Those therapists and clients who agreed to participate in her study told Kelli that it would be too intrusive for her to set up video equipment. Rather, they wanted to continue using their computers to record the sessions and then transfer the video data to a hard drive for her research purposes. Once Kelli received approval from her ethics committee, Kelli relied upon the therapists to record the sessions and then transfer the recordings to her on a weekly basis. She had to work closely with the therapists to find the best position for the computer, so that she could capture as much of the verbal and non-verbal interaction as possible.

However, the quality of these recordings may not be as good as those made on a device designed exclusively for recording.

Another recording option are Smartpens, which contain an audio-recording device and an ocular recorder to recognize and store handwritten text. This device can be used to take notes whilst recording and to transmit data to other devices through a wireless Internet connection. The quality of the recording is high, and it synchronizes seamlessly with writing done on special paper. See Vignette 5.2 in which Lisa Scherff and Boon Lim share their experiences with smartpens.

Vignette 5.2 — Using Smartpens in Educational Research

Lisa Scherff and Boon Lim, Florida State University

Our interest in the Livescribe Smartpen™ was driven by our need to be able to create a record of discussions between preservice teachers and the adolescents they were tutoring, as well as what they wrote down during their tutoring sessions.

The Smartpen both audio-records and saves what was written via a program called Livescribe. Using special paper, you simply tap the record mark on the paper and the pen automatically begins recording. You can stop and start recording by simply touching the appropriate marks on the paper. Once a recording session is complete, you plug the pen into a computer and all the data is saved. The Livescribe website offers multiple applications, such as pen casting, integration with Google Docs and Evernote synchronization.

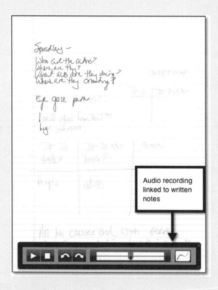

Our research team used the pens to document the extent to which the preservice teachers were incorporating particular teaching strategies into their tutorials. We wanted to be able to record impromptu conversations and semi-structured interviews between the teachers and the students. The preservice teachers were encouraged to use the pens during their interactions with the students. Some data were collected, but we found out that not all preservice teachers used the pens. For example, if the teachers were working with magazine articles or novels the pens were of little use. Next time, we will show teachers how they can print text (worksheets, informational text, poems, etc.) on to the dot paper using the free software. The best advice we can give is to provide enough of the special paper and ensure that all team members know how to use it.

Regardless of how you choose to record your data, it is important to spend time consulting with those who have collected similar types of data to find out what tools worked for them. Table 5.1 highlights some of the things you should consider when selecting a recording device.

Table 5.1 Questions to consider when selecting a recording device (adapted from Phelps, Fisher and Ellis, 2007)

- Can an external microphone be used?
- Will the participants view the size of the recorder as intrusive?
- Does the recorder clearly indicate battery life and recording time?
- What is the default file format and size of the recording?
- Does the recorder have any features that enhance the sound quality?
- Is it possible to easily erase the files when needed? To protect from accidental erasure?
- Is it possible to attach text or images to the converted file?
- Can files easily be transferred to a computing device?

Visit Web Resource 5.3 for tips on selecting and using recording equipment.

Now turn to Reflexive Practice 5.3.

REFLEXIVE PRACTICE 5.3

Select a recording device and collect some naturally occurring (e.g. conversational) data. How was the quality of the recording? What might you need to do differently next time?

Online Communities

The Internet has created a new type of naturally occurring data: online communities. Discussion groups, blogs, social networking sites and virtual worlds are all sites of interaction that are important for social scientists to understand. Qualitative researchers have been using ethnographic methods to study these online communities since the 1990s. Hine (2000, 2007, 2008) suggested that ethnographies of the Internet involve virtual, rather than face-to-face, travel to the research site, resulting in an 'experiential rather than physical displacement' (Hine, 2000, p. 45). Kozinets (2010) referred to this specialized form of ethnography as 'netnography', suggesting that an adapted ethnographic approach be used to study these unique digital spaces.

Visit Web Resource 5.4 to read Derya Kulavuz-Onal's vignette on the unexpected challenges of netnography.

Visit Web Resource 5.5 to review a special issue of *Forum: Qualitative Social Research* focused on virtual ethnography.

Researching online communities can raise ethical concerns. McKee and Porter (2009) suggested that whether or not online spaces are treated as *text* or as *people* may guide decisions around whether or not informed consent is needed before entering the community as a researcher. Treating spaces as texts, while possibly eliminating the need to obtain informed consent, still requires attention to copyright and other legal requirements for interpreting texts which have been generated by others. Viewing the Internet as a place populated by *people* will often require the informed consent of those potential participants. McKee and Porter noted that online communities are more welcoming and open to researchers who are already members of the community and who approach research in a transparent and collaborative manner. They emphasized the importance of establishing credibility and building trust with the community you wish to study, which is no different from what is necessary to study offline communities.

REFLEXIVE PRACTICE 5.4

Including direct quotations from an online community in your research report may make it very easy, with Internet search engines, to trace the data back to its original source. How might this impact the community?

Figure 5.1 is a heuristic that McKee and Porter (2009) provided to guide decisions around informed consent in online communities. The more private a conversation is considered to be by the participants (regardless of whether it actually *is* private), the more sensitive the topic, the more interaction the researcher intends to have with the participants and the more vulnerable the subject, the more likely informed consent should be sought.

Public vs Private	Topic Sensitivity	Degree of Interaction	Subject Vulnerability	Is Consent Necessary?
Private	High	High	High	Likely
↕	↕	↕	↕	↕
Public	Low	Low	Low	Not Likely

Figure 5.1 Heuristic for making informed consent decisions in Internet research (adapted from McKee and Porter, 2009, p. 88)

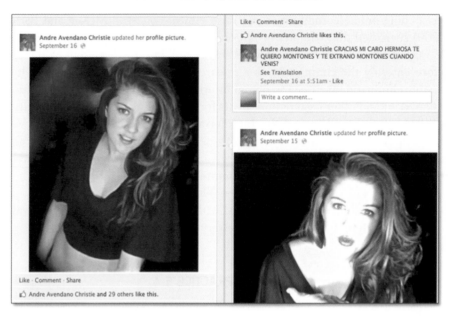

Figure 5.2   Images and posts on Facebook

Social networking sites, such as Twitter and Facebook, are the most recent type of online community. Unlike participants in earlier online communities, members of these sites often use their real names and identities. Social networking sites can be viewed as sources of qualitative data and/or a means by which to interact with research participants. For instance, you might use Facebook to study the ways in which young girls construct their identities through their status updates and profile photos (see Figure 5.2). Such data could be analysed over the course of several months or years to show changes over time.

Facebook can also be used as a way to verify your emergent interpretations of other data sources, as is described by Ron Hallett in Vignette 5.3.

| Vignette 5.3 | Facebook Posts as Data Source |

Ronald E. Hallett, University of the Pacific

In my study of college students who did not have documentation of legal immigration status, I sought to understand how social and institutional policies framed students' participation in the educational process. I developed a data collection plan that involved interviews, observations, document analysis and journalling. As the students became more comfortable with me in the researcher role, I began receiving 'friend' requests from them through the social networking site Facebook. I accepted without much thought about how this might influence data collection.

The value of these virtual connections soon became evident. I abandoned my original plan that involved asking the participants to keep journals because it was clear they were already reflecting on life through their Facebook posts. I found that these posts affirmed and challenged themes that emerged from interviews and observations. Social networks emerged as an important component of their experience as undocumented students. While my face-to-face observations involved only campus-based networking, online the participants engaged with regional, state and national networks of undocumented students. Facebook posts allowed me to see individual needs for books and food, as well as expression of emotional highs and lows. Finally, participants conducted much of their organization through Facebook. I had to follow posts to know if a meeting time had changed, a rally had been organized or a social event had been planned. Joining the students online widened and deepened my understandings of the social phenomenon.

However, entering this virtual space raised ethical questions I had not anticipated, particularly around consent. I took a fairly strict stance that participants needed to consent to my treating their Facebook posts as data. I met individually with each participant to discuss utilizing their posts in place of asking them to keep a written journal. Although I was technically able to view any post participants had made since they joined Facebook, I chose only to treat as data the posts made after they consented to my doing so. My interest in virtual spaces remains pragmatic. If my participants are interacting in online spaces, I should join them in order to more fully understand their experiences.

Visit Web Resource 5.6 for a discussion of how Facebook might be used for data collection purposes.

As noted in Vignette 5.3, studying online communities, or the online interactions of in-person communities, brings into focus new ethical concerns. McKee and Porter (2009) noted that whether or not online conversations should be considered public or private depends in part on whether the *participants* themselves consider it to be so. Consider Case Study 5.3 and examine the ways that you might respond to this ethical dilemma.

CASE STUDY 5.3	Ethical Dilemmas and Research in Online Communities

Geraldine desired to study an online forum in which grieving individuals share their experiences of loss. She wanted to find out how these sites might be used to help counsellors better support the bereaved. Geraldine's university ethics board said that she did not need to ask for permission to study the forums because they were publicly visible to anyone with

(Continued)

(Continued)

an Internet connection. Yet, as she began reading through the forums she became a bit uncomfortable, realizing that she was not viewing the data as just words, but as the words of real people who were in a vulnerable state and may not be aware that their words were publicly visible. She considered contacting each participant individually and asking for their permission, but feared that contact from a stranger might cause more pain and anxiety. She also considered contacting the site's moderator, a licensed counselling professional, but was unsure whether the moderator could really speak on behalf of the thousands of participants on the site. What would you do if you were Geraldine?

Visit Web Resource 5.8 (and Vignette 7.2) for information on tools that can be used to extract online interaction data.

Another type of online community is the virtual world, defined as 'places of human culture realized by computer programs through the Internet' (Boellstorff, 2010, p. 126). *Second Life*, a 3-D virtual world where you can engage in day-to-day living (e.g. buy homes, go to language classes) is one example of such a community. Vignette 5.4 presents an example of Doug Canfield's journey into *Second Life*.

| Vignette 5.4 | Collecting Data in *Second Life* |

Doug Canfield, University of Tennessee

For two years, I worked for a company who taught languages to students from all over the world in *Second Life*. I had a front-row seat to see how a virtual world could touch most every facet of our lives, from learning to entertainment to the consumption and production of popular culture. I began to reflect upon how virtuality transforms and questions core ideas about identity and relationships. This ultimately led to my initial foray into *Second Life* as a researcher. The ability to conduct research with persons in multiple worldwide locations was appealing to me.

Understanding a virtual space like *Second Life* requires, at a minimum, a consideration of the multiple demographics, cultures and modes of communication that exist there. To speak specifically of the multiple modes of communication, one can simultaneously text chat, voice chat, instant message, private voice chat, and file share. This speaks only to verbal communication. The ability to communicate non-verbally via gestures, clothing, the embodiment of the avatar itself (which can take any form) and *rezzing* (the creation or incarnation of objects in *Second Life*), complicates the collection of data.

To capture data from *Second Life* I tested out a few screen capture programs before deciding on FRAPS. This software captures audio and video up to 7680 × 4800 with custom frame rates up to 120 frames per second. The resulting videos were stunning. I could see and hear everything with clarity and take camera shots from any angle or distance from participants without being intrusive (see Figure 5.3). The trade-off was that the higher-quality video requires one gigabyte of hard drive space per minute, with recorded sessions saved in separate files of 4GB each. Since some of these recorded sessions were three hours long, I ended up having to buy several terabytes of hard drive memory, with no possibility of it being portable across machines. I now use FRAPS for initial recording and first-pass analysis, eventually exporting only selected scenes for further analysis.

Figure 5.3   Doug Canfield's avatar making a participant-observation in *Second Life*

Internet Archives of Multimedia Data

In addition to online communities, the Internet is rich with multimedia data such as professionally curated archives, amateur-created YouTube and Vimeo videos and photo-sharing websites. The Internet Archive, for example, contains a variety of cultural artifacts that are freely available and downloadable. CADENSA, an online archive of the British Library *Sound and Moving Image Catalogue*, and Britain's BBC archives are useful resources for researchers interested in reviewing documentary film and political speeches.

Visit Web Resource 5.8 for links to the Internet Archive, CADENSA and Britain's BBC archives.

Videosharing sites such as YouTube and Vimeo are good sources for understanding social life. For example, you might be interested in how adolescent mental health disorders are represented in this media. For those interested in the ways in which images are produced and disseminated by individuals, photo-sharing websites such as Flickr, Picasa and PBase are potential sources for building a collection of images.

Next, consider Reflexive Practice 5.5.

REFLEXIVE PRACTICE 5.5

Identify an online community and/or some online archival data that may be of interest for your research study. Consider how you might extract the data for further analysis and whether informed consent will be needed.

Digital Tools for Researcher-Generated Data

We now discuss digital tools that can support the collection of researcher-generated data such as interviews and focus groups, walk-alongs and images.

Interviews and Focus Groups

Whether structured, semi-structured or unstructured, many qualitative researchers have positioned interviews as a primary means of gaining access to human experience. Just like with recording naturally occurring data, there are many decisions to make around how to best record interview and focus group data. Vignette 5.5 illustrates the ways in which the video recorder itself shaped Art Herbig and Aaron Hess's research process.

Vignette 5.5 — **Data in the Visual Context**

Art Herbig, Indiana-Purdue University Fort Wayne, and Aaron Hess, Arizona State University

As part of our investigation into Americans' memories of 9/11, we quickly learned that the camera places a literal and figurative barrier between the participants and the researcher. Particularly while in the field, there are very few opportunities to create a stable camera setup. More often than not, there is a person behind the camera. In our work, we have chosen to address this concern by working together: one person behind the camera and another conducting the interview. How we use the camera to frame an interview has a lasting impact on how that data will become part of our research. Basic camera techniques and bits of context become ways of depicting people, not just as participants in research, but as characters in our story. The camera almost feels like a

---

translator taking content that existed in a particular time and context and reframing it as something to be part of a new project and often a very different conversation.

Working with that translator often provides challenges for the interviewer. In more typical fieldwork, interviews and observations are not bound by the norms of a medium that expects a three-act storytelling structure and clean audio tracks. For these reasons, the norms of film have the power to alter how the interviewer behaves. Those verbal cues that reassure the person that you are listening now have the power to replace that person's audio and make the shot unusable. Instead of choosing to conduct an interview in a private space out of the way, we look for visual contexts that will help frame who this participant is for the audience.

Capturing a participant's image for reproduction and distribution also changes that participant's relationship to both the research and the researcher. So much of qualitative research is grounded in our ability to mask the identities of our participants, but in visual work they appear onscreen for all to see. This requires an entirely different type of consent and sensitivity on the part of the researcher to know what would make good data and what would be exploitative. The participants who are willing to stand in front of a camera and pronounce their perspectives are often being very brave, and that act of bravery deserves to be treated with respect. Sometimes we have to acknowledge that what we have captured with the camera should never become data, and often those decisions are made while still in the field.

Thus, many decisions need to be made when constructing a video interview situation. While professional grade video cameras are necessary for the type of work described in Vignette 5.5, smartphones and other mobile devices can also be used to record interviews. See Vignette 5.6 for Everett Painter's description.

| Vignette 5.6 | Utilizing Mobile Devices in the Field: Interviews |

Everett Painter, University of Tennessee

I recorded my interviews using a smartphone (iPhone) since it had the same recording and storage features as a standalone digital recorder. I also opted for a small, external condenser microphone. This improved the sound quality and recording levels over the built-in microphone. While these devices also include basic recording software, I chose to use an

(Continued)

(Continued)

application called iTalk. A plethora of third-party recording applications are available that offer extended control over file formats, recording quality and playback features. These options allow for adjustments and recordings that can easily be used with transcription software. This combination worked well and produced recordings that were loud, clear and free of background noise. Additionally, I used the iPhone to document the environment through photos and scans of site artifacts.

I found the benefits of this approach to be accessibility and organization. It was helpful to have continuous access to my data when opportunities for reflection and analysis presented themselves. Collecting data in this way afforded convenience and allowed me to carry fewer items. Organization was improved by replacing paper data with easily manageable digital files. However, as all of the data is in a digital format, backups are essential. This is easily accomplished by synchronizing data across computing devices or using cloud-based storage such as Dropbox. Using passwords, encrypting data when possible and setting up the devices so they can be remotely erased in the event of loss or theft is crucial for keeping data secure and protecting the identities of participants. Even with these safeguards in place, I took the additional step of moving sensitive data to a more secure computer as soon as possible after collection.

Mobile devices can be an efficient way to collect interview data while in the field. Talking with others who have done similar types of data collection and reading reviews of new applications are good steps to take when considering this option.

Visit Web Resource 5.9 for information about the potential pitfalls of mobile interviewing.

The videoconferencing tools such as Skype and Google Hangouts described in Chapter 3 can be used for data collection as well as engaging in research team meetings. Travelling to remote communities to engage in research can be costly and is not always feasible, so the ability to talk in real time with visual cues can be of great benefit when conducting interviews or focus groups at a distance (Gratton and O'Donnell, 2011). It is important to be sure that all participants have a robust Internet connection to support the video. Tools such as Pamela (see Web Resource 3.5) and TechSmith's Camtasia (described later in the chapter) allow you to record these videoconferences.

An alternative to video conferencing to reach participants at a distance is to use online text-based asynchronous or synchronous interviews; see Table 5.2.

Table 5.2 Affordances and limitations of asynchronous and synchronous online interviews (adapted from O'Connor et al., 2008, p. 273)

	Asynchronous Online Interviews	Synchronous Online Interviews
Venue	Email and discussion board	Text chat, instant messenger
Time Restrictions	Non-real time; no time constraints	Real time; constrained by time
Software Requirements	Simple and likely familiar	May be more complex
Technical Abilities	Low	Medium
Speech of Response	Includes time to reflect	Spontaneous
Disadvantages	Easy to ignore or delete emails/discussion posts and lack of visual cues	May have more technical issues and lack of visual cues

With asynchronous tools, such as email interviews, participants can respond when it is most convenient for them to do so, decreasing the chances that people will leave the study due to time constraints. The participants will also likely have more time to reflect upon their responses, potentially resulting in richer data sets. While email is a familiar tool for many, it is important to remember that not everyone has access to it and some might find typing to be difficult due to a variety of impairments.

In contrast, synchronous tools, such as instant chat focus groups, retain the spontaneity inherent to an in-person interaction. With little time to edit or redraft responses, as might be done in email interviews, participants' responses in synchronous interviews are often viewed as more honest. A disadvantage to the synchronous interview is that you may have to work hard to keep up with the discussion, particularly if your interview is unstructured and you are required to make a quick interpretation of what is being written. Further, the synchronous discussions may appear somewhat disjointed, especially if you ask a new question prior to the participant fully responding to the previous one. One advantage to both synchronous and asynchronous text-based tools, however, is that you will not have to transcribe your interviews, as the conversations are automatically archived.

Visit Web Resource 5.10 to read Janet Salmon's blog, *Vision2Lead*, where she provides tips for engaging in online interviews as well as ethical issues to consider.

See Vignette 5.7 for an example of how text chat was used to conduct synchronous interviews.

Vignette 5.7	Using Synchronous Chat Tools to Conduct Interviews

Trena Paulus, University of Tennessee

A few years ago I was collaborating on a research study with a colleague in Oregon, three time zones away from where I live in Tennessee. We were studying how social networking sites could be used as part of a teacher education course. I was responsible for conducting the interviews and knew it would be a challenge with the time difference. Face-to-face interviews were not an option as we did not have funding for me to travel out of state. Telephone interviews could be a bit stilted since I had not met the participants face-to-face and it could be difficult to establish a rapport. Skype or videoconferencing interviews were considered, but I was not certain that all participants would have a webcam and microphone. The asynchronous nature of email wouldn't allow for much probing or many follow-up questions. We decided to use text chat because it would allow some of the advantages of email – in that participants could reflect before typing, and the synchronous nature would allow me to ask follow-up questions as needed.

Since the participants had recently experienced text chat as part of their class, we knew that they were familiar with the medium. Some chose to use Skype text chat, others Yahoo Messenger and others Gmail chat. Much of the hour-long interview time was spent waiting for the participant to type out their answers. The typing speed of the participants vastly impacted the duration and depth of the conversations. As is typical with synchronous chat, answers often spanned several turns, interspersed with my affirmation turns ('right', 'okay', 'sure'), making the conversations somewhat interesting to decipher when reviewing the transcripts.

An advantage of this approach is that the transcripts are automatically archived – eliminating the need for transcribing. However, the responses to the questions were likely shorter than they would have been had we been talking face-to-face, or even through email. I did not find much variation across the synchronous chat tools, as all work in very similar ways. You do have to keep in mind the potential risk of losing data (e.g. closing the chat box by accident or the window freezing). It is important, then, to save the chats carefully and in an ongoing manner.

Now turn to Reflexive Practice 5.6.

REFLEXIVE PRACTICE 5.6

Select one of the digital tools described thus far and use it to collect some sample interview data. After collecting the data, make a reflexivity journal post comparing the interaction with any past data collection face-to-face interview experiences you may have had.

Walk-Alongs

Beyond the traditional sit-down interview, a 'walk-along' interview is a data collection technique in which the researcher 'walks and talks' with the participant at the research site. This approach has the added benefit of building rapport with your participants (Carpiano, 2009). A walk-along serves as a concrete way to 'map' the spatial location of what is being shared in the interview, especially in conjunction with the use of GPS/GIS (Geographic Information System) technologies. Often, the audio or video recording will include soundscapes from the area (see Chapter 8 for a further discussion of soundscapes). Furthermore, the technique allows for the environment itself to serve as the prompt for the discussion. Video recording can be somewhat cumbersome during walk-alongs, with the use of mobile devices being more effective.

Jones and Evans (2012), in the 'Rescue Geography' project, used GPS technology and walk-alongs in which people's feelings about their environment were linked to the location in which they shared them. Participants were asked to choose their routes to generate stories about the spaces in which they navigated, using mobile devices to record their stories and aspects of the environment. Eventually, much of their data set resulted in the production of a transcript in which every 10 seconds of the audio recording was linked to a GPS record.

Visit Web Resource 5.11 to see the 'Rescue Geography' project.

We have seen several ways of collecting interview and focus group data. We now turn to another type of researcher-generated data – images.

Images

Anthropologists and other qualitative researchers have experimented with giving cameras or video recorders to participants with the aim of understanding the world through 'their eyes'. Photo-elicitation (also called photo-interviewing or projective interviewing) is a technique in which the researcher uses photographs or other images, either generated by the participant or the researcher, within an interview or focus group (Norman, 1991). The photographs are presumed to serve to expand the interactions between the researcher and participant, even serving to elicit latent memories and/or decrease the potential for misunderstandings (Harper, 2002).

Photovoice is a data collection method in which the participants themselves are involved in producing images that speak to their day-to-day lives (Baker and Wang, 2006). This particular approach has been conceptualized as a type of participatory action research with participants being directly involved in the production and, in many cases, interpretation of the images. The visual images typically accompany the everyday stories of participants; as described by Fanny Yeung in Vignette 5.8.

| Vignette 5.8 | Using Photography in Educational Research |

Fanny P.F. Yeung, University of California, Los Angeles

My research aims to better understand how students' family relationships, immigrant histories and responsibilities influenced their post-secondary experiences. In combination with in-depth interviews, photovoice was selected to provide participants with the opportunity to participate in the data collection process and document aspects of their lives from their own perspectives. In addition, photovoice enabled participants to continue to think about the themes during the interviews and enabled me to triangulate the various data sources. I was excited about the idea of using photographs to capture family dynamics, a perspective not often observed in educational research, and intrigued by the idea that students could actively participate in the data collection process.

There were three main components of the photovoice data collection phase: a photography guide, consent forms, and a photography log. The guide facilitated the photovoice process and asked students to reflect on artifacts at home related to their education and family responsibilities. Students returned with photographs of academic and co-curricular awards that they had not discussed in their interviews. Others documented their roles as care providers to younger siblings or their grandparents. Many times, the details and depth of the examples provided in the photographs far exceeded the information provided verbally in the interviews.

While participants were provided with disposable cameras, approximately a third of the participants requested to use their personal digital cameras instead and emailed their photos to me. In hindsight, there were advantages to both approaches. The disposable camera captured photos that were imperfect and in some ways more authentic. While all photos were staged to some extent, pictures taken with the disposable camera were more likely to include landscape pictures of rooms, rather than individual objects or sets of items. Disposable camera photos were more likely to capture parts of the room they had not initially intended to (and were often less organized). Some photos also had poor lighting, poor resolution and were blurry. In contrast, photos from digital cameras were more polished and of greater quality, i.e., objects were often framed and centred and had fewer distractions. Polished photographs provided limited opportunities to capture unexpected patterns or objects in students' thought processes.

The consent form was an important component for protecting the participants' identities and personal details. It was important to communicate how the photos would be used in scholarly presentations and publications. Students first consented to participate in the project and later provided consent for me to use the photographs in my study findings. The multiphase consent process was challenging due to time constraints; however, it was invaluable because it required participants and I to meet at least two to three times throughout the study.

Visit Web Resource 5.12 for tips on collecting photographic data.

Methods like photo-elicitation and photovoice can be particularly useful for engaging in research with individuals who may not express themselves verbally or may be less apt to share in the context of a formal interview (Banks, 2007). In Mizen's (2005) study of children's work life in England and Wales, he provided 50 children with inexpensive cameras and asked them to create a photo diary of their work experiences. As one of many data points, the photo diary was used to consider 'what the children had to tell us about their work [rather] than the usual preoccupation of researchers with what the work has to tell us about the children' (Mizen, 2005, p. 125).

Visit Web Resource 5.13 for examples of photovoice research projects.

Collecting images may require investment in disposable cameras and/or more expensive equipment to ensure adequate quality. When deciding what digital tools to use to capture images, consider the questions suggested in Table 5.3.

Table 5.3 Questions to consider when collecting images

- What level of quality is needed in the collected images?
- How will you acquire the consent of individuals in photographs who may not be part of the study?
- What will you use the image for? What types of analysis will you conduct?
- Will your participants be capturing the images?
- What level of technological abilities will be required in order to capture the images?
- How will you save the images?

One of the most straightforward ways of editing digital still images is to use the Snipping tool that is automatically included in the Windows operating system. Another option is TechSmith's Snagit 11, a very versatile image processing software package. With it, you can capture and annotate images from multiple sources. Beyond screen capture of images, you can also use it to capture text from a PDF, for example. A final tool that is particularly useful is its video capture tool. You can use this to capture screen activity, zero in on items playing on your computer, and/or create simple screencasts.

TechSmith's Camtasia software is also an image-based tool, primarily designed for making screencasts and presentations. It is powerful enough to use for editing video, yet simple enough to add images and voice-overs to video or static images. It is particularly useful for capturing actions on your computer screen and producing them as videos; if you design research that results in collecting interactions, you can capture the action and any speech occurring at the same time.

Visit Web Resource 5.14 for links to TechSmith's Snagit and Camtasia software programs.

Keep in mind that when capturing still or moving images it is important to think carefully about how the images will be used and the ways in which participants' identities will be protected, as highlighted in Reflexive Practice 5.7.

REFLEXIVE PRACTICE 5.7

Collect some image-based data – stills or video – that may be relevant for your research. What might be some ethical challenges resulting from making your participants and their locations visible in this way?

Visit Web Resource 5.15 for data management tips.

Final Thoughts

New digital tools make possible new types of methods such as walk-alongs and photovoice techniques, but bring with them new logistical and ethical challenges. Devices such as mobile phones, Smartpens and GPS tools can be used to collect data in less obtrusive ways than traditional recording devices. Online conversations and communities, in combination with mobile devices and the prevalence of video and image sharing sites, make it easier to capture social life as it is happening. Engaging in research in these spaces can result in large amounts of data, so when embarking on a new study, make a data generation plan and regularly evaluate the data that you have. Consider both naturally occurring and researcher-generated data that might help you answer your research questions. When necessary, modify your initial plan systematically and thoughtfully. While you might be initially interested in one type of data, be open to other types that may better represent the social life of your participants. Remember, too, that logistics matter. If you are interested in classroom talk, you will need to not only gain permission to access a classroom setting but also find a way to clearly record the talk of large groups. Remember too that capturing images and entering online communities carry with them new ethical dilemmas that must be handled carefully.

Chapter Discussion Questions

1. What are the differences between naturally occurring and researcher-generated data sets?
2. Give examples of the ways in which the Internet can be both a *source of data* as well as a *tool* for data collection.
3. What are some online communities you are a part of? What social interactions occur in those communities that might be of interest to qualitative researchers?
4. How can you ensure ethical practices as you generate data for your research study?

Suggestions for Further Reading

Fielding, Lee and Blank (2008) include sections on the ethics of Internet research, virtual ethnography and the Internet as an archival resource. Hesse-Biber (2011) provides chapters on emergent data collection methods and the use of audiovisual, mobile and geospatial technologies. For an overview of the various ways that blogs can be used as part of a qualitative researcher's toolkit, see Hookway (2008). Salmons' (2010) *Online Interviews in Real Time* is an excellent resource for conducting online interviews, and comes with a companion case study volume. Kozinets (2010) offers practical guidelines as well as an overview of studies that have examined online communities. Markham and Baym (2009) bring together well-known scholars to speak to Internet research issues such as the changing nature of privacy and how to evaluate quality in Internet studies.

References

Ashmore, M. and Reed, D. (2000) 'Innocence and nostalgia in Conversation Analysis: the dynamic relations of tape and transcript'. *Forum: Qualitative Social Research*, 1(3). Available at: http://www.qualitative-research.net/index.php/fqs/article/viewArticle/1020 (last accessed 17 July 2013).

Attenbourough, C., and Stokoe, E. (2012). Student life; student identity; student experience: Ethnomethodological methods for pedagogical matters. *Psychology Learning and Teaching* 11(1), 6–21.

Baker, T. and Wang, C. (2006) 'Photovoice: Use of a participatory action research method to explore the chronic pain experience of older adults'. *Qualitative Health Research*, 16, 1405–13.

Banks, M. (2007) *Using Visual Data in Qualitative Research*. Thousand Oaks, CA: SAGE.

Boellstorff, T. (2010) 'A Typology of Ethnographic Scales for Virtual Worlds', in W.S. Bainbridge (ed.) *Online Worlds: Convergence of the Real and the Virtual*, Human–Computer Interaction Series. London, UK: Springer-Verlag.

Carpiano, R.M. (2009) 'Come take a walk with me: The "go-along" interview as a novel method for studying the implications of place for health and well-being'. *Health & Place*, 15(1), 263–72.

Christensen, P., Mikkelsen, M.R., Nielsen, T.A.S. and Harder, H. (2011) 'Children, mobility, and space: Using GPS and mobile phone technologies in ethnographic research'. *Journal of Mixed Methods Research*, 5(3), 227–46.

Creswell, T. (2004) *Place: A Short Introduction*. Malden, MA: Blackwell Publishers.

Fielding, N., Lee, R.M. and Blank, G. (eds) (2008) *The SAGE Handbook of Online Research Methods*. London, UK and Beverly Hills, CA: SAGE.

Gratton, M. and O'Donnell, S. (2011) 'Communication technologies for focus groups with remote communities: A case study of research with First Nations in Canada'. *Qualitative Research*, 11(2), 159–75.

Harper, D. (2002) 'Talking about pictures: A case for photo elicitation'. *Visual Studies*, 17(1), 17–26.

Helfenbein, R.J. and Taylor, L.H. (2009) 'Critical geographies in/of education: Introduction'. *Educational Studies*, 45, 236–9.

Hesse-Biber, S. (2011) *Handbook of Emergent Technologies in Social Research*. Oxford, UK: Oxford University Press.

Hine, C. (2000) *Virtual Ethnography*. London, UK: SAGE.

Hine, C. (2007) 'Connective ethnography for the exploration of e-science'. *Journal of Computer-Mediated Communication* 12(2), article 14. Available at: http://jcmc. indiana.edu/vol12/issue2/hine.html (last accessed 17 July 2013).

Hine, C. (2008) 'Internet Research as Emergent Practice', in S. Nagy Hesse-Biber and P. Leavy (eds) *Handbook of Emergent Methods*. New York, NY: The Guilford Press, pp. 525–41.

Hookway, N. (2008) '"Entering the blogosphere": Some strategies for using blogs in social research'. *Qualitative Research*, 8(1), 91–113.

Jones, P. and Evans, J. (2012) 'Rescue Geography: Place making, affect and regeneration'. *Urban Studies*, 49(11), 2315–30.

Kozinets, R.V. (2010) *Netnography: Doing Ethnography Research Online*. London, UK: SAGE.

McKee, H.A. and Porter, J.E. (2009) *The Ethics of Internet Research: A Rhetorical, Case-Based Process* (Vol. 59). New York, NY: Peter Lang Pub Incorporated.

Markham, A. and Baym, N.K. (2009) *Internet Inquiry*. Thousand Oaks, CA: SAGE.

Mizen, P. (2005) 'A little "light work"? Children's images of their labour'. *Visual Studies*, 20(2), 124–39.

Norman, W.R. (1991) 'Photography as a research tool'. *Visual Anthropology*, 4, 193–216.

Ochs, E. (1979) 'Transcription as Theory', in E. Ochs and B. Schieffelin (eds) *Developmental Pragmatics*. New York, NY: Academic Press, pp. 43–72.

O'Connor, H., Madge, C., Shaw, R. and Wellens, J. (2008) 'Internet-Based Interviewing', in N. Fielding, R.M. Lee and G. Blank (eds) *The SAGE Handbook of Online Research Methods*. London, UK: SAGE, pp. 271–89.

Phelps, R., Fisher, K. and Ellis, A. (2007) *Organizing and Managing Your Research: A Practical Guide for Postgraduates*. London, UK: SAGE.

Rapley, T. (2007) *Doing Conversation, Discourse and Document Analysis*. London, UK: SAGE.

Sacks, H. (1984) 'Everyday Activities as Sociological Phenomena'. in J.M. Atkinson and J. Heritage (eds) *Structures of Social Action: Studies in Conversation Analysis*. Cambridge, UK: Cambridge University Press, pp. 411–29.

Sacks, H. (1992) *Lectures on Conversation*. Oxford, UK: Blackwell.

Salmons, J. (2010), *Online Interviews in Real Time*. Thousand Oaks, CA: SAGE.

Silverman, D. (2001) *Interpreting Qualitative Data: Methods for Analysing Text, Talk and Interaction*. London, UK: SAGE.

Spradley, J.P. (1980) *Participant Observation*. New York, NY: Holt, Rinehart & Winston.

SIX
Transcribing Audio and Video Data

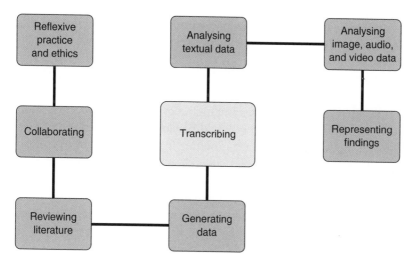

Companion website materials available here:

www.uk.sagepub.com/paulus

Learning Objectives

- Reflect upon the ways in which transcription is a situated act.
- Compare and contrast four approaches to transcription (verbatim, Jeffersonian, gisting and visual).
- Select and critique appropriate digital tools for transcribing audio and video data.
- Have strategies to ensure ethical practices when transcribing data.

Introduction

In Chapter 5, we discussed the various ways in which digital tools can be used for collecting both naturally occurring and researcher-generated data, such as recording conversations and interviews in new ways. In this chapter, we turn to digital tools that can support transforming recorded data into transcriptions for further analysis. We discuss how transcription itself is a situated act, describe four different types of transcription (verbatim, Jeffersonian, gisted and visual) and discuss features of four software packages (Express Scribe, Audio Notetaker, InqScribe and F4/F5). We also explore using voice recognition software (Dragon Dictate) and the video analysis tool Transana.

Transcription as Situated Act

Today's recording devices allow us to record vast amounts of audio and video data that must somehow be made sense of. Instead of being limited by the amount of information that could be documented by hand, we are now limited by how much recorded information we can process (Lee, 2004). As Ochs (1979) suggested, simply recording everything without making decisions about what is important results in these decisions being pushed to the transcription phase.

There are many approaches to transcription, depending on your field and understanding of what the transcript represents. For example, if you are interested in the way government officials' language is gendered you may be collecting, recording and transcribing data very differently than if you are looking at the use of turn-taking in conversations amongst doctors and their receptionists. What and how you choose to transcribe should be closely connected to your research focus and methodological approach, resulting in certain types of transcripts.

As you transcribe, you make particular choices, and those choices are related to your theoretical stance (Kvale, 2007). When creating a verbatim (word-for-word) transcript, for example, you make frequent decisions such as whether and how to include informal speech, non-word utterances, repetitions, stuttering, interruptions and background or other incidental sounds; see Figure 6.1.

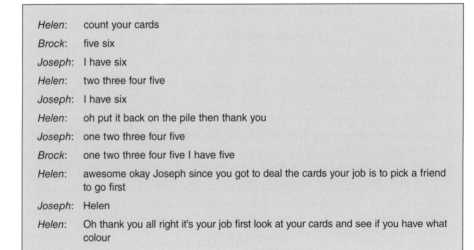

Helen:	count your cards
Brock:	five six
Joseph:	I have six
Helen:	two three four five
Joseph:	I have six
Helen:	oh put it back on the pile then thank you
Joseph:	one two three four five
Brock:	one two three four five I have five
Helen:	awesome okay Joseph since you got to deal the cards your job is to pick a friend to go first
Joseph:	Helen
Helen:	Oh thank you all right it's your job first look at your cards and see if you have what colour

Figure 6.1 Example of a verbatim transcript

The interaction in Figure 6.1 included three young boys (Joseph, Brock and Luke) and their therapist (Helen). However, only three speakers (Helen, Joseph and Brock) are represented in the transcript, as Luke was non-verbal and used body language to communicate. Choosing to only transcribe spoken words, and exclude physical movement or non-verbal behaviour, flattens the data and has consequences for how the interaction is being represented. Because it is impossible to document all features of social interaction, all transcripts should be considered *partial* representations, *selective* and *situated* in relationship to the goals of a particular study (Davidson, 2009; Lapadat and Lindsay, 1999).

Because transcription can be approached from a variety of perspectives, it is important that you engage in reflexive practice around your transcription choices. One view is that transcription can be seen as a form of analysis itself (e.g. Hammersley, 2010). Another is that qualitative data analysis software is making full transcription obsolete (Evers, 2011). Those who don't think about their approach in advance may end up with transcripts that do not align with their research goals (Oliver, Serovich and Mason, 2005). Thus, we encourage you to take a moment to complete the Reflexive Practice 6.1 activity.

REFLEXIVE PRACTICE 6.1

Consider the study you are designing in conjunction with this book:

- What kind of audio or video data might you collect and transcribe?
- What information in the recording do you need to attend to?
- Will features such as rate of speech, pitch and/or overlapping speech be important?
- How might you capture such features in your transcript?
- How might you represent laughter, pauses and gestures?

Transcription requires an investment of time, money and other resources. It takes a minimum of four hours to create a verbatim transcript for one hour of a high-quality recording (Dempster and Woods, 2011; Evers, 2011). Recordings of poor quality or of multiple overlapping speakers will take longer to transcribe. Case Study 6.1 illustrates some factors to consider in deciding on a transcription approach.

CASE STUDY 6.1

Jimmy is interested in interviewing nurses that have left the profession. He is considering conducting and audio-recording in-depth interviews, lasting about two hours, with 25 or more nurses, ex-nurses and other health workers. He realizes that it will take him around six hours to transcribe a one-hour interview. Based on this calculation, he would be under-taking 300 hours of transcription. After thinking about the resources he has, he decides to redesign his study to ask some of the questions in an online form that will allow participants

(Continued)

(Continued)

to respond at length, reducing the number of questions to be asked in the interview itself. He can then compare the participants' online responses with their interview transcripts, analysing across the data. Further, he decides not to transcribe the audio files in their entirety. Rather, he uploads his audio files into a software program that allows him to directly code and memo the audio files as well as transcribe selected portions.

We next discuss several ways to transcribe, each of which represents the data in a unique way. First, consider Reflexive Practice 6.2.

REFLEXIVE PRACTICE 6.2

Replacing real names with pseudonyms is standard practice in qualitative research. Deciding when and how to remove this identifying information often poses a dilemma for researchers. How might digital tools make it easier, yet more difficult, to anonymize your data? When will you apply pseudonyms – during or after transcription?

Types of Transcription

In this section, we discuss four types of transcription: verbatim (representing word-for-word what is said), Jeffersonian (representing additional features of the talk beyond the words), gisting (representing just an essence or condensed version) and visual (representing meaning with images).

Verbatim Transcription

A verbatim transcription involves typing everything you hear (in an audio recording) and/or see (in a video recording). This includes representing all utterances made by all participants without changing non-standard language usage (e.g. 'he don't care about me') or dialect (e.g. Doric Scots usage of 'fit like?' for 'how are you?') and without skipping over repetitions ('and-, and-'), false starts ('uh-, well, I mean') and backchannels ('mm-hmm'). Creating a verbatim transcript from video data should also include all of the non-verbal communicative behaviours (e.g. yawning, raising hands, throwing hands up in the air). While in theory a verbatim transcript is one that captures 'everything', it is never really possible to capture all that is communicated. To capture as much as possible, however, you will need to engage in several cycles of transcription, reviewing the recording multiple times. Foot pedals and shortcut keys can help with this.

Jeffersonian Transcription

Anyone who has attempted to create a verbatim transcript will have encountered the difficulty of representing features of the talk such as the rate of speech, volume and overlapping speech. In research traditions such as conversation analysis these features are assumed to carry meaning and so it is important to note them. There is a variety of notation systems (e.g. Du Bois, 1991; Gumperz and Berenz, 1993) that provide a way to represent these features. We focus here on Jefferson's (2004) notation system (see Figure 6.2 for a modified version of the notation system and Figure 6.3 for a modified Jeffersonian transcript).

↑	Upward arrows represent marked rise in pitch.
↓	Downward arrows represent a downward shift in pitch.
> <	Text encased in 'greater than' and 'less than' symbols is hearable as faster than the surrounding speech.
=	Equal signs at the end of a speaker's utterance and at the start of the next utterance represent the absence of a discernible gap.
the	Underlining represents a sound or word(s) uttered with added emphasis.
[ ]	Extended square brackets mark overlap between utterances.
(7)	Numbers in parentheses indicate pauses timed to the nearest second. A period with no number following, (.), indicates a pause which is hearable, yet too short to measure.

Figure 6.2   Modified Jeffersonian (2004) notation system

> 1 *Bria*: Okay so (.) what do you think on a scale of one to ten↑ is (.) the whole
> 2 grace situation for you at summer school right now↑ (.)
> 3 *Devin*: Well like (.) with one being handling it good or handling it bad↑
> 4 *Bria*: Uh (.) let's make one handling it bad and ten (.) handling it excellently↓ (2)
> 5 *Devin*: Well then it's probably a (.) somewhere between two and four↑=
> 6 *Bria*: Yeah that's that was kind of my impression in fact I'm not=
> 7 *Devin*: =Somewhere between two and four and a half probably↓ (.)

Figure 6.3   Excerpt from a modified Jeffersonian transcript from Lester and Paulus (in press)

Visit Web Resource 6.1 for more on transcription notation systems.

Jeffersonian transcripts must be created in rounds (ten Have, 2007), in which the transcriber focuses on different features of the talk each time. For instance, in the first round you might focus on the pauses between conversational turns, while during the second you might focus on intonation. Overall, this transcription approach involves multiple listenings, identifying analytically interesting sections for in-depth transcription, and using notation symbols to capture features which would not be included in other transcript types.

Case Study 6.2 illustrates how a researcher moved from hundreds of hours of video data to focused Jeffersonian transcripts. Further, the researcher decided to use Transana, a software program designed specifically for video transcription and analysis, because it supports Jeffersonian notations. Transana is discussed later in this chapter and further in Chapter 8.

CASE STUDY 6.2

Abraham has a corpus of video data from a youth therapy centre. Each therapy session lasted 30 minutes. Prior to transcribing his data, he listened to each recording once to become familiar with it. After completing one round of verbatim transcription with approximately 25 hours of data, he listened to the therapy sessions again and refined the transcriptions. As he gained a deeper level of familiarity with the data set, he began to attend only to those sections that focused on 'dealing with reported problems' (e.g. hitting a teacher). He used Transana to pull out just those sections and transcribed them using Jeffersonian notations. Transana was ideal for this as he was able to use the symbols already included within the software while listening and re-listening to capture detailed features of the talk such as interruptions and overlapping speech. He could easily take a few seconds of the talk and listen repeatedly to interpret where the overlapping speech occurred.

Visit Web Resource 6.2 for a Jeffersonian transcription tutorial.

Gisted Transcription

On the other end of the spectrum are researchers for whom gisting may be a viable option. A gisted transcript is similar to news show reports sharing the highlights of a politician's speech at the Houses of Parliament. Figure 6.4 defines the two types of gisted transcript: condensed and essence.

The process of creating a condensed transcript involves listening to the recording and leaving out 'all the utterings which do not seem relevant to the research question' (Evers, 2011, p. 13). All backchannels ('umm', 'er') are left out. Here is an example (the dots '…' indicate omitted speech):

> 90% of my communication is with … the sales director. 1% of his communication … with me. I try to be one step ahead, I get things ready … because he jumps from one … project to another. This morning we did Essex, this afternoon we did BT. (Evers, 2011, p. 13)

One of the most challenging issues with the condensed transcript is deciding what to leave out, while still retaining enough context for analytic purposes.

The second type of gisted transcript is the essence transcript (Dempster and Woods, 2011). While the condensed transcript captures the exact words, the

The condensed transcript	The transcript is condensed by removing unnecessary words and phrases, leaving a simplified version but with exact words. No additional text is added.
The essence transcript	The transcript retains the essence of the event through paraphrasing. It may even have single-word sections. Often used in tandem with software which hyperlinks back to the original media file. It can also include pictures in the transcript (visual transcript) instead of or in addition to words.

Figure 6.4 Types of gisted transcript

essence transcript retains only a paraphrased version of the recorded data. Dempster and Woods (2011) described this type of gisting as creating:

> a summary transcript that captures the essence of a media file's content without taking the same amount of time or resources as a verbatim transcript might require. Typically, a transcriber … may take four or five hours to create a verbatim transcript of the spoken word in a typical hour-long media file, while such a file can be gisted in one to two hours. (p. 22)

For instance, say that data was collected from a mathematics class in which children are studying patterns, similarity and symmetry. Some used actual quilt square patterns and others used a computer simulation. Figures 6.5 and 6.6 (where 'T' is the teacher, 'S' is the student) illustrate the differences between a verbatim transcript and an essence transcript.

Six turns in the verbatim transcript are represented as simply 'alternate explanations' in the essence transcript. Essence transcripts rely on your ability to adequately summarize the data based on your research purpose. This type of approach means that a heavier layer of interpretation is occurring whilst transcribing. What is kept in and left out becomes a more overt analytical act.

Using a tool such as InqScribe or Transana can be useful for gisted transcripts. These tools allow you to synchronize the transcripts with the media file. In this way, portions of the full recording can be revisited later if they become important. This means that you can be much more selective with what you transcribe, without losing access to other parts of the data.

T: Why do you think it is that the computer with the quilting software, since it's, since that software is for us to use to design quilts, why won't it let us do something we found out about quilts, which is diagonal flip?

S: Maybe they've never [heard of them.]

S: [Maybe the turtle…]

T: Maybe they've never heard of them.

S: Maybe the [turtle…]

T: [Do you think] that's possible?

S: Yeah.

S: [Maybe there is no, maybe there…]

S: [Maybe the people didn't, just didn't know] Maybe the people that, um, put the, um, the, um, the thing in didn't know about diagonal flips yet.

S: Or maybe, like, there wasn't any, like, CC, like C…G, or like, or any code thing.

T: Any command? There's not a [command.]

S: [Like D.]

S: Maybe they didn't get the right computer chip for that.

Figure 6.5 Verbatim transcript

> T: Why doesn't computer know diagonal flips?
>
> S: Maybe they've never heard of them.
>
> T: Do you think that's possible?
>
> S: Yeah.
>
> S: Alternate explanations

Figure 6.6 Essence transcript

Visual Transcription

Essence transcripts will often contain images to represent the action. This kind of 'visual transcription' uses still images taken from a video recording to represent the meaning. In Figure 6.7, still images taken from a video are combined with the descriptions in the transcript.

Synchronizing the media file with the transcript, you can click on the image to go directly to that point in the video file. This makes it possible to 'bookmark'

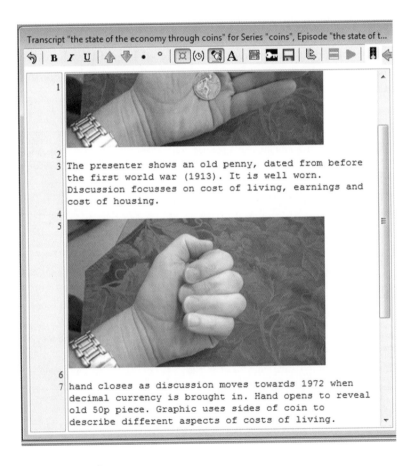

Figure 6.7 Visual transcript

hours of video and stay close to the original data. This approach, described more fully in the last section of this chapter, allows the researcher to analyse the audible layer, the visual layer and the interaction between these two layers (Dempster and Woods, 2011). See Reflexive Practice 6.3.

REFLEXIVE PRACTICE 6.3

Which of the transcription types do you have experience with? What type of transcription will be useful in the study you are designing?

Digital Tools to Support the Transcription Process

The development of recording technologies has impacted qualitative research in ways that few could have foreseen. The advent of reproducible sound recordings in the late nineteenth century did not mark the end of written field notes, as sound recordings remained a fragile technology. Indeed, researchers often made use of professional note takers (stenographers), which limited where interviews could be conducted. For example, the Chicago School researchers would access bureaucratically defined populations, such as prisoners, and interview them in office locations. 'The use of stenographers presumably fitted rather easily into this kind of "fieldwork of the office." While stenography involved a shift towards real-time recording, it was inevitably spatially constrained' (Lee, 2004, p. 874). Later, compact cassette tapes became popular devices for recording interviews and dictations. Specialized transcribing machines and foot pedals made the process even more efficient.

Kelle (2007) noted that the rise of informal qualitative interviewing coincided with the technological development of the portable tape recorder, transforming the 'non-recurring encounter' (p. 444) between the participants and researcher into an event that could be re-examined numerous times by the researcher (p. 444). With tape recorders, interviewing techniques such as focus groups became easier to manage. More diverse examples of data collection became possible, such as the 'walk-along' (Pink, 2007; 2009), described in Chapter 5, and soundscapes (Hall, Lashua and Coffey, 2008), described in Chapter 8. Recording, then, has moved qualitative research well beyond the bureaucratic spaces of the Chicago School into everyday life.

We discuss next four transcription software packages: Express Scribe, Audio Notetaker, InqScribe and F4/F5.

Express Scribe by NCH Software

Express Scribe, which works alongside a word processor, is a cost-effective and simple program. It works with both Windows and Apple operating systems and provides keyboard shortcut 'hot keys' to stop, start, rewind and fast forward the recording (see Figure 6.8). The professional version supports the use of foot pedals, templates and email file exchange. It does not, however, provide a way to visually conceptualize your data or synchronize the media file with the transcript.

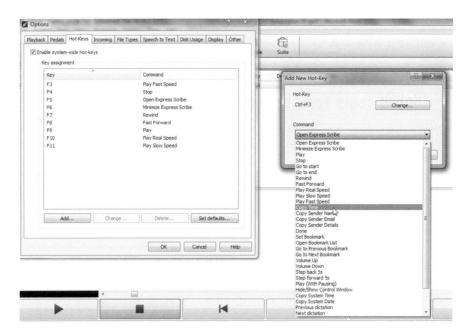

Figure 6.8 Express Scribe shortcut keys

Visit Web Resource 6.3 to watch a screencast introduction to Express Scribe.

Sonocent™ Audio Notetaker 3

Audio Notetaker supports audio data and works with both Windows and Apple operating systems. Audio Notetaker also works well in combination with voice recognition software, such as Dragon Dictate (described later in this chapter). A novel feature is its visual representation of the audio file as colour-coded blocks. This allows you to identify key parts of the recording and, with a click, return to that section of the data. Clicking on the colour-coded bars allows you to copy, paste or delete sections of the recording. Another useful feature is its ability to split the audio into sections and highlight blocks in different colours to mark analytically important speech that needs to be transcribed. This can also be done while recording live on your computer, which can be useful if you want to mark important parts of the audio data in real time. Unfortunately, these 'blocks' are not linked to the final transcript. In Figure 6.9 the blocks on the right link directly to places in the media file.

Figure 6.9 Audio blocks in Audio Notetaker 3 transcript

Visit Web Resource 6.4 to read case studies of researchers using Audio Notetaker.

Audio Notetaker transcripts are searchable, and you can export them along with the audio file to your portable computing device and/or iTunes. Cleverly, the audio file can be exported as an album, with the notes that you have taken becoming the track name and any images that you have included becoming the album art. Overall, the software provides a number of different ways to organize your media files visually and textually, making the transcript somewhat interactive and speeding up the transcription process. Case Study 6.3 illustrates this.

CASE STUDY 6.3

Dorothy is an ethnographer, working on a busy hospital ward. Unable to take extensive written field notes, she uses a recorder to dictate her initial notes, elaborating upon them later when back in her office. She uses a 'debrief file', which involves her talking to the recorder on her commute home. These musings are loaded into Audio Notetaker. When later listening to the recordings, long pauses, such as when she was concentrating on the road, can be quickly skipped by looking at the visual representation of the media file (the blocks). Once she has finished transcribing the notes these are imported into a word processor.

Inquiriam's InqScribe 2.1.1

InqScribe is transcription and subtitling software that works with both audio and video data and is compatible with both Windows and Apple operating systems. Unlike Express Scribe, which works with a word processor to create the transcript, with InqScribe you transcribe directly into the provided window using media file playback controls. Its key features include shortcut keys to control playback, the ability to create macros ('snippets') and synchronization of the media file with the transcript.

Synchronizing the media file with the transcript can lead to a more transparent, rigorous study, as it makes it possible to review the original data recording rather than rely solely on the transcript (Ashmore and Reed, 2000). The original source of data can be made available not only to all members of the research team, but also to the participants and even the reader, providing new opportunities for member checking and strengthening the trustworthiness of the study. This may also, however, raise some ethical concerns, which we ask you to consider in Reflexive Practice 6.4.

REFLEXIVE PRACTICE 6.4

What ethical dilemmas might be raised when synchronizing the media files with the transcript and then making them available to participants and/or consumers of your research findings?

Table 6.1 outlines some examples of how a synchronized transcript may be useful.

Table 6.1   Uses of synchronized transcripts

Synchronized transcripts can …

… make it easier to listen again to particular points in the recording, rather than relying only on the transcript during analysis.

… make it easier to navigate from one section of a long transcript to another.

… be useful for reviewing the full portion of a media file that was gisted.

… serve as a point of reference for other researchers in the team who were not involved in transcription.

In Vignette 6.1, David Woods of Transana discusses how moving seamlessly between gisted transcripts and the original media allows researchers to stay close to their data.

Vignette 6.1 ┤ Transcription, Transcripts and Software

David Woods, University of Wisconsin-Madison, Developer of Transana

Recorded data can be described as a selected abstraction of reality, and transcription is a further selected abstraction of the recording. Further, analysis is a selected abstraction of the transcript, and writing up your findings is often yet another selected abstraction of the analysis. This successive step-wise abstraction (also known as layers of interpretation) is often necessary in the process of moving from raw data to theory, but often comes at the cost of increasing distance between the researcher and the original data. The challenge for the researcher is to be careful to remain 'close' to the data at all stages of the analytic process. This can be accomplished rather well in the transcription and transcript review phases of analysis by using software that links and synchronizes the original media file data with the transcript, allowing the researcher to hear (and in the case of video, to see) the data being referred to while looking at the associated transcript. The written representation of the data (the transcript), is useful for many analytic tasks, but there is no true substitute for listening to the inflection and tone of how the words were said, or seeing the facial expression and body language of the speaker. Having the transcript linked to the media file gives the researcher significantly more analytic and interpretive power than working from the transcript alone.

Synchronizing transcripts in InqScribe is quite simple with the use of time stamps. When the media file is playing, or paused at a point where you want to add a time code, you simply press the Ctrl-+ shortcut which inserts the time into the transcript. Figure 6.10 shows time stamps at the end of each speaker's turn (e.g. [00:00:29:22]) Clicking on the time stamp replays the recording at that point in the transcript.

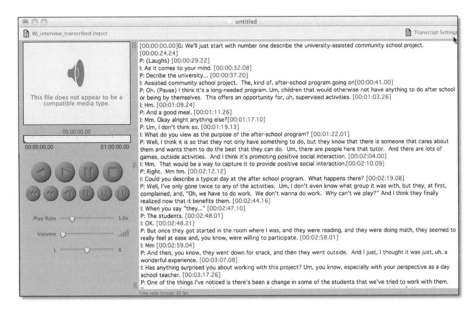

Figure 6.10   Transcript with time stamps in InqScribe

InqScribe also supports the use of shortcuts and customizable macros called 'snippets' to make transcribing easier (see Figure 6.11). In Vignette 6.2, Joshua Johnston discusses his use of snippets to support transcription.

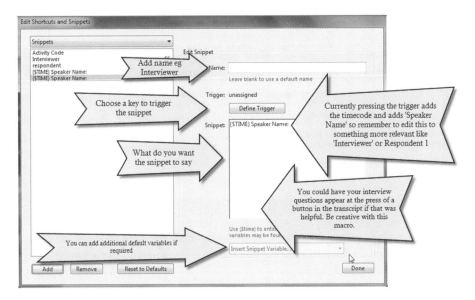

Figure 6.11   Creating snippets in InqScribe

Vignette 6.2	Creating and Using Customizable Shortcuts with InqScribe

Joshua P. Johnston, University of Tennessee

As a discourse analyst, I rely on InqScribe to prepare working drafts of my transcripts. What makes the program especially helpful are the 'snippets' – key combinations that insert commonly used words or phrases.

I use snippets in two ways to speed up my transcribing. First, I assign commonly used phrases and verbal tics of the participants to keys that I don't use otherwise. I assign [0] to 'umm', [-] to 'like' and [=] to 'yeah'. Second, I use snippets to aid in the formatting of my transcript. For example, I create snippets to alternate among speaker names and to insert a double space before participants' pseudonyms with the push of a single button. I create snippets named for each participant and assign each one to a [Function] key. Once defined, I simply press the corresponding [Function] key when I come to the end of one participant's utterance and the beginning of another's.

Understandably, you may feel like remembering all the snippets would be unmanageable, but you can keep the names and triggers visible in a box at the side of your screen. The snippets serve to maintain confidentiality by inserting pseudonyms rather than real names into the transcript.

F4 (Windows Version) / F5 (Apple Version)

F4/F5 supports audio and video data. It also supports adding time stamps to the data, as shown in Figure 6.12 (e.g. #00:00:04-6#).

Shortcut keys in F4/F5 can be used to insert the name of the speaker automatically at the beginning of a new paragraph and to support Jeffersonian or

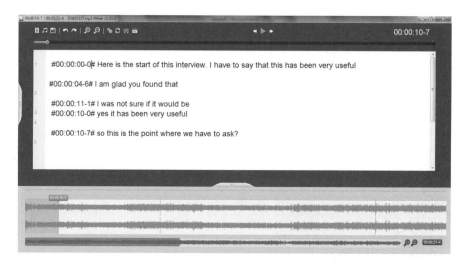

Figure 6.12   F4/F5 transcription software main screen

other notation systems. One of the greatest benefits of this software is that the transcripts will load straight into the qualitative data analysis software packages MAXQDA and ATLAS.ti without losing the notation symbols or time codes.

One other approach to transcription is to directly type into one of the major data analysis software packages, described in Chapter 7, which also support transcription and synchronization of the media files. In Vignette 6.3 Susanne Friese describes the use of ATLAS.ti for doing so.

Vignette 6.3 ─ Associated Documents in ATLAS.ti

Susanne Friese, Support Specialist, ATLAS.ti

The associated documents function allows you to transcribe your audio or video data and link documents to each other so that you can view them synchronously. This means you can mark a segment or a quotation in an associated document and instantly listen to the original audio or view the video.

As shown in the figure below, you can highlight a piece of text in the associated file and press the key combination Ctrl-P to play the linked video segment. The associated recording will be played back from the correct position. Playback stops at the end of the selection. You can also use the association points as a navigation device, either to enter at a particular point in the file or to easily jump around.

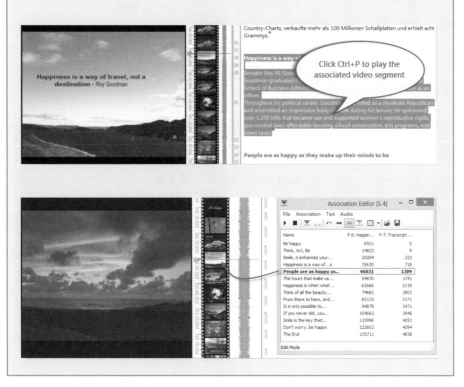

Table 6.2 provides a summary of features across the four transcription software packages that have been discussed so far.

Table 6.2 Transcription software features compared

Express Scribe	• Free version (does not expire) • Mac/PC platform • Supports audio and video data • Fee-based version supports foot pedal use • Hotkeys to control playback • Integrates with word processing programs • Works with voice recognition software
Audio Notetaker 3	• 30-day fully functional free trial version; offers site licences • Mac/PC platform • Supports audio data only, but can import PowerPoint slides • Supports foot pedal use • Audio represented visually with coloured bar segments for navigation, editing and organizing • Works well with voice recognition software
InqScribe 2.2.1	• 30-day fully functional free trial version with academic discounts • Mac/PC platform • Supports audio and video data • Supports foot pedal use • Can insert time codes for transcript/media file synchronization • Can create macros (snippets) for repeated words and phrases • Works with voice recognition software
F4 / F5	• Free version very limited • Mac/PC platform • Supports audio and video data • Supports foot pedal use (in pro version) • Hotkeys to control playback, add timestamps and other shortcuts • Integrates with word processing programs and with CAQDAS tools • Does not work well with voice recognition software

Now take a look at Reflexive Practice 6.5.

REFLEXIVE PRACTICE 6.5

Take some of your recorded data from the Chapter 5 reflexive practice activities, choose a transcription approach and a transcription tool. Practise transcribing your file. Reflect on your experience researching and testing out the selected transcription tool.

Other Approaches to Transcription

We next explore two other approaches to transcribing – using voice recognition software (such as Dragon Dictate) and generating multiple transcripts to represent complex audio and/or video data (using Transana).

Voice Recognition Software

Another particularly useful way to transcribe for those who cannot or should not spend long amounts of time typing is by using voice recognition software. Voice recognition software typically works by being trained to recognize one person's voice, so for transcription purposes the researcher must listen to the recorded data and re-voice it into the voice recognition software package. Transcribing in this way has been discovered by a growing number of researchers (Johnson, 2011; Matheson, 2007), including Paul who uses it for all forms of writing. With Dragon Naturally Speaking (Windows version) or Dragon Dictate (Apple version) voice commands function in the same way that foot pedals and keyboard shortcuts do in other programs.

Visit Web Resource 6.5 to read about Paul's experience of using Dragon.

Using this software will require an investment of both time (to learn the commands and to train the program to recognize your voice) and money (to purchase the software and invest in a quality headset) to get the best results. When it works, however, it is quite impressive. Case Study 6.4 describes how a researcher can use voice recognition software for transcription.

CASE STUDY 6.4

Samuel is a daily user of Dragon Dictate Professional, so it made sense for him to use it for transcription. He mainly does verbatim transcription, using Dragon to type and navigate through the recording. While at his computer, he simply plays the file, and speaks back what he hears. The secret is not to correct as he goes along, but to wait until he has completed three or four paragraphs. Then he uses the playback function, checking what is written on screen with what he hears. Samuel inserts headings into the transcripts using the voice macros. Samuel also used Dragon to make gisted transcriptions by speaking into a Dictaphone. The quality of the headset and the recording device can substantially impact the accuracy of the transcription.

Visit Web Resource 6.6 to learn tips on choosing headsets, eliminating repetitive transcription tasks and setting up macros in Dragon Dictate.

Use of Multiple Transcripts

As audio and video technologies advance, researchers are able to collect ever more complex data sources. Transcription decisions likewise become more complex, as there are additional layers of interaction to represent. For example, to analyse data from a live multi-player computer video game, four separate transcripts would be required to capture 1) the audio interaction, 2) the video feed of the game action, 3) text messages and 4) audio messaging/voiceover, each of which may be of analytic interest. Software such as Transana, which will be discussed in more detail in Chapter 8, allows multiple video/audio streams and multiple transcripts to be loaded simultaneously for analysis (see Figure 6.13). In addition to capturing the complexity of video game play, these multiple transcripts could be used for analysing focus group data, making it easier to identify speakers and non-verbal behaviour.

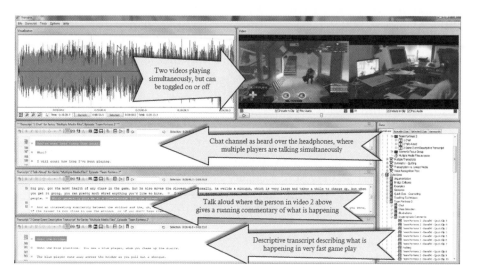

Figure 6.13 Multiple video and transcript features of Transana

Halverson, Bass and Woods (2012) described how they used multiple transcripts to analyse youth films through a variety of analytic lenses: scenes, sound, editing and cinematography.

The first transcript detailed the scenes with, for example, descriptions of where people were standing. The second transcript was a verbatim transcript of everything that was said. The third showed various editing decisions such as camera cuts, zooms and fades. The final transcript highlighted cinematography details such as framing. These transcripts together provided a detailed, nuanced and multi-faceted view into the video file within Transana.

The multiple transcripts in this particular study allowed a depth of analysis that would have been considerably more difficult to achieve without the use of Transana. Their work represents an example of how digital tools can broaden the definition and use of transcripts in qualitative analysis. Take a look at Reflexive Practice 6.6.

REFLEXIVE PRACTICE 6.6

Download the free trial version of Transana and use it to practise transcribing your recorded data. Write an entry in your reflexivity journal about your experience testing it out. How might multiple transcripts be useful in your study?

Final Thoughts

The work of the qualitative researcher often includes transforming audio and/or video files into texts through the process of transcription. Each approach to transcription brings with it a certain set of assumptions, and results in a unique representation of the data. Transcription is always a situated act that is selective and representational. The ability to synchronize the transcript with the original media file ensures the transparency and trustworthiness of the research process. While there have been many technological developments to support transcription, there is still no way for a software program to transcribe a media file *for* you unless you are the only speaker. You still have to invest the time in listening and typing or dictating what you hear and choose to represent in the transcript. The development of mobile computing devices has coincided with the development of computer-assisted qualitative data analysis software (CAQDAS) such as NVivo, ATLAS.ti, MAXQDA, Elan and Transana, which will be explored further in Chapters 7 and 8. Many of these programs support direct transcription of media files as well as enabling direct coding of the media files. This has sparked discussions among researchers about whether it is even necessary to transcribe media files prior to analysis (Evers, 2011). While CAQDAS tools certainly have implications for transcribing, they can also have steeper learning curves and be more expensive than the tools described in this chapter which are tailored specifically for transcription.

Chapter Discussion Questions

1. In what ways is transcription a situated act?
2. Compare the four types of transcription – what are the affordances and constraints of each?
3. How might the ability to synchronize the transcript with the audio or video file impact the trustworthiness of the study? How might the ability to represent the recording with multiple transcripts do the same?
4. How can you ensure ethical practices as you transcribe recordings for your study?

Suggestions for Further Reading

To read more about the transcription process, consider beginning with Davidson's (2009) review which reviews over 30 years of literature on transcription practices. Och's (1979) seminal article focuses on the ways in which the transcription process itself is theory driven and is reflective of a researcher's methodological commitments. Poland (1995) is considered a classic text on transcription. To acquire a more thorough understanding of the link between technological development and qualitative methods, including transcription, Lee's (2004) article is a useful beginning point. Evers (2011) is particularly helpful for those who are interested in exploring the possibilities and limitations related to bypassing the transcription process.

References

Ashmore, M. and Reed, D. (2000) 'Innocence and nostalgia in conversation analysis: The dynamic relations of tape and transcript'. *Forum Qualitative Sozialforschung / Forum: Qualitative Social Research*, 1(3).

Davidson, C. (2009) 'Transcription: Imperative for qualitative research'. *International Journal of Qualitative Methods*, 8(2).

Dempster, P. and Woods, D. (2011) 'The economic crisis through the eyes of Transana'. *Forum Qualitative Sozialforschung / Forum: Qualitative Social Research*, 12(1), Article 16.

Du Bois, J.W. (1991) 'Transcription design principles for spoken discourse research'. *Pragmatics*, 1(1), 71–106.

Evers, J. (2011) 'From the past into the future. How technological development change our ways of data collection, transcription and analysis'. *Forum Qualitative Sozialforschung / Forum: Qualitative Social Research*, 12(1), Article 38.

Gumperz, J.J. and Berenz, N. (1993) 'Transcribing Conversational Exchanges', in J.A. Edwards and M.D. Lampert (eds) *Talking Data: Transcription and Coding in Discourse Research*. Hillsdale, NJ: Lawrence Erlbaum and Associates, pp. 91–122.

Hall, T., Lashua, B. and Coffey, A. (2008) 'Sound and the everyday in qualitative research'. *Qualitative Inquiry*, 14(6), 1019–40.

Halverson, E., Bass, M. and Woods, D. (2012) 'The process of creation: A novel methodology for analysing multimodal data'. *The Qualitative Report*, 17(21), 1–27.

Hammersley, M. (2010) 'Reproducing or constructing? Some questions about transcription in social research'. *Qualitative Research*, 10(5), 553–69.

Jefferson, G. (2004) 'Glossary of Transcript Symbols with an Introduction', in C.H. Lemer (ed.) *Conversation Analysis: Studies from the First-Generation*. Philadelphia, PA: John Benjamins, pp. 13–23.

Johnson, B.E. (2011) 'The speed and accuracy of voice recognition software-assisted transcription versus listen-and-type method; A research note'. *Qualitative Research*, 11(1), 91–7.

Kelle, U. (2007) 'Computer-Assisted Qualitative Data Analysis', in C. Seale, G. Gobo, J. Gubrium and D. Silverman (eds) *Qualitative Research Practice*. London, UK: SAGE.

Kvale, S. (2007) *Doing Interviews*. London, UK: SAGE.

Lapadat, J. and Lindsay, A. (1999) 'Transcription in research and practice: From standardization of technique to interpretive positionings'. *Qualitative Inquiry*, 5(1), 64–86.

Lee, R. (2004) 'Recording technologies and the interview in sociology, 1920–2000'. *Sociology*, 38(5), 869–89.

Lester, J. and Paulus, T. (in press) '"That teacher takes everything badly": Discursively reframing non-normative behaviors in therapy sessions'. *International Journal of Qualitative Studies in Education*.

Matheson, J.L. (2007) 'The voice transcription technique: Use of voice recognition software to transcribe digital interview data in qualitative research'. *The Qualitative Report*, 12(4), 547–60.

Ochs, E. (1979) 'Transcription as Theory', in E. Ochs and B. Schieffelin (eds) *Developmental Pragmatics*. New York, NY: Academic Press, pp. 43–71.

Oliver, D.G., Serovich, J.M. and Mason, T.L. (2005) 'Constraints and opportunities with interview transcription: Towards reflection in qualitative research'. *Social Forces*, 84(2), 1273–89.

Pink, S. (2007) *Doing Visual Ethnography: Images, Media and Representation in Research*. London, UK: SAGE.

Pink, S. (2009) *Doing Sensory Ethnography*. London, UK: SAGE.

Poland, B.D. (1995) 'Transcription quality as an aspect of rigor in qualitative research'. *Qualitative Inquiry*, 1(3), 290–310.

ten Have, P. (2007) *Doing Conversation Analysis: A Practical Guide* (2nd edition). London, UK: SAGE.

SEVEN
Analysing Textual Data

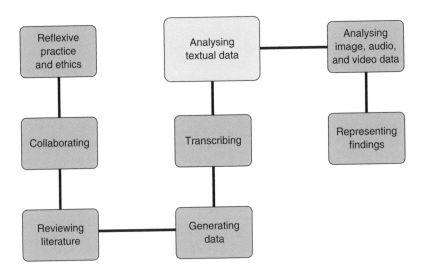

Companion website materials available here:

www.uk.sagepub.com/paulus

Learning Objectives

- Describe the variety of approaches to data analysis.
- Select and critique appropriate features of the major data analysis software packages for how they support the analysis process.
- Name various criteria with which one could evaluate and choose a software package.
- Have strategies to ensure ethical practices when analysing textual data.

Introduction

In Chapter 6, we discussed transcribing audio and/or video recordings. In this chapter, we turn to how digital tools, in particular features of computer-assisted data analysis software (CAQDAS), can be used to analyse textual data. In Chapter 8, we will deal specifically with issues related to the analysis of audio and video data, including the use of Transana, a software package developed specifically for video analysis.

Approaches to Data Analysis

There are many different approaches to data analysis. Tesch (1990), one of the earliest scholars to discuss data analysis software, identified 26 approaches to qualitative research and illustrated how they could be supported by software programs. Saldana (2013) discussed 25 first-cycle coding methods and six second-cycle coding methods for qualitative analysis. Ideally, data analysis *methods* are to be grounded in particular *methodologies*, such as the five introduced by Creswell (2013): narrative, phenomenology, grounded theory, ethnography and case study. Other qualitative research methodologies include, but are not limited to, life history or biographical research, discourse analysis, conversation analysis and ethnomethodology, action research, critical/feminist approaches, action research and visual or semiotic methodologies. Because the choice of research methodology and specific data analysis methods are beyond the scope of this book, we refer you to Saldana (2013), Grbich (2013), Gibson and Brown (2009) and Gibbs (2007) for helpful overviews of qualitative data analysis methods.

Visit Web Resource 7.1 for a review of different qualitative methodologies.

The use of computers to help analyse data has been a complex journey. In the 1980s, qualitative researchers developed software to assist them with their data analysis (with Ethnograph and NUD*IST being two of the earliest packages). As desktop computing became more prevalent and powerful, so too did the use of these packages – see Davidson and Di Gregorio (2011), Fielding (2008) and Hesse-Biber and Crofts (2008) for more comprehensive discussions of the history of software use for qualitative research.

The CAQDAS Networking Project in the UK, funded from 1994 to 2011 by the Economic and Social Research Council (ESRC), has served as a sort of meeting place for discussions around the use of qualitative data analysis software and remains a useful source of information.

Visit Web Resource 7.2 to explore the University of Surrey's CAQDAS networking project.

Even though CAQDAS packages were initially developed by qualitative researchers and were updated regularly based on user feedback (only later becoming commercial products), there has historically been scepticism and resistance towards the use of computers for data analysis (Davidson and Di Gregorio, 2011). Given the variety of approaches to analysis it is not particularly surprising that the idea of using computers to support analysis would generate debate. Over the years there has been a persistent, but mistaken, perception that CAQDAS most easily, or only, supports one methodology, namely grounded theory (Lonikila, 1995), and one analytic method, namely coding – see Coffey, Holbrook and Atkinson (1996) and the response by Lee and Fielding (1996). This is in part because grounded theory as a methodology was popularized at around the same time as the initial CAQDAS packages were (Davidson and Di Gregorio, 2011).

Visit Web Resource 7.3 to read more about the debates around the use of software for qualitative research.

We agree with the view of Lewins and Silver (2007) that far from *imposing* a particular analytic structure or approach to the data, CAQDAS tools *afford* a variety of functions and features which can be intentionally used (or ignored) by the researcher based on their analytic needs. Whether software is used or not, the researcher remains in charge of decisions around how to handle, analyse and interpret the data. In recent years, researchers have begun to publish more thorough descriptions of how they are using software to support their analysis. These studies have been mainly descriptive or comparative, with sometimes contradictory outcomes. For example, Goble et al. (2012) concluded, after exploring NVivo 8, that CAQDAS in general was not appropriate for phenomenological work, because they believed that coding was the primary analytic feature that the software offered. Nonetheless, numerous phenomenological studies have been published in which data analysis software was used (e.g. Mitchell, Silver and Ross, 2012; Mitchell and Kuczynski, 2010). In Vignette 7.1, Monique Mitchell discusses her use of MAXQDA for phenomenological research.

| Vignette 7.1 | **MAXQDA for Phenomenological Research** |

Monique B. Mitchell, The Center for Child and Family Studies, University of South Carolina

As a researcher examining the lived experience of various phenomena, I have found MAXQDA to be an invaluable qualitative research tool that has assisted me in exploring youths' lived experiences of transitions within the foster care system.

In addition to its highly intuitive colour-coded categorical system, MAXQDA provides an opportunity for users to view the document system, the code system, the document browser and retrieved segments windows simultaneously. This is particularly helpful when identifying, establishing and positioning parent and child codes within and between documents.

The 'edit' function is another useful feature of MAXQDA. While activated, this feature allows the user to edit the original document as a means to ensure the accuracy of all the data in the system. Users are not able to code while the 'editing' function is active to prevent accidental modification or deletion of the original document during the coding process. Fortunately, the editing function is deactivated in the default mode, prioritizing the coding and categorizing process in data analysis.

One my favourite features of MAXQDA is the logbook. This wonderful feature allows the user to document each step and key turning points during the analytic process. Thoughts associated with the study's design, concepts

---

and categories emerging from the data, relevant background literature, and/ or initial presuppositions can be exhaustively reflected upon in the logbook. The logbook is also a valuable tool for documenting an audit trail that can capture the daily events and decisions related to the research process.

We tend to agree with Schoenfelder's (2011) observation that perceived limitations of CAQDAS packages are 'based on the individual analytic approach rather than on principal methodological incompatibilities' (Section 1). Most users are not fully aware of the capabilities of the software and may therefore be disappointed with their experience.

Digital Tools That Support Qualitative Data Analysis

While some have advocated the use of non-specialized tools for analysis (Hahn, 2008), such as word processors (LaPelle, 2004) and spreadsheets (Meyer and Avery, 2009), mastering one of the major commercial software packages may be well worth your time. These packages are updated regularly, provide user support and are likely to be used by your collaborators. The initial investment of time and effort required to learn the tools will pay off handsomely over the course of your research career.

Weitzman and Miles (1995), and later Weitzman (2000), categorized software packages according to their functionality as text retrievers (able to retrieve all examples of particular word(s) across the data), text base managers (able to store and organize data sets), code and retrieve programs (able to apply codes to data and retrieve and display coded text), code-based theory builders (able to represent or create links and relationships between codes, create categories and write memos to annotate data) and conceptual network builders (able to create and analyse graphic representations of relationships between concepts). However, over the years the boundaries between these categories have blurred, with the major packages now supporting all of these functions.

ATLAS.ti 7, MAXQDA 11 and NVivo 10 are three popular qualitative data analysis software packages. ATLAS.ti was developed as a research project at the Technical University of Berlin in 1989, with the first commercial version released in 1993. Version 7 was released in 2012, with a mobile application released in 2013. The Apple version is scheduled for release in 2014. ATLAS.ti supports analysis of not only text but also images, audio and video data, allowing you to either directly code the media files and/or transcribe the files. You can also synchronize your transcript with the media file (the benefits of which were described in Chapter 6). ATLAS.ti can link to Google Earth coordinates for geodata analysis. It also supports importing survey data for mixed methods studies and provides bundling and merging features for teams to share analysis, although not in real time. Figure 7.1 shows a new feature in ATLAS.ti 7 – multiple data document windows. You can see, from left to right, an image data document, video data document and text document all open simultaneously in their own workspace for analysis.

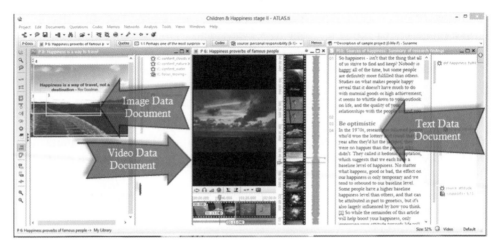

Figure 7.1 Multiple documents open in ATLAS.ti 7 (screenshot adapted courtesy of Susanne Friese)

Visit Web Resource 7.4 for a link to the companion website for *Qualitative Data Analysis with ATLAS.ti* by Friese (2012), which includes sample data and analysis activities.

MAXQDA released Version 11 in late 2012, with the Apple version scheduled for release in 2013. The first version was released in 1989 by creator Udo Kuckartz. The company, based in Berlin, offers a free MAXReader program with limited functionality that allows you to view and handle the data (but not code it). This can be useful for sharing analysed data with non-MAXQDA users. MAXQDA offers a free mobile device application, MAXApp, which supports data collecting, tagging and some coding. It is also the only one of the three to offer an 'emoticode' feature, as illustrated in Figure 7.2. Instead of choosing words, symbols can be selected to describe the data.

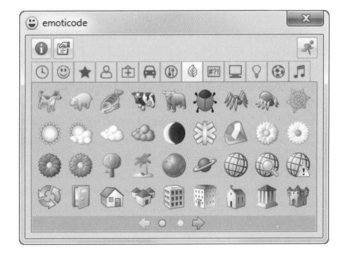

Figure 7.2 MAXQDA emoticodes

Like ATLAS.ti, MAXQDA supports direct audio and video file coding, transcription and media file synchronization, Google Earth integration and importing of survey data. MAXQDA is able to import bibliographic data from citation management software (such as Zotero) to support writing literature reviews from within the software.

Visit Web Resource 7.5 for a link to the companion website for *Basics of Qualitative Research* by Corbin and Strauss (2008), which includes a set of exercises to be conducted in conjunction with MAXQDA.

QSR International, the Melbourne-based company that distributes NVivo, was established in 1995. The earlier version of the software, NUD*IST, developed by Tom and Lyn Richards, was released in 1981. NVivo 10 was released in 2012, with the first version for Apple operating systems scheduled for release in 2013. Like the other two packages, NVivo supports multimedia file coding, transcribing and media file synchronization, Google Earth integration and importing of survey data. Like MAXQDA, NVivo will import bibliographic data from citation management software, such as Zotero, to support literature reviews. Unlike the other two packages (but similar to Transana), the NVivo for Teams server version allows collaboration in real time. The OneNote add-in imports content from Microsoft OneNote.

A unique feature of NVivo is its NCapture add-on – a web browser extension specifically designed to capture web and social media data, as described by Marcus Ogden, a product manager for QSR International, in Vignette 7.2.

Vignette 7.2	**Analysing Web Data with NVivo's NCapture Tool**

Marcus Ogden, Product Manager, QSR International

The wealth of qualitative information available on the web has become an increasing focus in recent years for researchers and for QSR International, the developers of NVivo. As well as research papers and journal articles (in PDF format) and web pages (such as blogs), social media sites such as Twitter and Facebook have become important to qualitative researchers as sources of data for analysis. For example, social media data can be analysed to examine how online communities interact (see Chapter 5), how public opinion changes during election campaigns or how people respond to public events or crises such as the 2011 UK riots.

Social media data often contains tags identifying topics or individuals, and structures representing the flow of information between people (replies, retweets). QSR's NCapture tool for NVivo 10 allows researchers to capture online content directly from their web browser, for import into NVivo. All

(Continued)

(Continued)

web pages can be imported as PDFs, but, additionally, data of interest from Twitter, Facebook and LinkedIn can be imported as structured data sets. These data sets can then be 'autocoded' to create NVivo node structures representing (for example) tags, users or conversations. Videos from YouTube can also be imported for analysis, along with their comments.

To help researchers understand what's going on in their social media data, NVivo offers a range of visualization features. For example, researchers can view charts for their Twitter data, showing how the incidence of particular hashtags – or of particular nodes arising from the researcher's own coding – vary with time. Or researchers can view cluster analysis diagrams for their Facebook data, showing which people are talking about similar topics. These visualizations can help researchers come up with new questions about the data for further investigation, and from the visualizations researchers can easily access the underlying qualitative data to help them investigate these questions.

Visit Web Resource 7.6 for a link to Bazeley and Jackson (2013) *Qualitative Data Analysis with NVivo.*

As you can see from these brief overviews, the three packages offer similar features with some unique differences. As competitors, new versions of one software package can often be found to have incorporated features of the other two packages; so it will be important for you to explore the most recent version of the software (or the version you have access to). Lewins and Silver (2007) have provided a comprehensive and comparative overview of these three packages, as well as descriptions of four additional packages (HyperRESEARCH 2.6, QDA Miner 2.0, Qualrus and Transana 2).

Visit Web Resource 7.7 for a more comprehensive list of data analysis software tools.

In Reflexive Practice 7.1, you will begin the process of exploring one of the CAQDAS packages. Your access to a software program, available training and support, and personal preferences around interface design are likely to be the factors that impact which package you ultimately choose.

Visit Web Resource 7.8 to read a vignette by Dr. Jonathan Pettigrew reflecting on the use of both NVivo and MAXQDA in his qualitative work.

REFLEXIVE PRACTICE 7.1

Which of these three packages, if any, are you familiar with? Have you already selected a package to use in your work? If so, what factored into that decision? If not, take some time to explore each product website, watching the introductory video tutorials and even downloading the trial versions of the software to see how well they run with your system. Make an entry in your reflexivity journal about your decision-making process and select one of the packages in which to try out the features that will be explored in this chapter. You should also by now have some text and audio/visual data that you collected in Chapter 5 and transcribed in Chapter 6. Use this data as you learn one of the data analysis software packages in this chapter.

Organizational Features

One of the most obvious benefits of using software is that it can serve as the 'textual laboratory' (Konopasek, 2008) for all of your data and the documents related to your study (e.g. literature review sources, institutional review board/ ethics committee forms and analytic notes). Di Gregorio and Davidson (2008) provide a fuller description of how to begin building your entire project within a software package, including detailed examples from all three major packages. Being able to read, annotate, code, visualize and interpret in one space, within reach of your theoretical literature, research proposals and ethics guides, drastically improves your ability to systematically document all the decisions that you make throughout the research process and allows others to view those processes. In this way your thinking is made visible in ways that it could not have been prior to the use of software (Konopasek, 2008). Consider now Reflexive Practice 7.2.

REFLEXIVE PRACTICE 7.2

CAQDAS tools make is easier to share your analysis process in an ongoing manner. However, there are certainly ethical dilemmas inherent in sharing unfolding interpretations with others. What are some of the ethical concerns and challenges with using CAQDAS tools in this manner?

As your data and documentation increases, letting computers do what they do best can free up your time to focus on the interpretations and analysis, rather than the management of your data. See Vignette 7.3 for a description of how Carlos Galan-Diaz and his colleagues used NVivo for a large data set.

| Vignette 7.3 | Using Nvivo for Handling Large Data Sets |

Carlos Galan-Diaz, Anna Conniff and Tony Craig, The James Hutton Institute, Aberdeen, Scotland

As part of an ESRC funded project [RES-000-22-1397] (Conniff et al., 2010), we collected the verbal commentary of 81 participants while they either watched a seven-minute walkthrough of a virtual environment

(Continued)

(Continued)

model (passive condition) or navigated themselves through the same virtual environment (active condition). After viewing two different versions of the same virtual environment, participants were asked to choose which one they preferred, with a particular onus on describing how the environment looked and felt using a 'think aloud' protocol. One of the main research questions was whether the navigation mode (active versus passive) would cause a qualitative difference in people's perceptions of the virtual environment.

Given the volume of material generated, the use of NVivo was necessary to analyse the data. As each of the two versions of the virtual environment model had three distinct areas where participants had to focus, we used NVivo (Version 9) in two ways. First, all transcripts were auto-coded according to the distinct moments at which participants talked about the different areas, thus creating a self-organizing structure at import. Second, word frequency queries were run against each of the desired output areas so as to identify (and corroborate) that participants were indeed describing the physicalities of the virtual world (i.e. that what they were reporting was commensurate with what they were doing). This was paramount as each of the three main areas had overall outputs in excess of 10,000 words. Once the data was structured, the actual qualitative analysis started.

Our research study would have been much more laborious to structure had we only used word processors, spreadsheets or pen and paper. With NVivo, we were able to store, archive and manage a large amount of text data. Searching and coding for particular sections of interest in the transcripts across 81 participants allowed for easy identification of emerging data trends, as well as testing for a priori research questions.

All three programs support organizing the data by 'known characteristics' (Lewins and Silver, 2007), that is, attributes of the data that are important to the study (e.g. demographic data). NVivo may have the best functionality in this area through its 'cases' for organizing the data, in combination with the attributes and queries features for searching. ATLAS.ti offers 'families' as an organizing tool, with query and explorer tools for searching. MAXQDA uses 'document variables' and 'sets' to group data, and the matrix coding query and code relations browsers for searching. These search tools are explored later in the chapter.

ATLAS.ti allows you to segment the data prior to coding by creating 'quotations' which can be manipulated separately from codes. This provides greater flexibility than the other two packages for creating a priori units of analysis as well as for the micro-analysis of data. Turn now to Reflexive Practice 7.3.

Analysis Features

We next describe in more detail a few of what Lewins and Silver (2007) called the 'main tasks of analysis', and illustrate how the packages support them. While not every approach to data analysis incorporates all of these tasks, and no two researchers are likely to perform these tasks in exactly same way, we consider these to be common analytic tasks. These tasks include annotating, linking, searching, coding, querying and visualizing.

Visit Web Resource 7.9 for tutorials and resources for exploring the relationship between analysis and software use.

Annotating

'Before computers, many researchers did not code segments of text', but rather 'felt through, explored, read and re-read ... compared and systematically built upon data records, keeping growing memo records about the accruing evidence and their exploration of its narrative' (Richards and Richards, 1998, p. 214). Reading through the data repeatedly, while noting its interesting aspects, is a common first step across data analysis approaches. While researchers used to do this with a highlighter and/or writing in the margins of printed documents, software tools now connect your annotations directly to the data.

In NVivo, an annotation can be displayed as a footnote within a document, with the relevant text highlighted. ATLAS.ti allows you to attach explanatory 'comments' to any segment of your data, to codes or to entire data documents. This can be useful but can also make it difficult to remember where you may have written a particular annotation. In both MAXQDA and ATLAS.ti, hovering the mouse over the comments allows you to see what is written. Figure 7.3 shows how the memo tool in MAXQDA is being used to more fully describe Student Interview #3.

Memos are a type of annotation tool that serve a more analytical function and are often more complex in structure and length than comments. In NVivo, each document and code can only have one memo linked to it, and memos can only be linked to one other item. Individual parts of a memo can be multiply linked to other project items. In contrast, MAXQDA and ATLAS.ti have more flexible memo functions, with the ability to link to multiple documents. In Vignette 7.4, Julia Schehl, Senior Manager at MAXQDS, describes the use of its memo tool.

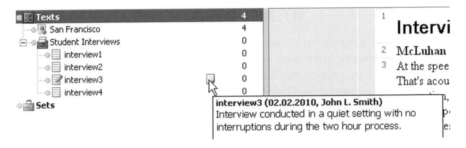

Figure 7.3 Memo tool in MAXQDA

| Vignette 7.4 | Using the Memo Feature in MAXQDA |

By Julia Schehl, Senior Manager, MAXQDA (VERBI Software)

In MAXQDA, the user can create 'Post-it'-like notes of insights and attach them immediately to segments of the data, codes or entire data documents. These notes are called memos. Memoing is extremely helpful for immediately recording your ideas, as well as communicating with team members. Memos can be tagged with different icon types, so that without having to open and read a memo the user immediately knows if it contains, for example, an open question, the beginning of a theory or a case summary.

In the figure below, memos were used to keep track of early thoughts and theories that came up during the beginning of the analysis which still needed to be proven by further information. Here, the researcher identified what might be the life strategy of the interviewee, but by using a symbol he notes that this is not yet a final conclusion. The memo tagged with 'L' is a literature memo and contains some important quotes from related articles.

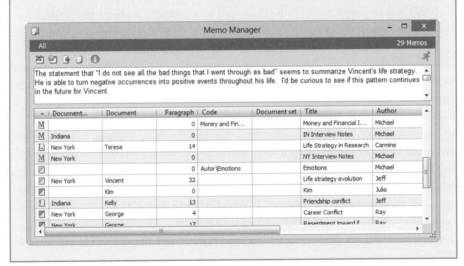

Code memos can be used to document code definitions like 'use this code if interviewee describes health issues that affect his or her day-to-day routine'. They may also contain actual quotes which can help clarify the coding category. In this way the memos can enhance the reliability of the coding process.

Thanks to the Memo Manager, all of these thoughts and questions are stored in a sortable table, which makes it possible to quickly call up memos with a specific icon or title at any time. Clicking on a memo in the Memo Manager opens up the original document, image or media file to which the memo is attached.

MAXQDA also allows free memos, which are not attached to a specific element (document, code or segment) but rather to the whole project. They can be used to store information or instructions for the whole team, such as interview guidelines.

Beyond annotating the data, there is a good bit of writing involved in qualitative research, including keeping a research journal (see Chapter 2), documenting decisions made around coding, making connections with the theoretical literature and writing up your interpretations after coding (see Chapter 9). All of this can be done using the memo tools in ATLAS.ti, MAXQDA or NVivo, with each memo incorporating a computer-generated date stamp. Eventually, you can export the memos into a word processing program as you finalize your reports. Turn now to Reflexive Practice 7.4.

REFLEXIVE PRACTICE 7.4

Create a memo that describes your research questions and the focus of your study. If necessary, read or view the online tutorial information about creating a memo in the software program you are using.

Then, read through your data and capture your initial thoughts using the comment, memo and other annotation tools available in the package you are using. Reflect in your journal on what this experience was like.

Linking

As part of your initial data exploration, and throughout the analysis process, it may be useful to make note of relationships you are seeing between your data sources, the ideas you have captured in memos, the theoretical literature and/or the codes you create. Prior to the advent of the computer, qualitative researchers could be found cutting their data into strips of paper or creating handwritten indexing systems to reflect relationships they were noting in the data. Now this can be done with linking tools in the software packages. For example, Figure 7.4 is a screenshot of the hyperlink tool from ATLAS.ti 7 in which two quotations that support each other are linked to reflect this relationship. Here we see a relationship link between a segment of a video clip coded as 'attitude' (#1) and a section of a newspaper article coded in the same way. The researcher used a hyperlink to show the 'supports' relationship (#2) in the data. This hyperlink then showed up in the margin (#3) of both primary documents (the video and the newspaper).

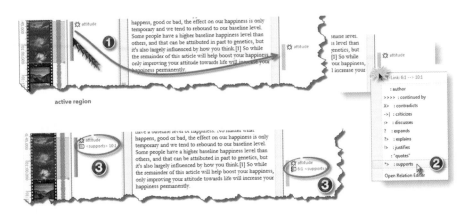

Figure 7.4 Hyperlink tool in ATLAS.ti (from http://www.atlasti.com/uploads/media/WhatsNew_a7.pdf, last accessed 18 July 2013).

The linking features of the software packages allow you to represent processes (e.g. storylines, sequences of events, causes and effects, steps in a procedure) and make connections between various aspects of the data or your study as a whole. These can be particularly important in research traditions such as narrative analysis, conversation analysis and discourse analysis.

Each package supports creating links in different ways. ATLAS.ti has a very flexible linking tool that allows multiple links to be established and quickly navigated, especially with the use of the multiple document windows, whereas MAXQDA allows only pairs of linked segments. Navigation between linked segments in NVivo is a bit more cumbersome than in the other two programs, requiring multiple mouse clicks. Turn now to Reflexive Practice 7.5.

REFLEXIVE PRACTICE 7.5

Within your sample project, practise creating links within or between your data sources. If necessary, read or view the online tutorial information about creating links between data. Then reflect on this experience in your journal.

Searching

Search tools can be used to find particular words or phrases (much like the 'find' tool in Microsoft Word), as well as provide word frequency counts. Searching can be a useful starting point for thinking about coding. For example, doing a word frequency search can easily show the most commonly occurring phrases across transcripts, but on closer examination you may see that it was the interviewer bringing up a particular phrase repeatedly in interviews rather than the interviewee. We would counsel researchers against putting too much stock in the numbers on their own, but they can serve as a useful starting point for further analysis; see, for example, Dempster, Woods and Wright (2013).

Coding

For many, but not all, researchers who work with textual data, coding is at the heart of the analytic process. Coding refers to the process of attaching a meaningful label to a specific portion of the data. In more deductive approaches to analysis, coding may come quite early in the process, with some or all codes established in advance. For more inductive approaches, codes may emerge only after initial exploration has been done through memos and linking. Codes can be created at any point during the process – prior to or during analysis – again depending on your methodological approach.

Prior to the use of software, coding was done by hand, for example through writing in the margins, colour-coding with highlighters and/or using index cards. The 'hands-on' nature of this very laborious process gave some researchers the sense of being 'immersed in' or 'close to' their data. There may still be value in engaging in the tactile experience of sorting the data by hand, both conceptually and as a learning experience. At the same time, it is very easy to get lost in piles of data and lists of codes with no way to 'see' patterns emerging across the data in a systematic way. In contrast, software packages can easily support your ability to 1) create and assign codes to data; 2) retrieve all data which has been assigned a particular code; 3) review the coded data in its original context; and 4) make decisions about renaming codes, deleting codes, recoding data, merging codes, creating hierarchies and groups of codes, and so on.

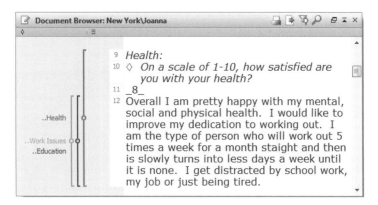

Figure 7.5   Coded data with margin view in MAXQDA (from MAXQDA 11 manual)

The mechanics of assigning codes to your data involves highlighting a portion of your data and clicking to attach a code. All of the software packages allow you to 'see' how the data has been coded through a margin view, often incorporating colour coding, as well as quick retrieval of all data segments that have been coded in a certain way. In Figure 7.5 you can see how the coded data appears in MAXQDA with coding stripes in the left-hand margin. Three codes (health, work issues and education) have been attached to this section of the data.

One of the main differences between the software packages in regards to coding has to do with the presence or absence of a hierarchical structure for the codes. ATLAS.ti is unable to provide code hierarchies by default in the way that MAXQDA and NVivo do. Figure 7.6 illustrates how coding hierarchies appear in NVivo.

Nodes			
Name		Sources	References
Economy		24	277
Agriculture		8	20
Fishing or aquaculture		18	168
Jobs and cost of living		15	76
Tourism		7	12

Figure 7.6   Nodes in NVivo

We see a coding 'node' ('Economy') with several subcodes (agriculture, fishing or aquaculture, jobs and cost of living, tourism). The 'sources' column indicates how many of the data sources contain the code (e.g. 18 sources have the code 'fishing or aquaculture'). The references column indicates how many times the code appeared in the data (e.g. 'fishing or aquaculture' has been applied across the data 168 times).

In contrast, ATLAS.ti hierarchies must be created by the researcher through code labelling devices, such as adding prefixes. The researcher would start with a flat coding structure first (e.g. 'agriculture', 'fishing or aquaculture', etc.), after which they would group the codes into the larger category of 'economy' (see Figure 7.7). The numbers after the code ({0,0}) will increase as codes are applied

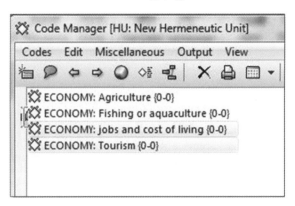

Figure 7.7   Prefix hierarchies added in ATLAS.ti

to the data to show their frequency of use. While this coding hierarchy can be created at the start of the study, its default 'flat' coding structure affords a more inductive approach to coding. The extra step needed to create hierarchical coding, or to change it later, can be frustrating for some.

One way that NVivo (Versions 9.2 onwards) supports the coding process is through its framework analysis tool. Framework analysis was developed in the 1980s by Ritchie and Spencer (1994) for policy research and involves five stages: 1) familiarization with the texts; 2) identifying a thematic framework; 3) coding the data; 4) charting the data; and 5) mapping and interpreting the data. See Vignette 7.5.

Vignette 7.5	**Using NVivo to Conduct Framework Analysis of Interview Data**

Paul G. Dempster, University of York

Framework analysis follows a process of data reduction where coding is represented across different cases and themes in a table format. The goal is to reduce data to manageable amounts. Having worked out the codes you wish to pursue, you assign codes to your data. By providing a summary of your coded data in cells on a chart, you can quickly see patterns and explore and map themes across the data. NVivo supports the ability to link individual cells back to their original data source. The following excerpt from an interview shows the affordances of using software to help manage the process of developing a framework analysis. In this study the researchers were exploring how bad news is shared and received with patients in hospital. This segment of the data had been assigned two codes ('who told bad news' and 'reaction to bad news').

Instead of retrieving all of the data which had been coded with these two codes into one document, which may run to a number of pages, framework analysis puts the result of the analysis into a chart organized by case.

(Continued)

(Continued)

Case number	Code 1: Who told you the bad news?	Code 2: What was your reaction?
Case 1	Told news by doctor (diagnosis), follow up by nurse.	Cried for long period. Devastation.
Case 2	Doctor gave diagnosis, left, then nurse explained.	Cried, then angry. Disbelief.

Simply clicking on the cell will bring up all the coded material relevant to that case, making the process more accurate and efficient. The methodology allows you to explore large amounts of data across a large number of cases with relative ease.

The summary grid and grid table features in MAXQDA 11 work in a very similar way to the framework analysis tool in NVivo and can be used to summarize and reduce data across multiple cases.

Visit Web Resource 7.10 for more resources on framework analysis.

Querying

Coding is a time-consuming process and requires extended engagement with the data, even with the assistance of software. Once the codes are entered, however, the hard work pays off. Querying tools provide powerful ways of systematically exploring relationships between the codes. Lewins and Silver (2007) refer to this as 'interrogating the dataset'. Queries can be used to find relationships and patterns between key attributes of the data.

Visit Web Resource 7.11 for guidance on moving beyond initial coding using CAQDAS packages.

For example, in ATLAS.ti, data that has been coded in a particular way can be retrieved by running queries with Boolean, semantic and proximity operators. The lower right window in Figure 7.8 shows the 24 results of a query that used the Boolean operator 'and' to identify all data coded with two codes (the 'overall stance: anti-supplement' code and the 'pre-lecture stance: beliefs' code). This data is from a study in which undergraduate nutrition students made blog posts related to their previous experiences and/or beliefs with dietary supplements.

Clicking on each of the results would then take you to where that quotation appears in the data set.

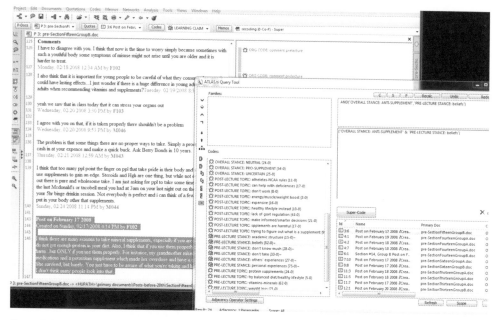

Figure 7.8   Results of query in ATLAS.ti

The co-occurrence explorer in ATLAS.ti, and similar tools in NVivo and MAXQDA, show which codes co-occur together in the data, as illustrated in Figure 7.9.

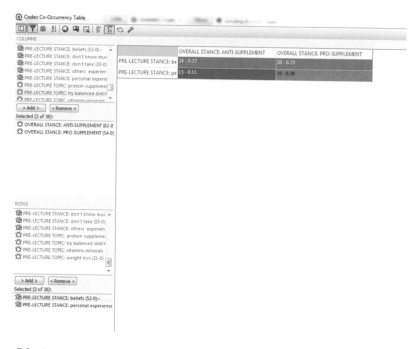

Figure 7.9   Results of co-occurrence inquiry in ATLAS.ti

131

Here we see that when students used personal experience to back up their claims about dietary supplements, nearly twice as many (29) took a pro-supplement stance than an anti-supplement stance (15). However, when students used beliefs to back up their claims, they were more or less equally divided between taking a pro- (20) or anti-supplement stance (24). While these numbers do not carry much meaning on their own, they are a way to explore hunches about relationships in the data. NVivo's matrix coding query functions in a similar way to the co-occurrence tool in ATLAS.ti, and is described by Chad Lochmiller in Vignette 7.6.

Vignette 7.6 | **Using NVivo 9 for Matrix Coding Queries**

Chad Lochmiller, Indiana University

I am currently using NVivo to compare written reflections submitted by leadership coaches for school administrators. I import the Word or PDF data documents into NVivo, and apply codes through a hierarchical structure that maximizes the power of the matrix analysis. For example, I use codes that are related to the time, place, participant characteristics and other descriptive factors that could influence how coaches provide support to the principals. Matrix queries allow comparison of coded text to identify differences, similarities or contrasts in the participants' thoughts, statements or experiences.

In a recent analysis, I used the matrix query to compare the type of issues that coaches were discussing with the administrators in the fall with the issues they discussed in the spring. I was able to select an 'issue' code as one of the rows and then compare what the coaches were writing based on a 'time' code that related to the calendar year (i.e. Fall, Winter, Spring, Summer) as the columns.

In this way I can make empirically supported statements about the magnitude of any differences found through the analysis. For example, I discovered that coaches working with experienced (EXP) school leaders more often reported 'resistance' (RES) to coaching (232) than coaches working with less experienced (NOV = novice) school leaders (132), as illustrated in Figure 7.10. Clicking on the numbers reported in the matrix analysis brings up the coded text for each of the categories.

Matrix Coding Query - Results Prev		
	A : ACCEPT ... ▽	B : RES TO C... ▽
1 : NOV_PRI ▽	7	132
2 : EXP_PRI ▽	38	232

Figure 7.10 Results of NVivo matrix coding query

Now turn to Reflexive Practice 7.6.

REFLEXIVE PRACTICE 7.6

Within your sample project, practise searching the data and assigning some codes to the data. Practise renaming the codes, combining/merging codes and working with or creating hierarchies as necessary. If necessary, read or view the online tutorial information on searching, coding and querying. Use the query and/or co-occurrence tools once you have applied some codes. Be sure to reflect on your experience in your journal.

Visualizing

Qualitative researchers have long considered data displays and other visualization devices to be useful tools for analysis (Miles and Huberman, 1994). Being able to graphically represent the relationship between your data documents, quotations, memos, links and codes provides an opportunity for greater analytic insight. Tag clouds, for example, show the frequency with which a word appears in the data and can be a useful starting point for understanding your data. All three software packages allow you to easily create a tag cloud with your data (see Figure 7.11).

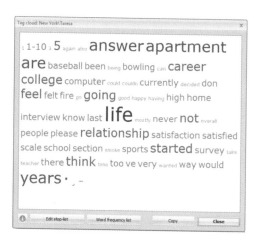

Figure 7.11   Tag cloud in MAXQDA (from MAXQDA 11 manual)

Vignette 7.7 illustrates several visualization tools offered by MAXQDA.

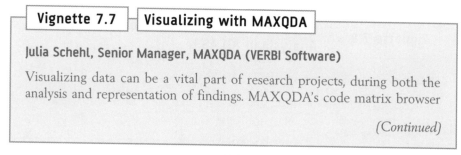

Vignette 7.7 ─ **Visualizing with MAXQDA**

Julia Schehl, Senior Manager, MAXQDA (VERBI Software)

Visualizing data can be a vital part of research projects, during both the analysis and representation of findings. MAXQDA's code matrix browser

(Continued)

(Continued)

provides a visualization of how often codes have been assigned to documents. The squares that visualize code occurrences are bigger, or smaller, depending on how often a code was used in a document, making it immediately clear which topics played a bigger or smaller role across the data. Looking at the figure below, it is easy to see that the interviews with Teresa, Milly and Jack have not been analysed yet. This is also a great way to check the progress of the research and stay on top of things.

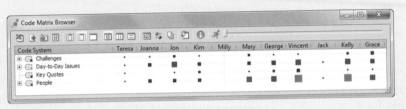

Sometimes it can be of great interest to know how often subcodes have been used in a project. If, for example, researchers in an evaluation study collected data on the software features users hope to see implemented in the future, it is important to know which features were mentioned most often. MAXQDA offers a tool that quickly pulls up the frequencies of subcode use, and can also create charts that could be used to present these results in a report or presentation.

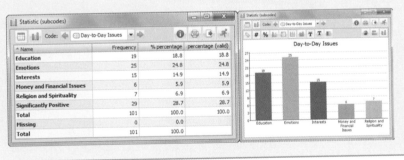

NVivo 'models', MAXQDA 'maps' and ATLAS.ti 'networks' all provide ways to visually explore data through creation of graphical representations and maps. In Vignette 7.8 Susanne Friese of ATLAS.ti explores the use of networks.

Vignette 7.8	Using Network Tools for Visual Analysis in ATLAS.ti

Susanne Friese, Support Specialist, ATLAS.ti

Network views in ATLAS.ti can be used for analytic purposes as well as for representing findings. A network view can display primary documents, codes, quotations and memos. In my study of the relationship between having children and happiness, I used the network view as a visual analysis tool to examine whether happiness is defined differently by parents and non-parents. The data includes blog posts made on this topic by adults with children and adults without children.

The analysis began by importing one of the codes ('don't have children') into an empty network view. The 'import co-occurring' codes option was used to see which of the happiness definition codes were provided by non-parents. As a result, two codes were imported. These two codes were linked using the 'is reported by' link.

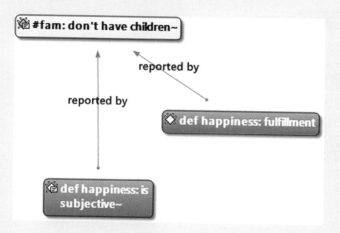

The process was repeated for the 'have children' code. The two network views were then brought together. The existing links between the codes were instantly visible.

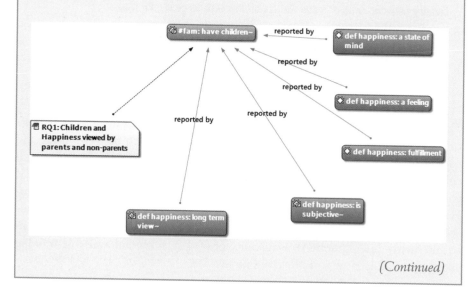

(Continued)

(Continued)

The next step was to bring the two network views together. The existing linkages with the definition codes were then instantly visible.

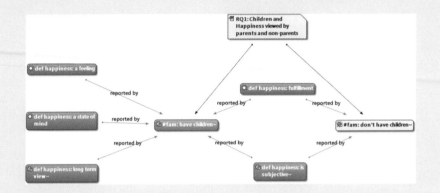

The network nodes were then arranged in a way that best reflected the answer to the research question. The actual data behind the nodes can be viewed by right-clicking on it.

Now turn to Reflexive Practice 7.7.

REFLEXIVE PRACTICE 7.7

Within your sample project, practise using the mapping/networking tool to display your initial memoing and coding. If necessary, read or view the online tutorial information about creating network views or maps. Reflect on this experience in your journal.

Visit Web Resource 7.12 for more resources on visualization tools.

Evaluating and Selecting a Package

There are several important questions to consider when deciding which package to adopt. First and foremost, it is probably a good idea to consider using the package that is supported at your institution and/or that is used by your research collaborators. For example, if everyone at your institution is using NVivo, then it will be an uphill battle for you to adopt MAXQDA. Of course, it is ideal whenever possible to choose the best tool for the job rather than according to availability. Other factors you will want to consider include operating system requirements, pricing options, availability of trial versions and available training and support. Turn now to Reflexive Practice 7.8.

REFLEXIVE PRACTICE 7.8

Reflect on your experience trying out one of the data analysis software packages as part of this chapter. Visit the websites for each of the software programs and fill out the information in order to make an informed comparison.

Program:	ATLAS.ti	MAXQDA	NVivo
Most recent version			
Operating system and mobile apps			
Pricing/licensing			
Trial version			
Training/support			
Recommended system requirements			
Other features			

Visit Web Resource 7.13 for links to the CAQDAS guides for engaging in teamwork and choosing the appropriate software.

Visit Web Resource 7.14 for an excellent list of questions to ask yourself when comparing software programs.

Final Thoughts

Choosing and learning a software package is a wise investment of time, as their features can be used to support other aspects of the research process beyond data analysis. The question of whether it is better to analyse data by hand or with software is reminiscent of the instructional technology 'media debates' of the 1990s. Kozma's (1994) view was that new technologies (media) undoubtedly would impact learning. Clark (1994) countered that it was always the *method underlying* the new media that impacted learning. Media comparison studies have consistently found no difference in learning outcomes when all variables are held constant except for the use of a particular technology. There have been similar studies comparing 'by-hand' qualitative data analysis techniques with 'software-supported' analysis techniques in an effort to decide which is better (Basit, 2003; Davis and Meyer, 2009; Welsh, 2002). These studies have concluded, as did the earlier media comparison studies, that what matters are the circumstances under which one is working. Digital tools are neither completely neutral, nor are they overly deterministic. While they may have a certain 'software architecture' (Salliard, 2011), with affordances and constraints that need to be understood, the features can be appropriated to support the kinds of analysis needed.

Visit Web Resource 7.15 for some words of advice on using data analysis software by Dr Ray Maietta, President of ResearchTalk.

Chapter Discussion Questions

1. What methodology are you using for the study you are designing? What approaches to data analysis are generally used in that methodology?
2. Which analysis features supported by the major software packages may be most useful in understanding your data?
3. Describe your experience creating a sample project and using the software features to explore the data. What additional training or resources will you explore to improve skills?
4. How might the use of a software package to share your analysis more easily with others add trustworthiness and transparency to your work? How might it create some ethical dilemmas?
5. How can you ensure ethical practices as you analyse the data for your study?

Suggestions for Further Reading

Recent chapters by Davidson and Di Gregorio (2011), Fielding (2008) and Hesse-Biber and Crofts (2008) are helpful in understanding the broader context of data analysis software in qualitative research. Konopasek (2008) provides an insightful description of how software helps us make our thinking visible as we engage in research. Lewins and Silver (2007) and Di Gregorio and Davidson (2008) provide a more thorough discussion of what we have only been able to touch upon in this chapter. For those who have selected ATLAS.ti, Friese (2012) is an indispensable resource; likewise, for those who have selected NVivo, Bazeley and Jackson (2013) will be your guide. MAXQDA users may be interested in Corbin and Strauss (2008), which integrates the software throughout the text. To learn more about data analysis and approaches to coding in general, see Saldana (2013), Richards (2009) (with its outstanding companion website), Richards and Morse (2013), Grbich (2013), Gibson and Brown (2009) and Gibbs (2007).

Visit Web Resource 7.16 for a link to Richards (2009) companion website.

References

Basit, T.N. (2003) 'Manual or electronic? The role of coding in qualitative data analysis'. *Educational Research*, 45(2), 143–54.

Bazeley, P. and Jackson, K. (2013) *Qualitative Data Analysis with NVivo* (2nd edition). London, UK: SAGE.

Clark, R.E. (1994) 'Media will never influence learning'. *Educational Technology Research and Development*, 42(2), 21–9.

Coffey, A., Holbrook, B. and Atkinson, P. (1996) 'Qualitative data analysis: Technologies and representations'. *Sociological Research Online*, 1(1). Available at http://www.socresonline.org.uk/1/1/4.html (last accessed 18 July 2013).

Conniff, A., Craig, T., Laing, R. and Galan-Diaz, C. (2010) 'A comparison of active navigation and passive observation of desktop models of future built environments'. *Design Studies*, 31, 419–38.

Corbin, J. and Strauss, A. (2008) *Basics of Qualitative Research: Techniques and Procedures for Developing Grounded Theory*. London, UK: SAGE.

Creswell, J.W. (2013) *Qualitative Inquiry and Research Design: Choosing Among Five Approaches* (3rd edition). London, UK: SAGE.

Davidson, J. and Di Gregorio, S. (2011) 'Qualitative Research and Technology: In the Midst of a Revolution', in N.K. Denzin and Y.S. Lincoln (eds) *The SAGE Handbook of Qualitative Research* (4th edition). Thousand Oaks, CA: SAGE, pp. 627–43.

Davis, N.W. and Meyer, B.B. (2009) 'Qualitative data analysis: A procedural comparison'. *Journal of Applied Sport Psychology*, 21(1), 116–24.

Dempster, P., Woods, D. and Wright, J.S.F. (2013) 'Using CAQDAS in the analysis of Foundation Trust hospitals in the National Health Service: Mustard seed searches as an aid to analytic efficiency'. *Forum Qualitative Sozialforschung / Forum: Qualitative Social Research*, 14(2), Article 1.

Di Gregorio, S. and Davidson, J. (2008) *Qualitative Research Design for Software Users*. Berkshire, UK: Open University Press/McGraw Hill.

Fielding, N. (2008) 'The Role of Computer-Assisted Qualitative Data Analysis: Impact on Emergent Methods in Qualitative Research', in S. Hesse-Biber and P. Leavy (eds) *Handbook of Emergent Methods*. New York, NY: The Guilford Press, pp. 655–73.

Friese, S. (2012) *Qualitative Data Analysis with ATLAS.ti*. London, UK: SAGE.

Gibbs, G. (2007) 'Analysing Qualitative Data', in U. Flick (ed.) *The Sage Qualitative Research Kit*, London, UK: SAGE.

Gibson, W.J. and Brown, A. (2009) *Working with Qualitative Data*. London, UK: SAGE.

Goble, E., Austin, W., Larsen, D., Kreitzer, L. and Brintnell, S. (2012) 'Habits of mind and the split-mind effect: When computer-assisted qualitative data analysis software is used in phenomenological research'. *FORUM: Qualitative Social Research*, 13(2), Article 2. Available at http://www.qualitative-research.net/index.php/fqs/article/view/1709/3340 (last accessed 18 July 2013).

Grbich, C. (2013) *Qualitative Data Analysis: An Introduction*. London, UK: SAGE.

Hahn, C. (2008) *Doing Qualitative Research Using your Computer: A Practical Guide*. London, UK: SAGE.

Hesse-Biber, S. and Crofts, C. (2008) 'User-Centered Perspectives on Qualitative Data Analysis Software: Emergent Technologies and Future Trends', in S. Hesse-Biber and P. Leavy (eds) *Handbook of Emergent Methods*. New York, NY: The Guilford Press, pp. 655–74.

Konopasek, Z. (2008) 'Making thinking visible with ATLAS.ti: Computer-assisted qualitative analysis as textual practices'. *FORUM: Qualitative Social Research*, 9(2), Article 12. Available at http://www.qualitative-research.net/index.php/fqs/article/view/420/910 (last accessed 18 July 2013).

Kozma, R.B. (1994) 'The influence of media on learning: The debate continues'. *School Library Media Research*, 22(4), 233–9.

LaPelle, N.R. (2004) 'Simplifying qualitative data analysis using general purpose software tools'. *Field Methods*, 16(1), 85–108.

Lee, R. and Fielding, N. (1996) 'Qualitative data analysis: Representations of technology. A comment on Coffey, Holbrook and Atkinson'. *Sociological Research Online*, 1(4). Available at http://www.socresonline.org.uk/1/4/lf.html (last accessed 18 July 2013).

Lewins, A. and Silver, C. (2007) *Using Software in Qualitative Research: A Step by Step Guide* (2nd edition). London, UK: SAGE.

Lonikila, M. (1995) 'Grounded Theory as an Emerging Paradigm for Computer-Assisted Qualitative Data Analysis', in U. Kelle (ed.) *Computer-Aided Qualitative Data Analysis*. London, UK: SAGE, pp. 41–51.

Meyer, D.Z. and Avery, L.M. (2009) 'Excel as a qualitative data analysis tool'. *Field Methods*, 21(1), 91–112.

Miles, M.B. and Huberman, A.M. (1994) *Qualitative Data Analysis: An Expanded Sourcebook* (2nd edition). London, UK: SAGE.

Mitchell, M.B. and Kuczynski, L. (2010) 'Does anyone know what is going on? Examining children's lived experience of the transition into foster care'. *Children and Youth Services Review*, 32(3), 437–44.

Mitchell, M.B., Silber, C.F. and Ross, C.F.J. (2012) 'My hero, my friend: Exploring Honduran youths' lived experience of the God–individual relationship'. *International Journal of Children's Spirituality*, 17(2), 137–51.

Richards, L. (2009) *Handling Qualitative Data: A Practical Guide* (2nd edition). London, UK: SAGE.

Richards, L. and Morse, J.M. (2013) *README FIRST for a User's Guide to Qualitative Methods* (3rd edition). London, UK: SAGE.

Richards, T.J. and Richards, L. (1998) 'Using Computers in Qualitative Research', in N. Denzin and Y. Lincoln (eds) *Collecting and Interpreting Qualitative Materials*. Thousand Oaks, CA: SAGE, pp. 211–45.

Ritchie, J. and Spencer, L. (1994) 'Qualitative Data Analysis for Applied Policy Research', in A. Bryman and R.G. Burgess (eds) *Analyzing Qualitative Data*. London, UK: Routledge, pp. 173–94.

Saldana, J. (2013) *The Coding Manual for Qualitative Researchers*, 2nd edn. London: SAGE Ltd.

Salliard, E.K. (2011) 'Systematic versus interpretive analysis with two CAQDAS packages: NVivo and MAXQDA'. *FORUM: Qualitative Social Research*, 12(1), Article 34. Available at http://www.qualitative-research.net/index.php/fqs/article/view/1518/3133 (last accessed 18 July 2013).

Schoenfelder, W. (2011) 'CAQDAS and qualitative syllogism logic: NVivo 8 and MAXQDA 10 compared'. *FORUM: Qualitative Social Research*, 12(1), Article 21. Available at http://www.qualitative-research.net/index.php/fqs/article/view/1514/3134 (last accessed 18 July 2013).

Tesch, R. (1990) *Qualitative Research: Analysis Types and Software Tools*. London, UK: Routledge.

Weitzman, E.A. (2000) 'Software and Qualitative Research', in N. Denzin and Y. Lincoln (eds) *The SAGE Handbook of Qualitative Research* (2nd edition). Thousand Oaks, CA: SAGE, pp. 803–20.

Weitzman, E.A. and Miles, M.B. (1995) *Computer Programs for Qualitative Data Analysis: A Software Sourcebook*. Thousand Oaks, CA: SAGE.

Welsh, E. (2002) 'Dealing with data: Using NVivo in the qualitative data analysis process'. *FORUM: Qualitative Social Research*, 3(2), Article 26. Available at http://www.qualitative-research.net/index.php/fqs/article/view/865/1880 (last accessed 18 July 2013).

EIGHT
Analysing Image, Audio, and Video Data

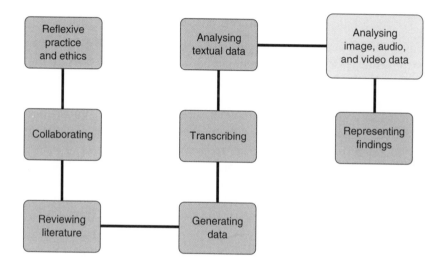

Companion website materials available here:

www.uk.sagepub.com/paulus

Learning Objectives

- Articulate ways in which image, audio, and video data can be used to enrich our understanding of social life.
- Describe analytical approaches to the analysis of image, audio and video data.
- Select and critique appropriate features of the major data analysis software packages for how they support the analysis of multimedia data.
- Have strategies to ensure ethical practices when analysing multimedia data.

Introduction

In Chapter 5, we focused on collecting data, including image, audio and video data. In Chapter 6, we discussed transcribing this data. Chapter 7 introduced three major qualitative data analysis packages and how they can be used to analyse textual data. We now discuss the features provided by digital tools that make working with multimedia data more feasible.

In this chapter, we discuss how synchronized transcripts, waveforms, time stamping, direct coding and geolinking can be used in the analysis of multimedia data. We give particular attention to the features of Transana, a program designed specifically for the analysis of video data.

The Importance of Image, Audio, and Video Data for Qualitative Research

Silverman (2007) suggested that 'qualitative researchers' almost Pavlovian tendency to identify research design with interviews has blinkered them to the possible gains of other kinds of data' (p. 42), including images, audio and video data. Multimedia data is often overlooked as an opportunity to deepen our understanding of social life. Sometimes the complexity of seeking ethical approval, the perceived lack of support by funding bodies or even the practicalities of working with audio and video recordings discourage researchers from their use. Further, it is often easier, or just more familiar, to manipulate and analyse data in textual form.

Analysis of recordings has typically, though not always, involved converting the media files into some form of textual representation (through transcription), and rarely, if ever, includes going back to the audio or video sources during the analysis process. Now, however, qualitative researchers seem to be rediscovering image, audio and video forms of data as digital tools become more robust. Quite a few special journal issues have been dedicated to the analysis of the visual.

Visit Web Resource 8.1 for a link to the International Visual Sociology Society and its journal, *Visual Studies*.

Visit Web Resource 8.2 for links to special journal issues on visual methodologies.

Mitchell (2011) suggested that 'there is no quick and easy way to map out the interpretative processes involved in working with visual research' (p. 11). Just as there is no blueprint for how to engage in fieldwork, there is no set way by which to use and analyse multimedia data (Pink, 2007). As we discussed in Chapter 7, your overall research methodology will inform how you approach data analysis. New methodologies that result in novel forms of data and enriched interpretations are being explored by researchers (Pink, 2007). For example, the 'walk-along' interview (described in Chapter 5), where people walk and talk as they interact with their environment, is one example of how audiovisual data might be used to explore how meaning is produced within and across space and place.

Multimedia data also poses a range of ethical dilemmas to consider, such as how to protect the identities of participants when their voices and faces are part of the data. Similarly, linking your data to the geographical space where it was collected can also compromise anonymity. Collecting video data requires developing higher levels of trust with research participants than is required when recording audio alone (Grant and Luxford, 2009). It also requires an ongoing conversation with participants about how the data will be used (Forsyth, 2009) or reused. Consider Reflexive Practice 8.1.

REFLEXIVE PRACTICE 8.1

Banks (2007) suggested that visual data could be perceived by participants as a tool for surveillance and control, particularly for participants living and working in potentially sensitive contexts. How would you respond to these concerns?

Visit Web Resource 8.3 for an exploration of ethical concerns specific to multimedia data.

Analysing Image, Audio, and Videos

There are a variety of ways to work with image, audio and video files in your research work. We first address issues around processing your files prior to analysis, and then introduce some considerations for the analysis of data.

Processing Multimedia Data

One of the first issues to be considered after collecting multimedia data is how it will be processed prior to analysis. The format in which the media was collected may or may not be compatible with the formats that are recognized by the digital tools. As such, you first need to ensure that the files are in a recognizable format, and if not, convert them.

Visit Web Resource 8.4 for information on preparing multimedia data for analysis in CAQDAS tools.

With images, you need to consider whether the resolution of the image is such that an analyst can clearly see what is being depicted for the purpose of analysis. It may be that a particular portion needs to be enlarged, in which case images may need to be cropped or otherwise manipulated prior to analysis. For audio and video files, noise reduction may be important for clarity and, if files are large, a smaller section of the audio or video may need to be clipped out for analysis purposes. Consider Case Study 8.1 for an example of a researcher who spent time preparing and narrowing her video data set prior to engaging in a more refined analysis process.

CASE STUDY 8.1	Using Digital Tools to Narrow the Analytical Focus

Lorena collected 200 hours of video data, specifically family therapy sessions. The focus of her research was on the ways in which families presented problems to their therapists and how these problems were then negotiated within the context of the therapy session. As she reviewed her data multiple times, she began to narrow the focus of her analysis to the initial moments in which problems were presented. Thus, prior to engaging in a more refined analysis, she created clips of these moments, resulting in 40 hours of data. She then engaged in a more refined discourse analysis of these clips.

Analysing Images

As part of your analysis it may be important to track where the images were produced, and the ways in which various audiences (e.g. participants) interact with the image (Rose, 2012). Art historians have developed conventions for describing photographs, looking at content, colour and spatial organization, light, and expressive content. Content analysis techniques can be helpful when exploring photographs and other images. Two classic studies exemplify this analytical approach. Richardson and Kroeber (1940) analysed women's dress length through the ages, and Robinson (1976) focused on shifting fashions in the shaving and trimming of men's beards. Looking at fluctuations in skirt length and facial hair styles allowed the researchers to illustrate a 50-year change cycle.

Digital tools ranging from simple image manipulation software to more comprehensive qualitative data analysis software packages can be used to analyse images. Often, digital cameras or computer operating systems come with basic image manipulation software (such as Microsoft Windows Paint) which can be used for improving lighting in shots, cropping images or rotating images. Of course, changing images has ethical implications, particularly as you consider the degree to which such changes impact the authenticity of the image. Take a moment to respond to the questions posed in Reflexive Practice 8.2 below.

REFLEXIVE PRACTICE 8.2

There are a variety of reasons that image data might be altered prior to or during analysis; for example, to have a clearer image or perhaps to protect the identities of individuals. What consequences might altering images have for the quality and value of the research data?

Visit Web Resource 8.5 for the guidelines for ethical practices established by the British Sociological Association, particularly the Visual Sociology group.

ATLAS.ti, NVivo and MAXQDA (introduced in Chapter 7) support the analysis of images. Some features to consider when selecting a package are its ability to zoom in on particular parts of the image, to code sections of the image and to annotate the images. Figure 8.1 is a still image of a church analysed in MAXQDA.

Analytically interesting portions of the image were segmented and coded (health and safety, posters, windows, etc.).

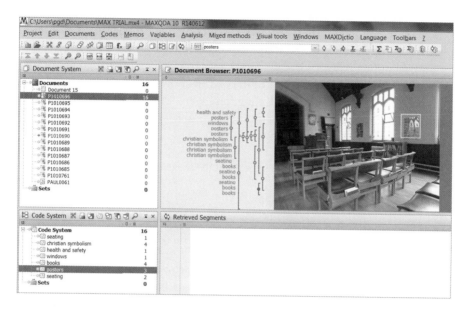

Figure 8.1 Example of an image coded in MAXQDA

Now turn to Reflexive Practice 8.3.

REFLEXIVE PRACTICE 8.3

Using one of the CAQDAS packages, practise importing and coding an image. Check the online tutorial for the program if necessary. How might you use image data in your own research?

Analysing Sounds

Sounds can be useful in qualitative research studies. 'Soundscapes', for example, give us insight into how a particular space is being used and how people interact with the environment around them. The term was originally coined by Schafer (1977), a composer, who was interested in the ecology of sound. Environments have not only important sounds but also background noise, and even annoying dins or potentially disagreeable rackets (Bauer and Gaskell, 2000). Hall, Lashua and Coffey (2008) argued that more researchers should re-engage with sound by walking around a research site and providing a narrative about the sounds they hear, or keep an audio diary recording the 'soundscapes' at different times throughout a day. These soundscapes can then be analysed for a variety of purposes.

Visit Web Resource 8.6 for how to conduct a soundscape.

Some sounds may be measurable in terms of quantity or levels. Yet a soundscape is also made up of qualitative interpretations of those sounds. A crackling fire, the clanging of table settings in a tearoom or the sound of children in a playground may engender a range of emotions and reactions. There may also be a variety of meanings ascribed to the production and interpretation of these sounds. Ultimately, how we go about capturing and analysing sounds can enrich our understanding of everyday life and the ways in which people go about making sense of it. The British Sound Library project has acquired a vast collection of sounds. People in the United Kingdom were invited to record and share sounds from their work, play or home environments for a one-year period, resulting in over 2,000 recordings.

Visit Web Resource 8.7 for more about the Sound Ethnography project.

Now turn to Reflexive Practice 8.4.

REFLEXIVE PRACTICE 8.4

Go to the companion website and access the next few web resources so that you can listen along as we describe some soundscapes. When you are finished reading and listening, reflect on what you noticed and how sounds might be incorporated into your own research.

Visit Web Resource 8.8 for the link to the 'Buying Bananas' soundscape.

The first sound example, 'buying bananas', is only 43 seconds long and comes from Argyll Street in Glasgow, Scotland. This soundscape captures an interaction with an automated till in a shop where individuals can scan and pay for items themselves. The beeps indicate the customer interacting with the till. As you listen, notice the accents of the automated assistants.

Next, listen to the soundscape entitled, 'The Beer Café in Glasgow'.

Visit Web Resource 8.9 for the link to the 'The Beer Café in Glasgow' soundscape.

Notice how there is not a great deal of sound that can be easily interpreted. However, if you were to collect recordings from a range of pubs, you might be able to compare and contrast these different soundscapes. As you listen again, notice the noise level of the music and people, and the way people seem to interact with their surroundings. Do they sing along to songs? Is there a fire crackling? Is there live music playing quietly in the corner, or is the music a central focus of the environment? Is there hustle and bustle from the kitchen and servers, or is this a quiet place where you could hear a pin drop as you contemplate your pint?

Finally, 'Glassford Street' was recorded along the roadside and provides a soundscape of a street.

Visit Web Resource 8.10 for the link to the 'Glassford Street' soundscape.

You can hear a small snippet of a conversation at the beginning and the flow of traffic. At 8.30 a.m., the number of lorries delivering to shops causes the buses bringing workers into the city centre to slow down, resulting in erratic traffic flow. You can hear the hiss of air brakes and the movement of traffic coming in waves, suggesting that traffic is smoothly flowing. Sampling the soundscape at different periods of the morning reveals a pinch point at 7.20–7.40 a.m., where the soundscape has the constant hum of engines. Imagine how this soundscape might build upon interview data collected at the same location.

As you begin to consider the ways you might go about analysing sounds within your own research, take a moment to explore how a soundscape shapes your orientation to a given song by completing Reflexive Practice 8.5.

Visit Web Resource 8.11 to listen to the track Suicide by the band Barclay James Harvest in conjunction with Reflexive Practice 8.5.

REFLEXIVE PRACTICE 8.5

A soundscape is included as the second part of the song. How does it change your view of the song? Do the sounds provide an additional layer of meaning? Can you hear the sounds of the built environment?

Analysing Videos

While video recordings are most often used to represent findings, video can also be analytically useful (Heath, Hindmarsh and Luff, 2010). For example, it may allow you to analyse non-verbal communication such as gesture and eye gaze or provide insights into the ways participants use artifacts in their everyday interactions.

Case Study 8.2 shows how video data was purposefully created in order to solve a problem identified during the research study.

CASE STUDY 8.2 | **Working with Video and Conversation**

When people in the National Health Service were interviewed about their informal networks as part of a funded research study, they would point to specific names from lists on the computer without voicing those names aloud. The researchers did not want to interrupt the participants as they were talking, so using screen capture software in conjunction with a touch screen laptop made it possible to capture their gestures on video. Spreadsheets were created with spaces for the names of people within the networks. The screen capture software was turned on at the beginning of the interview, and when people typed in names and talked this was captured as a video. Participants could show links by simply touching the screen. When participants said 'see that guy he was amazing in helping these people meet together, the screen would highlight the name of the person and the cursor would trace the

(Continued)

(Continued)

finger of the interviewee pointing to another group in the network. Treating the data as video was the easiest way to process the information. The spreadsheets with all the names could then be coded by making associations between groups of people, drawing out data from the video and adding it to the various coded networks.

Vignette 8.1 is another example of video data being collected in a creative way, in this case to meet pedagogical needs. Later the videos served as data for Craig Howard's research into this teaching activity.

Vignette 8.1 — Collaborative Video Annotations

Craig D. Howard, Indiana University, Bloomington

One of the tasks in my online class for preservice teachers is for them to observe a practising teacher, and then return to discuss their experiences in an online discussion forum. However, these observations occur all over campus, leaving the preservice teachers little common ground for sharing their observations with each other. I wanted to provide a way for everyone to be observing and discussing the same recorded teaching example. I could post a video link directly to the discussion forum, but I knew it would be difficult for the preservice teachers to reference the particular parts of the video they wanted to comment on. Using the comments section on a platform like YouTube or Vimeo would not work as they would still need to scroll through the video and include time stamps to reference their discussions. I wanted a

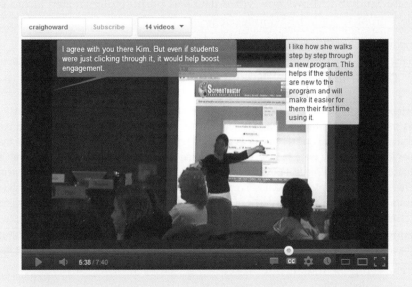

> more seamless discussion and viewing experience where the preservice teachers could watch the video and place annotations right on the video screen. Using Microsoft Movie Maker, Microsoft Paint and a PHP script written by a colleague, we developed what I call *Collaborative Video Annotations*, a way for people to talk asynchronously as they watch a video (Howard, 2012; Howard and Myers, 2010).

Workplace studies and studies of institutional talk rely heavily upon video recordings as ways to analyse the accomplishment of social action. Heath et al. (2010) suggested three levels of review – a *preliminary* review to describe and classify the data set, a *substantive* review to identify particular instances of the phenomenon for further analysis and an *analytic* review to create a collection of instances for comparison and contrast. They recommended beginning analysis by selecting and transcribing a brief video fragment of no more than ten seconds, mapping the action and attending to how each action is taken up by the participants as they in turn make subsequent actions.

Video and audio data can be used as a way to check findings with your participants or colleagues. By sharing the media files with participants, you are able to explore your initial interpretations further. Participants often have interesting reactions when they hear a recording of themselves, as Case Study 8.3 illustrates.

CASE STUDY 8.3 — **Using Sound Files for Member-Checking**

Paul included sound files as part of a presentation he made to his study participants to share his initial findings. Using the open source software Audacity, he created audio clips to illustrate the key themes. He embedded the clips into a presentation slide so that the participants could hear each other's responses. This allowed for member-checking of the emergent interpretations, and stimulated a lively discussion which was recorded for further analysis. The discussion changed the researcher's perception of his initial findings, highlighting that, in one case, the suggested theme was really a very isolated incident and should be considered an outlier, rather than representative of the entire data set.

Visit Web Resource 8.12 for information about Audacity as a tool to work with audio and video data.

Digital Tools to Support Multimedia Analysis

Qualitative data analysis software packages provide several features that can assist with analysis of multimedia data: 1) synchronized transcripts; 2) visual and waveform representation; 3) time stamping; 4) direct coding; and 5) geolinks and modelling tools.

Synchronized Transcripts

In Chapter 6, we discussed how synchronizing media files with a transcript can help you to conduct a more meaningful analysis. The transcript alone might not capture subtle nuances or non-verbal cues in the social interaction; thus, having your transcript linked to your media file can be analytically useful. For example, in Figure 8.2 an 'awkward' moment in a video interview is captured as a still photograph. The participant used a gasp, laughter and scratching (blocking his face) as he responded to the question. The transcript was synchronized with an image from the recording, along with a few seconds of the video interaction. This allowed the researcher to go back to the original media source at any time for further analysis, resulting in a fuller integration of audio, visual and text formats of data.

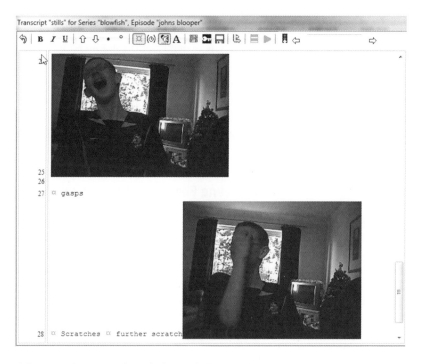

Figure 8.2 Transcript synchronized with images in Transana 2.50

The ability to return numerous times to a particular point in the media file means that the transcript can become a referencing tool to aid in the analysis of the original media file. Consider Reflexive Practice 8.6.

REFLEXIVE PRACTICE 8.6

Practise synchronizing a transcript with the media file in the software package that you have chosen. Reflect on how this might be useful in your own study.

Waveform Representations

Most of the data analysis software packages provide a navigable waveform to help you explore the data as you listen and view the media file. Figure 8.3 presents three different waveforms created using Audacity R.[1] The clips are short, around a few minutes in length. The height of the lines represents volume, with shorter lines representing quieter speech. A straight horizontal line represents silence. Just by looking at the three recordings below, you can start to make some analytic distinctions.

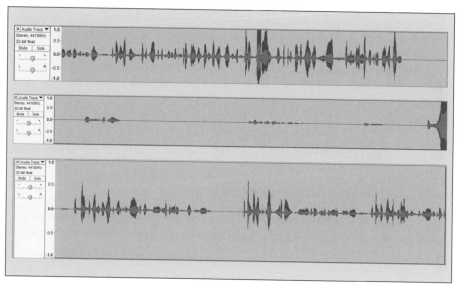

Figure 8.3 Waveform representation of audio files

Waveforms provide a way of attending to *how* things are said. For instance, rate and volume of speech, moments of laughter and episodes of crying all may have analytic implications, particularly when carrying out conversation or discourse analysis studies. In the first clip, there is no absence of sound (no horizontal lines) until the end. This speaker talked at length, very fast, and with increasing volume (as represented by the longer vertical 'waves'). The speaker was animated for a period of about three or four minutes and then paused for a break (as represented by the flat line at the end). In the second example, you can see longer breaks between the conversational turns. This interviewee was upset and tearful, explaining a hard moment in their life. The interviewee wavered for a few seconds, said a few words, and then, at the end of the clip, you can see a big splash. This is where the interviewee started to talk loudly, shouting a response with a loud 'argh'. before regaining composure and continuing with the interview. The third example shows a question and answer

---

1 Audacity R software is copyright © 1999–2013 Audacity Team.

sequence, with a visible pause between speakers. Consider Case Study 8.4 for an example of how waveforms might inform a given study.

CASE STUDY 8.4 — **The Value of Waveforms for Analysis**

Josh was investigating how bereaved people make sense of their loss. He interviewed 40 people who had experienced the loss of a family member. Each bereaved person was asked similar questions several times throughout the interviews. The study gave particular attention to whether the bereaved individuals rehearsed and prepared a conversation about their loss. He was able to analyse the waveforms of the video interviews, taking note of the ways in which the participants ended their interviews with what seemed like a rehearsed monologue about their loss. He noted that the last five to ten minutes of each interview was viewable as having little hesitation and few recognizable pauses. The waveforms allowed him to isolate the last few minutes of each interview as important data to return to for further analysis.

Turn now to Reflexive Practice 8.7.

REFLEXIVE PRACTICE 8.7

If your data analysis software package provides a waveform view, explore its functionality with your own media file. What do you notice about the data when viewed in this format?

Time Stamping

Adding time stamps during initial reviews of media files can help you identify key phrases, words or actions. In Figure 8.4, time stamps on the left have been added in NVivo 10. By clicking on any of the time stamps, you can easily replay that portion of the media file for further analysis.

Much like DVDs are split into chapters, time stamps segment data into useful chunks to assist you in moving more quickly to parts of the clips that are

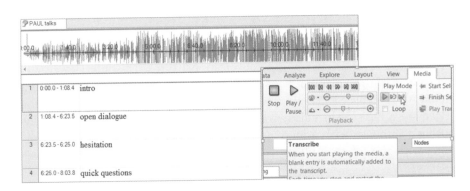

Figure 8.4 Time stamps in NVivo 10

somehow related without having to fast forward through hours of data. Time stamping alone never replaces more detailed coding; however, 'mapping' your data through time stamps can help you identify the important points. By taking note of these points, you can quickly see the landscape of your data. Take a moment to engage in Reflexive Practice 8.8.

REFLEXIVE PRACTICE 8.8

As you listen to and/or view a small segment of your audio or video data, take notes that highlight the sections that are most relevant to your research questions. Try to use as few words as possible to summarize the key points in a list.

Segmenting the data through time stamps can sometimes be done with the same recorder that was used to collect the data. Case Study 8.5 describes how Paul used his recording device to begin his data analysis through time stamps while still in the field.

| CASE STUDY 8.5 | Using a Recorder for Initial Analysis |

While riding the bus home after a day of fieldwork, Paul used his headphones to listen to his recordings and marked the interesting parts with time stamps. Time stamps were used to split up the interview to correspond with areas of his interview topic guide, which would later allow him to quickly skip to the relevant sections for further analysis. If he heard something on the tape that provoked an analytic memo, he inserted the memo directly into the recording at that point. He distinguished these memos from the original recording by:

- inserting a long pause (this allowed for the memos to be picked up by visually checking waveforms);
- stating 'start memo' with a title, thereby relating it to the audio; and
- finishing by stating 'end memo', along with a brief pause.

Paul's recorder was capable of adding these memos without overwriting the original record-ing. In this way, it was possible to time stamp and create memos within the original record-ing, without transcribing first. When this recording was typed up, his memos naturally flowed out of the text and were contextually located in the correct place for further coding.

Direct Coding

Direct coding of media files without a transcript is possible in ATLAS.ti 7, MAXQDA 11 and NVivo 10. It is, of course, important to reflect first on whether and how the ability to bypass the transcription process would be beneficial and/or disruptive to your analysis process (Evers, 2010). It may be beneficial to directly code the media files when the data is sensitive in order to protect the participants (Wainwright and Russell, 2010). Direct coding can also avoid some of the problems associated with feeling distanced from the original data through transcription.

The Eudico Linguistic Annotator (ELAN) is a free tool that allows you to annotate your audio or video files directly, with the annotations being saved in Unicode format. Up to four files can be associated with each annotation. In Vignette 8.2, Hannah Dostal shares her use of ELAN for directly coding video data.

Visit Web Resource 8.13 to learn more about ELAN.

| **Vignette 8.2** | **Using Eudico Linguistic Annotator for Video Analysis** |

Hannah Dostal, Southern Connecticut State University

In my research on writing interventions, I am interested in the potential for a signed-language intervention (an approach focused on developing knowledge of American Sign Language) to have a positive impact on second language use and acquisition (reading and writing in English). To investigate this, I collect video data of students' signed language use, as well as samples of their writing. I then store, analyse and make connections and comparisons between samples of students' language use in written English and American Sign Language.

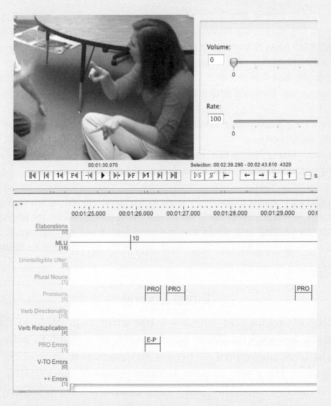

I use ELAN, a free language archiving software program from the Max Planck Institute for Psycholinguistics, to directly code my data.

ELAN allows me to store audio and visual data in a format that makes it easy to share files with collaborators without requiring large amounts of memory. In addition, it allows me to create multiple layers of coding and/ or transcription that are always visible and synchronized with the audio or visual file. One level of analysis (i.e., annotations) might include a gloss of how the participants are using American Sign Language, with another layer of analysis including time stamped annotations or direct coding of the interactions. Each level of analysis (i.e., annotation) is visible on the screen for easy analysis across layers. One potential drawback of ELAN is the need to remind all collaborators to save files in one compatible format (AVI), rather than the default format. In the figure above, video data has been coded directly, with codes such as 'elaborations', 'MLU' (mean length of utterance) and 'unintelligible utterance' listed on the left side of the screen.

The ability to directly code media files means that all of the features of the major data analysis software packages described in Chapter 7 are also available for the analysis of multimedia files. This includes annotating, coding, linking and visualizing relationships in the data. Figure 8.5 shows a video that has been directly coded in ATLAS.ti, with frames on the left and the analytic codes, links and comments on the right.

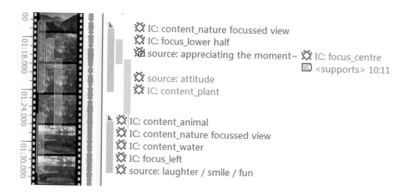

Figure 8.5 Coded video data in ATLAS.ti

Turn to Reflexive Practice 8.9.

REFLEXIVE PRACTICE 8.9

Import the audio or video file you recorded in Chapter 5 into a selected CAQDAS package and code the file directly. Watch the online tutorials if necessary. What differences did you notice between coding a transcript and directly coding the media file?

Geolinking

Multimedia data collected through approaches such as walk-alongs (introduced in Chapter 5) may include linking the data with specific GPS coordinates. Steinberg and Steinberg (2006) introduced methods for a GIS-based analysis approach that builds upon grounded theory. The steps include selecting a topic, determining a geographic location of interest; collecting qualitative, spatially linked social data; geocoding the data; physically visiting the location; analysing the data looking for spatial and social patterns; and, finally, engaging both spatial and social theory while representing findings.

Visit Web Resource 8.14 to review Steinberg and Steinberg's (2006) *Geographic Information Systems for the Social Sciences: Investigating Space and Place.*

The major data analysis software packages provide ways to easily create 'geolinks' between data sources and Google Earth place marks.

View Web Resource 8.15 for a description of MAXQDA's geolinking tool and a discussion of digital mapping tools.

Visit Web Resource 8.16 for a special issue of *Forum: Qualitative Social Research* on using visual data to explore migration and social division.

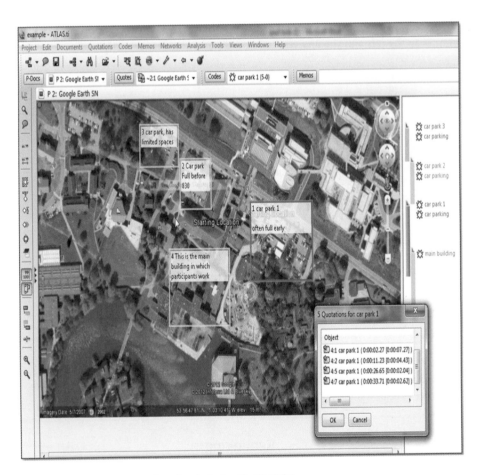

Figure 8.6 Coding a snapshot from Google Earth with ATLAS.ti 7

Figure 8.6 is an image of the campus of the University of York, taken in conjunction with an interview study of campus traffic volume. A snapshot was taken from Google Earth to create an image to be coded. Using ATLAS.ti, the three main car parks were highlighted and audio quotations from interviews were linked to the image and coded in relation to the car park mentioned ('car park 1', 'car park 2', 'car park 3' and 'main building'). When codes were retrieved, the audio could be listened to while examining the map.

In Vignette 8.3, James Dorough-Lewis describes his use of GIS to locate patterns in the locations discussed in interviews with members of a gay community in Chapel Hill, North Carolina.

| Vignette 8.3 | GIS as a Qualitative Research Tool |

James Dorough-Lewis, Jr, Nova Southeastern University

As a researcher in the field of conflict studies, I seek to understand how members of marginalized or underrepresented populations negotiate barriers to achieving their goals. Geographic information systems (GIS) can play a valuable role in managing and visualizing spatial relationships in raw data. A GIS essentially combines a computerized database management system with various means of analysing data and visualising results. This holds incredible potential for shaping my reading of texts that tease out new understandings I would have been unlikely to achieve otherwise.

While analysing transcripts from the Southern Oral History Project of several men discussing their experiences of being gay in Chapel Hill, North Carolina from the 1960s through the 1990s, I began using GIS to input locations that participants mentioned in their interviews, giving them attributes based on my readings of the transcripts, playing with various pattern detection tools, and then seeing how those patterns affected my re-reading of the texts. I first produced a graphic to demonstrate how the landscape of the city may be viewed through the aggregated visions of the interviewees. Tight, red blotches represented strong affinities with certain locations where participants congregated with other gay men and women (see Figure below). These blotches were surrounded by gulfs of empty space with little transition from one to the other. Returning to the texts I found a sense of isolation present in the participants' descriptions, accompanied by a sense of safety within the gay community.

I then ran a hot spot analysis based on individual texts to compare how they might reflect similarities or differences in how participants interpreted the geography of their experiences. Returning again to the texts, I found that the arrival of the AIDS epidemic of the 1980s and 1990s seemed to correlate with a dispersion of gay meeting places away from places associated with finding sexual partners and toward locations associated with

(Continued)

(*Continued*)

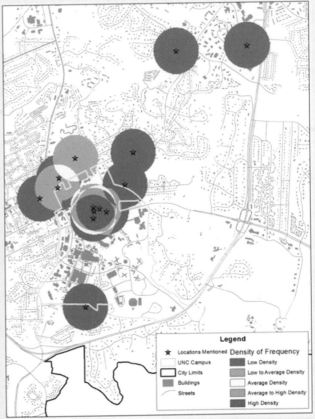

political activism. I then ran a density analysis to see if certain locations were mentioned more frequently across several transcripts, which affirmed the centrality of the University of North Carolina as a place of safety and self-discovery.

In my subsequent research I have found that these 'maps' – a term I use loosely – are less helpful than more traditional methods at facilitating my exploration of themes. But the advantage of GIS is that after some initial, albeit occasionally tedious, data management, I can produce an array of geovisualizations with very little cost in terms of time or energy that make the chance of finding nothing a negligible risk. The greater risk, in my experience, comes with failing to keep in mind that the 'maps' must not be given credit for being anything more than highly technical doodles. For this reason, I rarely produce maps as final products even while I often incorporate them into a recursive qualitative data analysis process.

Turn now to engage in Reflexive Practice 8.10.

REFLEXIVE PRACTICE 8.10

Practise creating a geolink to your data in the data analysis software package that you have chosen. How might this help your analysis?

Useful tools for analysing multimedia data, then, include synchronized transcripts, waveform representation, time stamping, direct coding and geolinking. We now turn to a discussion of Transana, a software package developed specifically for video analysis.

Transana for Analysing Video Data

Transana was designed around a television series metaphor. The top analytic level is a 'series' which consists of a group of related media files. Each 'episode' within the series is a single media file with its transcript. Interesting sections of the media file are made into video 'clips' by adding time stamps to synchronize the

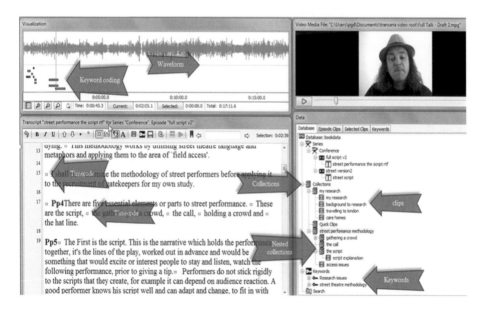

Figure 8.7 Screenshot of Transana's windows

transcript. These clips can be added to video clip 'collections', a set of data for further analysis. Keywords and notes can be added to clips. You can search for particular clips or notes throughout the process.

Visit Web Resource 8.17 for the Transana tutorial.

Transana has four main windows, shown in Figure 8.7.

The visualization window (on the top left) contains a waveform and keyword coding bars. The video window (on the right) has navigation controls and a snapshot button for creating still images from videos. Time codes can be added in the transcript window (lower left). The data window (lower right) is where clip management occurs, as keywords are created and applied to clips and organized into collections.

Media data must have a transcript associated with it before Transana can be used to analyse it. We described the benefits of synchronization in Chapter 6, as well as Transana's ability to connect multiple transcripts to one media file. We next discuss analysing video data with Transana. This is done by creating collections of video clips and applying keyword codes and notes to the clips.

Video Clips and Keyword Codes

In Transana, analysis begins by creating analytically interesting 'clips' of video data and compiling them into 'collections'. 'Clips' become the unit of analysis for your data. Keyword codes can then be applied to the clips in two ways – either starting with a list of a priori keyword codes (usually based on a theoretical framework) or by letting the keyword codes emerge from the data by, for example, using *in vivo* keyword codes. This is sometimes referred to as open coding (Strauss and Corbin, 1990).

Transana is designed to differentiate between these two approaches to coding. In the first approach, collections and keywords are created at the start of analysis, and interesting video clips are immediately assigned to collections and tagged with keyword codes. In the second approach, 'quick clips' are created when something interesting is noted in the data, but these clips are not assigned to collections or given keyword codes. Instead, the researcher decides on collection and code names as the data is reviewed. Case Study 8.6 illustrates how quick clips might be used.

CASE STUDY 8.6	**Example of Quick Clips Which Are 'Open Coded'**

Looking through video data of street performers from around the world, Mario starts to find interesting examples of different phases within and across street shows. No previous research study had yet noted different cultures of performance in street theatre shows, so the procedure of coding could be described as a 'messy' noticing of the different phases of the performances. Quick clips of key events were created (e.g. attracting a crowd, the big shout, opening effect, defining a stage on the pavement, main effects, the finale trick, collecting money). Iterative analysis and repeated viewings of these quick clips provided insights which were eventually reflected in the names chosen for them. For example, 'collecting money' was described as 'collecting a hat' by a number of performers. As such, 'collecting a hat' became a good keyword code and collection for some of the quick clips.

Groups of quick clips can be turned into collections as you begin to interpret your data. Clips can easily be moved from one collection to another as your analysis is refined. Further, keyword codes may be added or removed as your analysis develops, particularly as earlier findings may need to be revised or rethought in light of new findings. Throughout this analysis and coding process, you may also be writing memos to document your decisions, which we discuss next.

Creating Notes

Transana has a 'notes' feature that can be used to annotate the video clips, collections, transcripts and episodes. They can be used to document the emergent structure of keyword codes and collections and to chronicle changes in your research focus. Notes can be used at different levels of your analysis. For example, if you create a 'collection' of video clips, you will want to write a note that reflects how this collection fits into your overall analytic framework. You can easily search for notes you have created using the 'notes browser', as shown in Figure 8.8. Creating a note that contains the transcript makes it searchable as well. Adding notes to the data provides you with a means by which to create a clear and thorough audit trail.

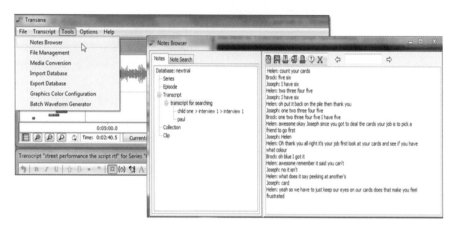

Figure 8.8 The notes browser in Transana

Transana also allows you to analyse up to four video files at the same time, and has several types of reporting features that can be useful for outputting the analysis.

Visit Web Resource 8.18 for a description of reporting features in Transana.

Now turn to Reflexive Practice 8.11.

──────────── **REFLEXIVE PRACTICE 8.11** ────────────

Continue the exploration of Transana that you began in Chapter 6, trying out the features described here. Are there ways that Transana may be useful in your work?

Final Thoughts

Images, audio and video can be a powerful source of data for understanding social life. While the analysis of such data posed challenges for researchers in the past, new digital tools such as mobile devices in conjunction with CAQDAS programs make it more feasible to implement methodologies such as photovoice, soundscapes and walk-alongs. The ability to directly code media files without initially transcribing them opens more possibilities for the analysis of audio and video recordings 'in the moment'. GIS technologies provide new ways to connect space and place with collected data. Programs such as Transana make it possible to connect more than one transcript to the same video, as well as viewing more than one video for analysis. This opens up new possibilities for understanding complex social environments such as large-group interactions. At the same time, the ability to easily alter digital images and sounds, as well as share them with others, raises ethical concerns about protecting participant privacy and retaining the integrity of the data.

Chapter Discussion Questions

1. In what ways might image, sound or video data be useful in the study that you are designing?
2. Which features for analysing multimedia data will be most useful for understanding your data?
3. When might it be appropriate for direct coding of audio or video data to replace transcription?
4. What social environments might be better understood through the use of multiple video cameras and layers of transcription?
5. How can you ensure ethical practices as you analyse multimedia data?

Suggestions for Further Reading

Pink (2007), Mitchell (2011), Spencer (2011) and Heath, Hindmarsh and Luff (2010) are good comprehensive texts for exploring the use of image, audio and video data in qualitative research. Banks (2007) draws upon sociology, anthropology and cultural studies while discussing visual methods. Silver and Patashnick (2011) present a conceptual frame by which to align software with researcher needs. Rose (2012) offers a thorough overview of visual methodologies, across various traditions and disciplines. Dempster and Woods (2011) and Woods and Dempster (2011) both provide a detailed look at the use of Transana. Finally, Wiles et al. (2011) discuss ethical issues around visual research.

References

Banks, M. (2007) *Visual Methods in Social Research*. London, UK: SAGE.
Bauer, M. and Gaskell, G. (2000) 'Qualitative Researching with Text, Image and Sound: Analysing Noise and Music as Social Data', in M. Bauer and G. Gaskell (eds), *Qualitative Researching with Text, Image and Sound: A Practical Handbook*. London, UK: SAGE, pp. 263–80.

Dempster, P.G. and Woods, D.K. (2011) 'The economic crisis though the eyes of Transana'. *Forum Qualitative Sozialforschung / Forum: Qualitative Social Research*, 12(1).

Evers, J.C. (2010) 'From the past into the future: How technological developments change our ways of data collection, transcription and analysis'. *Forum Qualitative Sozialforschung / Forum: Qualitative Social Research*, 12(1).

Forsyth, R. (2009) 'Distance versus dialogue: Modes of engagement of two professional groups participating in a hospital-based video ethnographic study'. *International Journal of Multiple Research Approaches*, 3(3), 276–89.

Grant, J. and Luxford, Y. (2009) 'Video: A decolonising strategy within ethnographic research into intercultural communication in child and family health'. *International Journal of Multiple Research Approaches*, 3(3), 218–32.

Hall, T., Lashua, B. and Coffey, A. (2008) 'Sound and the everyday in qualitative research'. *Qualitative Inquiry*, 14(6), 1019–40.

Heath, C., Hindmarsh, J. and Luff, P. (2010) *Video in Qualitative Research*. London, UK: SAGE.

Howard, C.D. (2012) *Higher Order Thinking in Collaborative Video Annotations: Investigating Discourse Modeling and the Staggering of Participation*, Doctoral dissertation. Bloomington, IN: Indiana University.

Howard, C.D. and Myers, R.D. (2010) 'Creating video-annotated discussions: An asynchronous alternative'. *International Journal of Designs for Learning* 1(1).

Mitchell, C. (2011) *Doing Visual Research*. London, UK: SAGE.

Pink, S. (2007) *Doing Visual Ethnography: Images, Media and Representation in Research*. London, UK: SAGE.

Richardson, J. and Kroeber, A. (1940) 'Three centuries of women's dress fashions: A quantitative analysis'. *Anthropological Records*, 5(2), 111–53.

Robinson, D. (1976) 'Fashions in the shaving and trimming of the beard: The men of the *Illustrated London News*, 1842–1972'. *American Journal of Sociology*, 81(5), 1133–41.

Rose, G. (2012) *Visual Methodologies: An Introduction to the Interpretation of Visual Materials* (3rd edition). London, UK: SAGE.

Schafer, R.M. (1977) *Tuning the World*. New York, NY: Alfred K. Knopf.

Silver, C. and Patashnick, J. (2011) 'Finding fidelity: Advancing audiovisual analysis using software'. *Forum Qualitative Sozialforschung / Forum: Qualitative Social Research*, 12(1), Article 37.

Silverman, D. (2007) *A Very Short, Fairly Interesting and Reasonably Cheap Book about Qualitative Research*. London, UK: SAGE.

Spencer, S. (2011) *Visual Research Methods in the Social Sciences: Awakening Visions*. New York, NY: Routledge.

Steinberg, S.J. and Steinberg, S.L. (2006) *Geographic Information Systems for the Social Sciences: Investigating Space and Place*. London, UK: SAGE.

Strauss, J. and Corbin, A. (1990) *Basics of Qualitative Research*. Thousand Oaks, CA: SAGE.

Wainwright, M. and Russell, A. (2010) 'Using NVivo audio-coding: Practical, sensorial and epistemological considerations'. *Social Research Update*, 60.

Wiles, R., Coffey, A., Robison, J. and Prosser, J. (2011) 'Ethical regulation and visual methods: Making visual research impossible or developing good practice?' *Sociological Research Online*, 17(1).

Woods, D.K. and Dempster, P.G. (2011) 'Tales from the bleeding edge: The qualitative analysis of complex video data using Transana'. *Forum Qualitative Sozialforschung / Forum: Qualitative Social Research*, 12(1).

NINE
Writing and Representing Findings

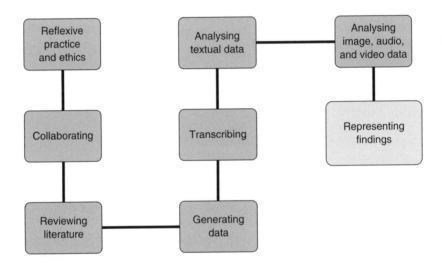

Companion website materials available here:

www.uk.sagepub.com/paulus

Introduction

In Chapters 7 and 8, we discussed the use of digital tools to support analysis of both textual and multimedia data. In this chapter, we examine how new tools have also changed our ways of writing and representing findings. We begin with an overview of the ways in which writing and representing findings have been understood in qualitative inquiry. We highlight the shifts that occurred as social scientists began to negotiate a crisis of representation. We then give attention to the ways in which digital tools such as presentation software and storyboarding might support the writing process. Then we turn to how findings might be represented in new, more accessible ways through digital ethnographies, digital storytelling, blogs and websites, online soundscapes and films, documentaries and videos.

Perspectives on Writing and Representing

How you represent your findings is integrally connected to ontological and epistemological assumptions underlying your work. If your goal is to represent an essence or overall structure of an experience, as in some forms of phenomenology, your findings may look different from representing a life history or a theory. Creswell (2013) outlined the 'overall' and 'embedded' writing structures inherent to five different approaches to qualitative

Table 9.1 Representing research across five qualitative research approaches (adapted from Creswell, 2013, pp. 221–2)

Approach	Overall writing structures	Embedded writing structures
Narrative	• Story chronologies • Temporal or episodic ordering of information • Reporting what participants said, how they said it or how they interacted with others	• Epiphanies • Themes, key events or plots • Metaphors and transitions
Phenomenology	• Traditional research report format • Themes; analytic analysis; essence; time, space and other dimensions	• Figures or tables reporting essences • Philosophical discussions • Creative closings
Grounded theory	• Results of open, axial and selective coding • Theory and arguments that support it	• Extent of analysis • Propositions • Visual diagrams
Ethnography	• Types of tale • Description, analysis and interpretation • Thematic narrative	• Tropes • Thick description • Dialogue • Scenes • Literary devices
Case study	• Vignettes • Types of case • Substantive case report format	• Funnel approach • Description

research (see Table 9.1): narrative, phenomenology, grounded theory, ethnography and case study. He highlighted how a given study's findings may 'look' different because of the particular assumptions that undergird the individual approach.

In recent years, many qualitative researchers have embraced the idea that there is not a neutral, objective reality 'out there' waiting to be discovered by a researcher and represented to others. Rather, even 'facts' require some degree of interpretation, and no interpretation can fully capture lived experience (Richardson, 1990). Historically, however, this understanding has not always been embraced. Beginning in the seventeenth century, a clear divide between literary and scientific writing emerged. Literary writing was associated with fiction and subjectivity, while scientific writing was associated with facts and objectivity (Clifford and Marcus, 1986). Fictional writing was positioned as false, presumably filled with invented realities. In contrast, scientific writing was assumed to be objectively reporting valid findings from scientific research studies. Take a moment to consider your own beliefs about representing research findings by completing Reflexive Practice 9.1.

REFLEXIVE PRACTICE 9.1

As you think about the study you are designing, consider the ways in which you have represented or plan to represent your research findings. How does your approach speak to your own beliefs about representation?

Table 9.2 The historical periods of qualitative research (Denzin and Lincoln, 2005)

Period	Time Period	Orientation to Writing/Representation
Traditional	1900s to World War II	Dominated by 'valid' and 'objective' accounts of field experiences.
Modernist	Post-war to 1970s	Dominated by post-positivism and a focus on giving 'voice' to society.
Blurred Genres	1970 to 1986	Included multiple paradigms, epistemologies and methods.
Crisis of Representation	Mid-1980s to current day	Mounting struggle between scientific and literary writing.
Postmodern Moment	1990 to 1995	Emergence of new forms of ethnography and representation, such as autoethnography.
Post-Experimental Inquiry	1990 to 2000	Growing sense of social consciousness brought to ethnographic texts in particular.
Methodologically Contested Present	2000 to present	Proliferation of methodological approaches.
Fractured Future	Future	Ongoing evolution around reconnecting social science to a social purpose and emphasis upon indigenous methodologies.

Denzin and Lincoln's (2005) description of the eight historical periods of qualitative research highlights well the shifting perspectives on how research findings should be represented, as well as the very meaning of 'scientific' versus 'fictional' writing. Table 9.2 presents an overview of the eight periods.

Outside the realm of visual anthropology or film, as well as some art-based approaches to research, findings are still represented through the printed word. Peer-reviewed journals, even those with an online presence, are still primarily paper based. With tenure and promotion being based in large part on one's publishing record in established journals, it is not surprising that few researchers have ventured far beyond text-based representations of their findings. Nonetheless, as we have come to recognize the multisensory nature of everyday life (Pink, 2007; 2009), some qualitative researchers have begun to explore how digital tools can expand how we engage in the act of writing and how we represent the findings.

Supporting the Writing Process

From field notes to annotating your data to reporting your findings, qualitative research requires you to spend a significant amount of time writing. Writing shapes our understandings and our understandings shape what we write. Whether you are a graduate student completing your thesis or a senior faculty member working on your hundredth manuscript for journal publication, the recursive and frequent act of writing is simply part of engaging in the research process (Ellis, 2004; Goodall, 2000; Wolcott, 2009).

Your professional community and disciplinary home, as well as the qualitative approach you use, will shape your style. None are neutral, as 'how we are expected to write affects what we can write about' (Richardson, 1990, p. 16). For instance, some research approaches place greater emphasis on reader evaluation (e.g. discourse analysis), while others employ more arts-based experimental forms of writing (e.g. autoethnography). As a reflexive researcher, it is important to write in a way that makes explicit your beliefs and assumptions, the theories that informed your work, and how you came to understand and interpret the data. Take a moment to consider Reflexive Practice 9.2.

REFLEXIVE PRACTICE 9.2

Consider the research study you are designing.

- Who are you writing for?
- Who should be involved in the writing process (e.g. just you, or the participants as well)?
- To what degree do you plan to write yourself into the research findings? Why?

While there have been a multitude of texts (e.g. Wolcott, 2009) and articles (e.g. Colyar, 2009) published about the writing process, there has been far less discussion around the digital tools that can support the writing process. Case Study 9.1 illustrates the use of ATLAS.ti to support the writing process from the very start of a research study to the completion of a journal manuscript.

| CASE STUDY 9.1 | Using ATLAS.ti to Support the Writing Process |

Drawing upon conversation analysis, Andrew was studying the ways in which an autistic identity was made real in parent support group talk. Early on, he decided to use ATLAS.ti 7 throughout the research process. Long before collecting data, he maintained a research journal using the memo tool. Further, he imported his ethics committee documents, research proposal and other notes related to his study into the software for easy referencing and reviewing. After transcribing his data in ATLAS.ti and beginning the analysis process, he used the memo tool to write the major sections of his findings. He also used the network view manager to create visual representations of his findings. Andrew used memos to generate the bulk of his manuscript, and was later able to export these to a word processor for further editing. Andrew felt that one of the benefits of such an approach was that his entire research process, shifting perspectives and even most of the writing process were documented in one location and in a transparent, easy to access way.

Digital Tools That Support Writing

We first explore how presentation software, such as Microsoft PowerPoint, can be used as a 'creative composition tool' for designing, analysing and creating texts. Then we highlight the possibilities for reading and writing using the storyboarding tool Scrivener.

Writing as Creative Composition: Presentation Software

Presentation software such as Microsoft PowerPoint and Apple's Keynote are often used when making presentations of research findings to funding organizations and/or at professional conferences. However, fewer researchers consider them to be 'creative composition tools' as described by Melanie Hundley and Teri Holbrook in Vignette 9.1 below. They highlight the potential for adapting these tools to meet unique writing needs.

| Vignette 9.1 | PowerPoint as Creative Composition Tool |

Melanie Hundley, Vanderbilt University and Teri Holbrook, Georgia State University

PowerPoint has earned the reputation as the death knell of presentations; however, through our inquiry into its inner workings we realized that it has uses beyond the linear presentation of prepared slides. Re-conceived as a 'creative composition tool', PowerPoint becomes a space for designing, analysing and creating texts (Hundley and Holbrook, 2013).

Melanie: PowerPoint as a Reshaper of Data Stories

I was interested in how composing for a digital media format reshaped my writing process and end product. I chose PowerPoint because it is ubiquitous; most computer labs have it. It also offered me a way to link between data stories, theory, interviews, videos and field notes. The hypertext linking feature of PowerPoint allowed me to create a visual document in which I could dig into a specific theme and link across content. I was able to colour code specific types of slides (reflections, theory, participants, etc.), allowing me to know, at a glance, the type of data I was seeing as I followed links through my 'presentation'; this visual sorting made the gaps in my thinking evident. Data sets that had not been theorized, or theory that had not been linked to participant data, were clearly visible. The program allowed me to embed clips from participant interviews on the slides alongside excerpts from the transcripts. I could hear the pauses, the hesitations or the excitement in their words. I could click on a link to the full transcript or follow a link to a different participant who made a similar or a contradictory statement. The below image is of a slide displaying data with associated hyperlinks.

Write Up #1

transcript
write up
emails
rewrite
comments

Felicity's explanation of her composing process focused on her starting point—an image—and moved through her developing the events and emotions of a hypertext fiction piece. In describing the writing of one of her more complex hypertexts, she said, "I had to have the image first. Every lexia, every screen had image and text...I was really surprised to find that I had to have the image first." She focused on her training as a print writer and said, "I am such a word person that I would have thought that my inclination would have been to have the image support the text even though my goal was...to have multimodality in which image and text had relations but one wasn't necessarily in support of the other". A contrast between her expectations as a print writer and her experiences as a hypertext writer occurred several times in her interviews. Like Claire, she spoke with relative sophistication when considering what the "technology could offer, the technological affordances" that could be utilized for the creation of her hypertext pieces.

PowerPoint as a compositional tool

Teri: PowerPoint as Visual Architecture

PowerPoint is often associated with word-heavy screens and linear, point-and-click movement. However, the program also provides a simple

(Continued)

(Continued)

hypertext linking function that, when coupled with its visual applications, provides alternative textual constructions. Instead of words on a flat page, screens can be re-imagined as image-filled spaces, allowing for hyperlinked materials that permit readers to move through a virtual landscape. One of my first hypermedia architectures was a virtual prison that housed fragments of philosophical texts used to theorize memoirs. In this architecture, each screen represented either a threshold or a space. An organizing screen featured a drawn schematic of the prison; by clicking on embedded hyperlinks, readers selected a cell block. At the entry screen to each cell block, readers found a series of photographed doors. Clicking through each door linked readers to a cell that contained texts and/or images (see Figure below). These visual architectures disrupted the notion of a linear text and suggested alternative ways of navigating, constructing and considering academic writing.

You have entered Cell Block 5.
In these cells you will find representations of scholastic power relations, the interplay of forces that tangle within and beyond the classroom. Front and center in these cells are the writings of Foucault; in the background, flitting in and out of view like a ghost, sometimes explicit, always implied, is the category of learning disability. The installations in these cells wrestle with what Foucault called "dividing practices," those processes which divide the subject within herself and from others.

PowerPoint as a representational tool

This vignette illustrates how digital tools not typically associated with writing might support the writing process in new and helpful ways. We next turn to consider the uses of a storyboarding tool in the writing process.

Writing as Storyboarding: Scrivener

While word processors make writing, revising and editing much easier than in the days of the typewriter, it can still be hard to navigate through a manuscript as it grows in length. Scrivener is a project management tool for organizing and writing long documents. It works on both Windows and Apple operating systems and offers a free trial version. Using a system of virtual index cards and outlines, Scrivener gives you the ability to easily 'shuffle' sections of your paper as you draft and organize your arguments and ideas. In lieu of having to work across multiple files and/or have papers scattered across your desk, Scrivener allows you to store everything in one place, making your process more efficient and systematic.

Visit Web Resource 9.1 for more information about Scrivener.

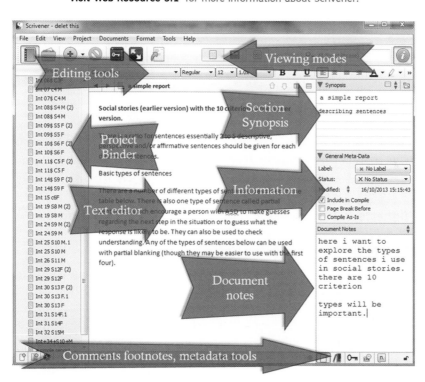

Figure 9.1 Main interface of Scrivener

The left pane of the Scrivener interface (Figure 9.1) is the 'binder' that has navigational tools to hierarchically organize all aspects of your project. 'Collections' (appearing as tabs) group related documents together. The editor includes tools for annotating, writing and formatting. The 'inspector' includes metadata, index cards, keywords and reference links.

Scrivener also allows you to block out your screen, editing your text on a black background, as displayed in Figure 9.2. This offers you a less distracting environment in which to write, while allowing quick access to all files and documents you might need.

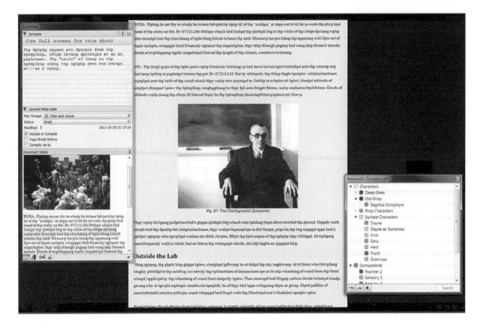

Figure 9.2 Scrivener's distraction-free full-screen mode

In Vignette 9.2, Doug Canfield describes his use of Scrivener to engage in academic writing, discussing the features that he found most useful.

| Vignette 9.2 | Using Scrivener for Academic Writing |

Doug Canfield, University of Tennessee

As with most researchers, I typically wrote papers and articles with a traditional word processor. I had separate folders on my computer desktop full of research articles, timelines, sections of my manuscript, snippets of mini-epiphanies, outlines, arguments and many other writings. It was chaotic. I had to have several files open when I worked so I could quickly access my notes, but spent most of my valuable time searching for the right file. As I began preparing my thesis research proposal, the realization that word processors are terrible for writing up these types of project was the source of much angst.

I first tried out Scrivener when I was looking for software that could facilitate some of the things I needed to do for my initial literature review and research workflow. I was addicted to it within days. Scrivener allows me to organize my manuscript, research, notes and media files easily and organically. I have a virtual 'binder' where I can see my chapters (which I can subdivide to any granularity I need), my research, my notes and even my 'corkboard' (a visual way of viewing and arranging the documents in my binder), and I was able to arrange these any way I pleased as my project progressed.

My favourite feature of Scrivener is being able to import research files, websites and other media so everything is together in one place. The ability to link these all together makes it easy for me to create a network of cross references that helps me to navigate my information quickly (no more lost notes!).

I also like the flexibility that Scrivener gives me in compiling my writing. I can use traditional formats (print, RTF, Word, OpenOffice, PDF), as well as compile my project to be reviewed on most e-readers (including iBooks), as a web page or even as a LaTeX file.

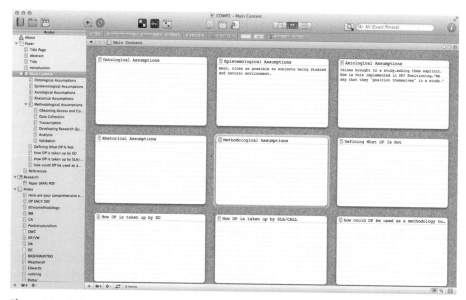

Figure 9.3 Scrivener corkboard view

Visit Web Resource 9.2 to review several articles related to using Scrivener for your dissertation/thesis work.

Digital tools can not only support non-linear writing processes but also provide opportunities for more engaging and accessible ways to represent our work to the public. Take time to consider Reflexive Practice 9.3.

REFLEXIVE PRACTICE 9.3

What are some challenges you face during your writing process? How might Scrivener or other tools help you overcome those challenges?

Representing Findings in New Ways

Relatively few researchers move beyond journal articles, technical reports or books when disseminating their research findings. Even as the number of published qualitative studies increases, the implications of their work remain mostly on shelves or etched within rarely opened journals (Finfgeld, 2003; Troman, 2001). With academic promotion and professional expectations often dependent upon publishing in traditional venues, few qualitative researchers have ventured into alternative and/or more public forms of research. Thus, research findings remain relatively inaccessible to the majority of people. Others may resist the idea of 'popularizing research' out of a 'fear of being popular', which could result in being misquoted and/or feeling that a complicated research study was 'dumbed down' (Vannini, 2012, p. 4). Yet, if we only speak or write to like-minded researchers, we are unlikely to reach the populace whom the research might actually be intended to impact.

Visit Web Resource 9.3 to read how Christopher Brkich and Tim Barko challenged the research status quo in their study of memes during the 2012 American presidential election.

Pursuing a more public form of research is not a new idea, as many anthropologists (e.g. Margaret Mead and Bronislav Malinowski) found ways to share their work with a broader audience. Today, scholars like Howley (2012), after producing an oral history of the life of Russell Compton (a professor of philosophy at DePauw University in the United States), worked with a radio station to share the audio documentary with a broader audience.

Visit Web Resource 9.4 for a link to the companion website for *Popularizing Research* (Vannini, 2012).

Arts-based approaches, which have been taken up particularly in educational research, are those that use art to generate, interpret and/or represent data (Cole and Knowles, 2001; Knowles and Coles, 2008). Arts-based research often embraces new forms of representation by crossing (presumed) disciplinary bounds. For instance, some have partnered with artists to generate performative texts and public performances of their research findings (Lester and Gabriel, 2012). Others have expanded how they share their text-based research reports, working to incorporate images and other sensory-rich representations. In Vignette 9.3, Teri Holbrook and Melanie Hundley offer one example of how qualitative researchers might learn from young adult literature to expand how their research is represented.

Vignette 9.3	**Young Adult Literature Novels as Predictors of Academic Texts to Come**

Teri Holbrook, Georgia State University and Melanie Hundley, Vanderbilt University

Academic texts look much the same as they have for 100 years – words on paper, linearly displayed, broken only by an occasional supporting chart or illustration. We offer that the conventional construction of academic texts is poised to shift, and we look to an unconventional source for our argument – young adult literature (YAL). Responsive to their Internet-raised adolescent readers, YAL authors are experimenting with literary formats that may point to the future of academic texts. Rather than crafting stories designed to be read word by word, page by page, some YAL authors are taking up the affordances of digital technology to create works that are multi-modal, interactive and hyperlinked.

- *Making Up Megaboy* (Walter, 2007) is a multi-modal novel that juxtaposes character voices to depict the multiple perspectives surrounding a 13-year-old murderer. Images and graphic design are used to construct the story while discomforting the reader. The author uses the ease of digital technology to create a mixed media narrative that challenges notions of truth and storytelling.
- *Skeleton Creek* (Carman, 2009), a series that employs two media formats, print novels and online websites, revolves around two teen characters – a writer and a videographer. Readers begin in the novel, which is formatted as a personal journal, and at key points are directed to videos posted on the videographer's webpage. Both formats are necessary to access the entire story.
- *Inanimate Alice* (Pullinger and Joseph, 2005) is an interactive, online multi-modal narrative constructed from the first person view of a young girl who aspires to be an online game developer. The story unfolds over a series of narratives set in the different places the child inhabits; as she grows older and her digital composing practices mature, so do the elements of the episodes. Readers control the pace of the story. Tension and atmosphere are developed through the creators' design that utilizes words, images, sound and animations.

Many academic journals have online components and/or make their articles available through online databases. Fewer are moving toward rethinking what an article or even a journal can be. YAL authors are experimenting with both the form and function of storytelling as they engage with the affordances of digital media. Some academic journals, also experimenting with the form and function of academic texts, are beginning to respond to the question: *What new and different forms and functions of academic writing and representing will digital technology make possible?*

Visit Web Resource 9.5 for links to journals that incorporate multimedia representations in their online venues.

Take a moment to consider Reflexive Practice 9.4.

In a comprehensive literature review of qualitative research studies where the findings were disseminated beyond a journal article and/or conference presentation, Keen and Todres (2007) identified ten modes for doing so:

1. Research-based ethnodrama, often including a video performance (e.g. Gray, 2000);
2. Ethnopoetics or poetic texts (e.g. Richardson, 1992);
3. Unperformed performative texts (e.g. Pifer, 1999);
4. Evocative storytelling (e.g. Gray, 2004);
5. Multimedia presentation (e.g. Cole and McIntyre, 2004);
6. Patchwork quilts, with audio and photographs (e.g. Brackenbury, 2004);
7. Documentary films (e.g. Woo, 2008);
8. Websites and DVDs (e.g. Rozmovits and Ziebland, 2004);
9. Workshops (e.g. Smith et al., 2000); and
10. Brochures (e.g. Hunt, Emslie and Watt, 2001).

Drawing upon performance studies, representational arts, folk and popular culture, these new forms of scholarship act to popularize research through 'genre-blurring, collaboration, and application to multiple social problems and issues' (Vannini, 2012, p. 7). With increasing access to multimedia sources and the Internet, as well as a commitment to expanding the impact of research findings, more and more researchers are experimenting with sharing their findings in new ways.

Digital Tools to Represent Findings

We discuss next various digital tools that can support you in representing your research to a broader audience through: digital ethnographies; digital storytelling; blogs and websites; online soundscapes and films; and documentaries and videos.

Representing as Digital Ethnographies

Ethnographers have experimented with representing their work through what Dicks and Mason (2008) refer to as 'hypermedia environments' (p. 572) that use clickable multimedia, often located on the Internet, to represent their research process and findings. Rather than simply representing findings in textual forms, field experiences are chronicled on the Internet. In the 1990s, prior to the days of prevalent high-speed Internet access, many of these hypermedia-based representations were distributed in the form of CD-ROMs or DVDs. For example,

Peter Biella's fieldwork among the Ilparakuyo Maasai of Tanzania resulted in an interactive DVD. Now, however, it is possible to develop interactive websites that provide opportunities for others to engage with research findings in ways that introduce them to sensory-rich aspects of fieldwork.

Visit Web Resource 9.6 to view Peter Biella's ongoing work in visual anthropology.

An excellent example of the potential of a digital ethnography is Michael Wesch's Nekalimin.net. His study explored how people in Papua New Guinea navigated new forms of development in society. Wesch shared his findings *only* on the Internet. On his website, he included field notes, videos, images and historical documents, both scholarly based expositions and actual voices (e.g. interviews) from his fieldwork. To protect the participants, interested viewers must first contact Wesch for access to the site.

View Web Resource 9.7 to see the Nekalimin digital ethnography project.

View Web Resource 9.8 to watch Michael Wesch's lecture on digital ethnography.

Representing as Digital Stories

Situated within narrative theory and community-based participatory research methods, digital storytelling is another way to represent and share life narratives. In this method, individuals, along with a researcher (or a researcher alone), generate a brief (3–5 minute) visual narrative that synthesizes images, video, voice and music to create a compelling story (Lambert, 2006). In many ways, this approach blurs the boundary between data collection and representation of findings, with the data collection process itself involving decisions and attention to how everyday experiences are represented. Some researchers have used digital storytelling to foster community-building and collaboration, with community members co-constructing digital stories that display their community concerns and/or generate dialogue around central social issues (Gubrium and Turner, 2011).

Visit Web Resource 9.9 to visit the Center for Digital Storytelling.

Representing as Blogs and Websites

Blogs, introduced in Chapter 2, can be used to share your research methods, findings and conclusions in a transparent way to reach a larger audience (Powell, Jacob and Chapman, 2012). They can be used as a way to encourage non-academic audiences to respond to findings, potentially strengthening relations with stakeholders and improving rigour. For instance, while working on her PhD research, Lilia Efimova (2009) used a blog, incorporating video, to share major findings from her research (see Figure 9.4).

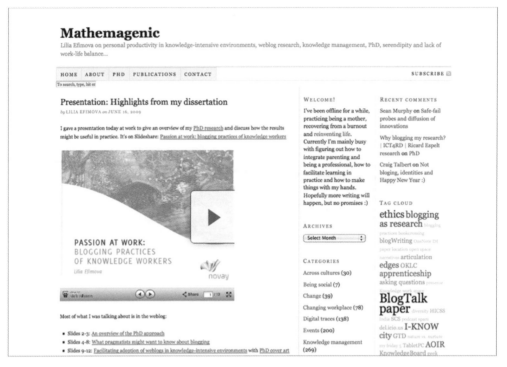

Figure 9.4 Lilia Efimova's PhD blog

Visit Web Resource 9.10 to see Lilia Efimova's Mathemagenic blog.

As another example, Noah Wardrip-Fruin, a computer science professor, created a group-authors blog, Grand Text Auto, to generate reviews for a book manuscript. He used both the comments on his blog and peer reviews received from his publisher to refine his work.

Visit Web Resource 9.11 to explore Grand Text Auto.

Deciding whether to limit access to and/or allow comments on your blog posts should be done with the goal of protecting your participants. Copyright is another issue to consider. Quite often, researchers who share their research findings on a blog use tailored copyright licences through organizations such as Creative Commons. Creative Commons offers free copyright licences that allow you to regulate the degree to which the public can use and share your work. Some blogging platforms, such as WordPress, have settings which can limit a reader's ability to copy the text and paste it elsewhere for their own use.

Visit Web Resource 9.12 to learn about the tailored copyright licences at Creative Commons.

Indeed, there are ethical concerns whenever you choose to make your work more public. Take a moment to consider Reflexive Practice 9.5.

REFLEXIVE PRACTICE 9.5

When using a blog to report research findings, a larger audience has access to your research process and conclusions. What might be some of the risks and ethical dilemmas of sharing your research findings within such a public venue?

Other kinds of websites can be created to display the life stories of everyday people. For example, the 1000 Voices project (see Figure 9.5) is a narrative-focused website that seeks to collect, share and analyse life stories of people with disabilities. Stories can be created and shared using images, film, audio, or text. This is an excellent example of using the Internet as the medium by which to not only collect and display data but also make findings accessible to the public. It also provides a way for researchers to collaborate with stakeholders in relation to how a given story is represented and shared.

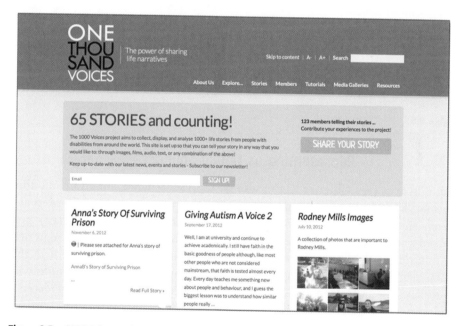

Figure 9.5 1000 Voices project website

Visit Web Resource 9.13 to see the 1000 Voices project.

Similar to the 1000 Voices project, Healthtalkonline.org (see Figure 9.6) is an award-winning website that stores the health-related experiences of more than 2,000 people. The site is arranged by medical condition (e.g. cancer), allowing individuals to enter the site and view videos and/or listen to audio clips from interviews with people experiencing the condition. The collected interviews are analysed by a research team and then shared within a platform that has allowed for dissemination to a larger audience, including the medical community.

View Web Resource 9.14 to see the award-winning website Healthtalkonline.

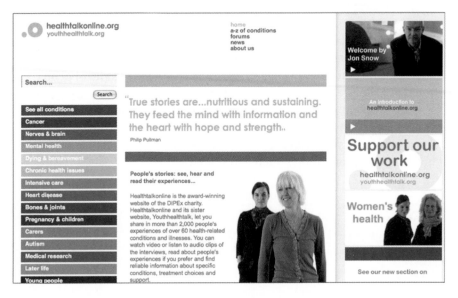

Figure 9.6   Healthtalkonline.org

Representing as Online Soundscapes

Soundscapes (see Chapter 8) can also be represented and shared in an online format. Researchers can produce a compilation of the sounds generated at a given site, often alongside narration of some kind. Neumann (2012) produced a sound portrait of the site of Jim Morrison's (an American songwriter and leader of the band The Doors) grave in Paris, France. His interest in this particular research site emerged as he found that it was full of people who were singing and playing Morrison's music. Neumann eventually created a sound portrait that layered the collected interviews and naturally occurring sounds, while also creating a website to store and disseminate the sound portrait.

View Web Resource 9.15 to listen to Mark Neumann's sound portrait of the site of Jim Morrison's grave.

Another example of an online soundscape is the Soundscapes and Cultural Sustainability ethnographic project funded by the Academy of Finland. The research team posts sounds on their blog, as shown in Figure 9.7. In this way, their unfolding findings are made publicly available, not only textually, but in an auditory manner as well.

23 APRIL 2012

Countryside frogs

It was a warm summer evening in May. I'm standing on a porch of a friend of mine. She's having a picnic party at her country house north of Istanbul. Behind me is the house and behind that a crowd of 50 people singing *türküs*, playing *baglamas*, eating salads, pies and *köftes* and skipping rope. On this side of the house you can only hear the frogs. It's strange. As if I was in a different place alltogether.

There must be some other creatures sounding out with the frogs. I spot the obvious dog. Somekind of insects maybe? Too bad I'm lousy with birds so I can't recognize the ones on this recording. An owl? I try to count the frogs when they stop for awhile and then start again, there is at least four. But there must be more hidden in the undergrowth...

Listen to the croaking:

Figure 9.7 Soundscapes and Cultural Sustainability project blog site

Visit Web Resource 9.16 to hear the Soundscapes and Cultural Sustainability project.

Representing as Films, Documentaries or Videos

Visual anthropologists have long produced films and documentaries to illustrate their findings. These can have both a pedagogical capacity and the ability to engage broad audiences, thereby potentially increasing the impact of research. The process of translating research findings into a feature film can seem daunting, particularly if you are not trained as a filmmaker. Woo (2008), who translated her research findings into a 105-minute narrative film, *Singapore Dreaming*, suggested that aspiring filmmakers create representations that spark conversation between the researcher, participants and broader audience members; encourage the audience to examine broader social issues; result in the audience identifying with the storyline and/or see themselves in the film; and keep the audience engaged with the storyline.

With these considerations in mind, Woo herself constructed a screenplay by compiling vignettes from her study which examined 'young people's sense of legitimate and illegitimate ways of spending their time ... and their sense of undesirable life paths' (p. 322). She provided an excellent example of how one might represent qualitative findings through film.

Visit Web Resource 9.17 for more information about *Singapore Dreaming*.

181

Visit Web Resource 9.18 to watch a video about visual ethnographies.

In Vignette 9.4, Art Herbig and Aaron Hess provide another example of moving from a data set to a documentary film, highlighting the ways in which they had to carefully consider the ethical implications of this particular medium. As noted in Chapters 2 and 5, Herbig and Hess studied people's memories of 9/11 in New York City during the tenth anniversary of the tragedy.

Vignette 9.4	**Documentary Process as Qualitative Research**

Art Herbig, Indiana University–Purdue University Fort Wayne and Aaron Hess, Arizona State University

As part of our study of how memories of the events of 9/11 have been shaped in the past decade, we made an active decision to incorporate different forms of information gathering and dissemination into our work. We began with the idea of making a feature-length documentary.

We have found that there is a different type of responsibility when using a participant's image as part of the research findings. The decisions about how to do this begin in the field with the camera. Where we chose to conduct our interviews, how we chose to frame a person and what we include in the frame with the person are all decisions that will impact how we present our findings. Working with the camera is a skill, and its role needs to be carefully considered while still in the field. While editing, decisions need to be made about how to best represent both your participants and your findings. Those decisions will not always be in sync. Because the use of audio/visual materials changes the relationship between the researcher and the participant in terms of anonymity, each edit requires the researcher to decide how to blend the participant's voice.

We made a number of calculated decisions while in New York about how we would represent our findings before data collection was complete. One specific decision was to not release interview footage as part of our video logging (vlogging) so as not to violate our relationship with our participants by rushing to judgement on what we had found. Instead, we treated those interviews as part of our longer written and documentary projects. By posting our work-in-progress to our Facebook page, we invited commentary and critique before we had something fully formulated in our own mind. This helped us to see things in new and different ways.

Visit Web Resource 9.19 to see how Dr Kip Jones' three-year research study of ageing and gay life in rural South West England and Wales was turned into a film.

Take a moment to consider Reflexive Practice 9.6.

REFLEXIVE PRACTICE 9.6

What are some ethical dilemmas that might arise by sharing video footage from a study on a social networking site and eliciting feedback from a broader audience?

While you might not produce an extensive film or professional-grade documentary as Woo or Herbig and Hess have, it is possible to generate shorter videos to represent and share your work. There are a number of tools that you may want to consider for this. Most simply, you might create a short video of your work with a built-in computer web camera and a movie-making program (e.g. iMovie). Probably one of the best tools, with a range of flexible features, is Camtasia by TechSmith. You can make videos, create screencasts and add elements such as audio, subtitles, images and graphics. This is particularly useful if you want to provide commentary or explanations about your research.

These videos can then be shared on YouTube or Vimeo (introduced in Chapter 5) with broader audiences. For instance, Margaret Wetherell, Emeritus Professor of Psychology at the Open University, shared findings from her research around racism and issues of social structure and power (Wetherell and Potter, 1993) on YouTube. YouTube's comment feature can be used to invite an audience response.

View Web Resource 9.20 to see Margaret Wetherell's YouTube video discussion of her discourse analysis study of racism.

Take a moment to respond to Reflexive Practice 9.7.

REFLEXIVE PRACTICE 9.7

As you consider how you might use online video sharing sites to engage a broader audience, what challenges might arise when inviting 'unknown' others to respond to your work?

Vignette 9.5 highlights how Rebecca Williams went about using Camtasia (see Chapter 5) to create YouTube videos, as well as a Prezi presentation to disseminate her research findings.

Vignette 9.5	Presenting Data Analysis Interactively to Elicit Emotional Response

Rebecca J. Williams, University of Florida

From 2009–2011, I served as a Peace Corps volunteer in Honduras. During the course of my service, I noticed that all the volunteers, including myself,

(Continued)

(Continued)

changed gender behaviors based on the culture of the place. These experiences led me to an interest in studying the relationship between gender roles and natural resources management as part of my PhD studies in Interdisciplinary Ecology. During my time in the doctoral program, I conducted a small qualitative study on how female Peace Corps volunteers serving in a machismo country perceive and enact gender as a result of their service.

My theoretical stance as a researcher is largely based in critical and feminist epistemologies that drive me to explore ways in which I can analyse and present my research to elicit emotional responses from readers and viewers. The purpose of this is to elucidate the issues facing my participants, their resulting actions, and how this has changed their behaviours in a manner that would represent their struggle and resonate with viewers. For this data analysis project I used Prezi, a web-based presentation tool, in conjunction with original artwork and YouTube videos, which combined images, narration and traditional folk music.

Prezi is a web-based tool that supports the embedding of images, videos and audio allowing for an interactive multimedia experience. I used Camtasia Studio to create YouTube videos that were embedded into an original drawing that was intended to depict the process and results as a tree. The roots represented the tools of discourse analysis; branches signified subjectivity, theoretical perspective, and literature review; the trunk represented the research question and participants; and the crown represented the results. See Figure 9.8.

The use of multimedia tools was intended to allow the viewer to engage in the research process and connect with its participants. Although the presentation has all of the elements of a traditional research paper, the multimedia version allowed the viewer to progress through the process experientially. My aim was to have the viewer experience the concept of machismo, gain an understanding of my subjectivity as a researcher, experience the challenges of discourse analysis, and ultimately experience the consequences of how my participants changed their gender behaviour during their Peace Corps service.

When working on this project and disseminating it to others, I learned that this manner of data presentation is a powerful tool that can elicit different types of emotional response. When deciding to present data in an interactive manner, it is important to know that this process is more time intensive than writing a traditional paper, and issues of copyright when choosing music and images must be considered if a project is to be submitted for publication.

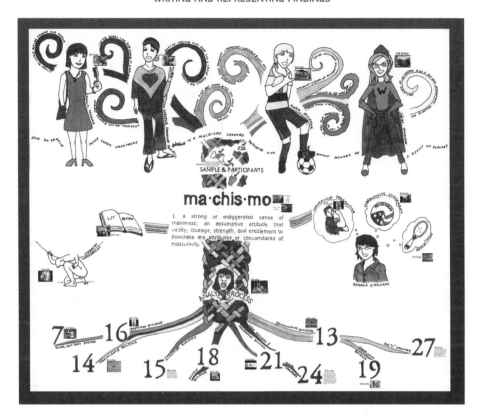

Figure 9.8 Rebecca William's representation of the research process

Visit Web Resource 9.21 for more information on Prezi and to view Rebecca William's presentation.

Take a moment to consider Reflexive 9.8.

REFLEXIVE PRACTICE 9.8

Choose one of the tools presented in this chapter and explore its use in the context of the study you are designing. Reflect on your experiences with these tools.

Final Thoughts

As Woo noted, it is important not to 'fall back on modes of representation that are familiar to us, especially if we know that those modes will not reach the audiences for whom the findings are truly intended' (2008, p. 325). Digital tools are one means by which to expand your research audience, opening up your work to new levels of critique and application. Because paper-based journals are rarely read outside of academia, there is a need to re-examine how we might invite the larger populace to make sense of and engage with our research findings. There are a variety of digital tools that can afford you opportunities to represent your findings in new, alternative ways – many of which move away from a sole reliance on text. Many tools also provide ways in which you can make your research more public, which could result in others both consuming and critiquing your work. As we move to expand how we represent our findings, it is critical to remain cognizant of how and who we choose to represent, acknowledging that whatever we share is always partial and positional.

Chapter Discussion Questions

1. How has the crisis of representation challenged what it means to report results of research studies?
2. How can new digital tools support a non-linear writing process?
3. In what situations might it be particularly important for your research findings to reach the public? How might this be accomplished?
4. How can you balance the desire to popularize your research with the need to protect your participants?
5. How can you ensure ethical practices as you write and represent your findings?

Suggestions for Further Reading

Richardson (1990) is a classic text on representing findings in qualitative research, and is worth reading. Wolcott (2009) offers practical advice for developing effective writing approaches. Dicks and Mason (2008) focus on the ways in which multimedia methods can be used to represent findings, focusing specifically on hypermedia environments. Powell et al. (2012) highlight how blogs can be used to rapidly share research methods and findings. Woo (2008) provides an excellent example of the ways in which art-based methods can be employed to expand the ways in which qualitative research is represented and disseminated.

References

Brackenbury, J. (2004) 'Pulling together the threads: Boundaries, silences and the continuum of care among women in families'. *Arts-informed*, 4(1), 19–20. Available at http://home.oise.utoronto.ca/~aresearch/artsinformed4.1pdfpdfpdf (last accessed 19 July 2013).

Carman, P. (2009) *Skeleton Creek*. New York, NY: Scholastic Press.

Clifford, J. and Marcus, G.E. (eds) (1986) *Writing Culture: The Poetics and Politics of Ethnography*. Berkeley, CA: University of California Press.

Cole, A. and Knowles, G. (2001) *Lives in Context: The Art of Life History Research*. Walnut Creek, CA: AltaMira Press.

Cole, A. and McIntyre, M. (2004) *Living and Dying with Dignity: The Alzheimer's Project* [online]. Available at http://home.oise.utoronto.ca/~aresearch/projects.html (last accessed 19 July 2013).

Colyar, J. (2009) 'Becoming writing, becoming writers'. *Qualitative Inquiry*, 15(2), 421–36.

Creswell, J.W. (2013) *Qualitative Inquiry and Research Design: Choosing among Five Approaches* (3rd edition). Thousand Oaks, CA: SAGE.

Denzin, N. and Lincoln, Y. (2005) *The SAGE Handbook of Qualitative Research* (3rd edition). Thousand Oaks, CA: SAGE.

Dicks, B. and Mason, B. (2008) 'Hypermedia Methods for Qualitative Research', in S.N. Hesse-Biber and P. Leavy (eds) *Handbook of Emergent Methods*. New York, NY: The Guilford Press, pp. 571–600.

Efimova, L.A. (2009) 'Passion at work: Blogging practices of knowledge workers'. *Novay PhD Research Series*, 24.

Ellis, C. (2004) *The Ethnographic I: A Methodological Novel about Autoethnography*. Walnut Creek, CA: AltaMira Press.

Finfgeld, D. (2003) 'Metasynthesis: The state of the art—so far'. *Qualitative Health Research*, 13(7), 893–904.

Goodall, H.L. (2000) *Writing the New Ethnography*. Lanham, MD: AltaMira Press/ Rowman & Littlefield.

Gray, R. (2000) 'Graduate school never prepared me for this: Reflections on the challenges of research-based theatre'. *Reflective Practice*, 1(3), 377–90.

Gray, R. (2004) 'No longer a man: Using ethnographic fiction to represent life history research'. *Auto/Biography*, 12, 44–61.

Gubrium, A. and Turner, K.C.N. (2011) 'Digital Storytelling as an Emergent Method for Social Research and Practice', in S.N. Hesse-Biber (ed.) *The Handbook of Emergent Technologies in Social Research*. Oxford, UK: Oxford University Press, pp. 469–91.

Howley, K. (2012) 'Engaging Communities Through Grassroots Media', in P. Vannini (ed.) *Popularizing Research*. New York, NY: Peter Lang, pp. 83–8.

Hundley, M. and Holbrook, T. (2013) 'Set in stone or set in motion? Multimodal and digital writing with preservice English teachers'. *Journal of Adolescent & Adult Literacy*, 56(6), 492–501.

Hunt, K., Emslie, C. and Watt, G. (2001) 'Lay constructions of a family history of heart disease: Potential for misunderstandings in the clinical encounter?' *Lancet*, 357, 1168–71.

Keen, S. and Todres, L. (2007) 'Strategies for disseminating research findings: Three exemplars'. *Forum: Qualitative Social Research*, 8(3), Article 17. Available at http:// www.qualitative-research.net/index.php/fqs/article/viewArticle/285 (last accessed 19 July 2013).

Knowles, G. and Cole, A. (eds) (2008) *Handbook of the Arts in Social Science Research: Methods, Issues and Perspectives*. Thousand Oaks, CA: SAGE.

Lambert, J. (2006) *Digital Storytelling: Capturing Lives, Creating Community*. Berkeley, CA: Digital Diner Press.

Lester, J. and Gabriel, R. (2012) 'Performance Ethnography of IEP Meetings: A Theatre of the Absurd', in P. Vannini (ed.) *Popularizing Research: Engaging New Media, Genres, and Audiences*. New York, NY: Peter Lang, pp. 173–8.

Neumann, M. (2012) 'Hearing Places and the Representation of Sonic Culture', in P. Vannini (ed.) *Popularizing Research*. New York, NY: Peter Lang, pp. 95–100.

Pifer, D.A. (1999) 'Small town race: A performance text'. *Qualitative Inquiry*, 5(4), 541–62.

Pink, S. (2007) *Doing Visual Ethnography*. London, UK: SAGE.

Pink, S. (2009) *Doing Sensory Ethnography*. London, UK: SAGE.

Powell, D.A., Jacob, C.J. and Chapman, B.J. (2012) 'Using blogs and new media in academic practice: Potential roles in research, teaching, learning, and extension'. *Innovations in Higher Education*, 37, 271–82.

Pullinger, K. and Joseph, C. (2005) *Inanimate Alice*. Available at www.inanimatealice. com (last accessed 19 July 2013).

Richardson, L. (1990) *Writing Strategies: Reaching Diverse Audiences*. Newbury Park, CA: SAGE.

Richardson, L. (1992) 'The Consequences of Poetic Representation. Writing the Other, Rewriting the Self', in C. Ellis and M. Flaherty (eds) *Investigating Subjectivity. Research on Lived Experience*. Thousand Oaks, CA: SAGE, pp. 125–37.

Rozmovits, L. and Ziebland, S. (2004) 'What do patients with prostate or breast cancer want from an internet site? A qualitative study of information needs'. *Patient Education and Counseling*, 53, 57–64.

Smith, P., Masterson, A., Basford, L., Boddy, G., Costello, S., Marvell, G., Redding, M. and Wallis, B. (2000) 'Action research: A suitable method for promoting change in nurse education'. *Nurse Education Today*, 20, 563–70.

Troman, G. (2001) 'Tales from the Interface: Disseminating Ethnography for Policy Making', in G. Walford (ed.), *Ethnography and Education Policy*. London, UK: JAI, pp. 251–73.

Vannini, P. (ed.) (2012) *Popularizing Research: Engaging New Media, Genres, and Audience*. New York, NY: Peter Lang.

Walter, V. (2007) *Making up Megaboy*. New York, NY: Delacorte Books for Young Readers.

Wetherell, M. and Potter, J. (1993) *Mapping the Language of Racism: Discourse and the Legitimation of Exploitation*. New York, NY: Columbia University Press.

Wolcott, H. (2009) *Writing up Qualitative Research* (3rd edition). London, UK: SAGE.

Woo, Y.Y.J. (2008) 'Engaging new audiences: Translating research into popular media'. *Educational Researcher*, 37(6), 321–9.

TEN
Looking to the Future

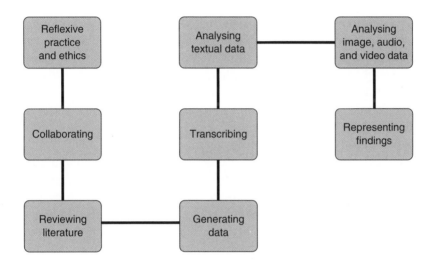

Companion website materials available here:

www.uk.sagepub.com/paulus

Introduction

We hope that you now have a better sense of how digital tools can be used in qualitative research. While digital tools are most often considered in the context of data collection and analysis, we have sought to highlight the ways in which digital tools might support you across the research process. We hope that the vignettes and case studies of how researchers have used various tools in their work might inspire you to try them yourselves, after first reflecting on the affordances and constraints of each tool. We particularly encourage our student readers to begin to explore these tools early in their research careers, and would encourage staff and faculty members to consider how digital tools might support if not transform their current practices.

The past decade has seen a massive increase in the mediation of our communication through networks (Castells, 2000). As our social interactions are increasingly intertwined with digital technologies, it becomes ever more important to attend to the digital layer of the human experience in our explorations of social life. Over the course of these chapters we have charted a number of 'technological shifts', where early technologies such as stenography determined the location in which research could be carried out, to audio-recording, which allowed moments in time to be captured and replayed indefinitely. With digital cameras becoming increasingly affordable, we have seen those who were once considered research subjects now able to take active roles in the creation of the data that is to represent their lives.

Murthy's (2011) description of his digital ethnographic toolkit synthesizes some of these technological shifts. He describes his use of a mobile device (which has an Internet connection, camera and recorder) to upload images and videos from the field to a free image sharing account. These images are ultimately posted on a blog that serves as his field notes. Murthy then organizes his entries and images through tags that can be shared with others, making it particularly useful for team-based research. Data analysis no longer has to take place only in an office, with a personal computer on a desktop, but can be extended to sharing field notes, recorded conversations or images through mobile devices, with opportunities for multiple digital onlookers to become part of the process.

Table 10.1 outlines some of the developments that we have discussed across the chapters.

Table 10.1 Technological shifts with digital tools in qualitative research

Reflexive practice and ethics	The emergence of cloud computing, mobile devices and social media, among other technologies, can afford greater transparency and collaboration in our research work, including our practices of reflection and ethical decision-making.
Collaborating	Creative conversations with colleagues, participants and consumers of our research are now possible at a distance, enabling us to network, meet, share and write with others in ways that we could not before.
Reviewing the literature	Digital tools enable us to retrieve, store, read and analyse resources in ways that are more transparent and systematic as we seek to join a particular scholarly conversation. The ability to go paperless in our work can help us more easily manage this process.

Generating data	Digital tools are making it easier to generate naturally occurring data as a complement to researcher-generated data. Mobile devices, GIS, online communities and the 'YouTube nation' are making it easier to capture social life as it happens, adding a layer of authenticity to our work.
Transcribing	The ability to share transcripts that have been synchronized with the recording and/or to use multiple transcripts to represent data can lend transparency to our work. Voice recognition software may also change the process of transcription and make it a less onerous task.
Analysing textual data	Data analysis software packages can serve as a 'textual laboratory' for our work, adding transparency and trustworthiness to the entire process. While these packages afford a variety of analytical features, it is up to the researcher to decide which ones to use and how.
Analysing image, audio, and video data	Analysis of multi-media data is increasingly feasible, including the analysis of multiple video streams and the ability to georeference data. The ability to bypass transcription entirely may have analytic consequences, but this combined with mobile devices and new methods such as soundscapes and photovoice can be powerful tools for understanding social life.
Writing and representing findings	Storyboarding tools can support a more non-linear writing process. Reaching larger audiences by popularizing research is becoming increasingly possible with the use of digital tools to represent findings in new, more accessible ways.

Turn to Reflexive Practice 10.1.

═══ REFLEXIVE PRACTICE 10.1 ═══

Review the entries you have made in your reflexivity blog as you have worked through this book. Which new tool are you likely to begin using first? Write a paragraph justifying your use of the tool for a particular phase of your study, including a discussion of its affordances and constraints.

We acknowledge that one's chosen methodology and associated epistemological beliefs should drive all decisions around methods, and this includes digital tool use. We encourage you to develop the habit of providing a rationale for the use of digital tools alongside your rationale for other design choices made when proposing or reporting a study.

In the remainder of this chapter, we share some recent innovations that we suspect, or hope, will continue to influence our qualitative research practice. As Fischer, Lyon and Zeitlyn (2008) noted, while it may be possible to guess at the *capabilities* of new technologies, we will likely not be able to accurately predict the precise form they will take. They noted that new inventions often take 15–20 years to be fully adopted by the general public. Certain segments of the population, such as those actively working in technology fields, adopt a bit earlier than others (within 2–3 years). They also argued that, increasingly, social scientists will be expected to be literate in digital tool use. Much of what we describe next is already possible, but has not yet been fully embraced.

Pervasive Computing Environments

As more people are able to access Internet networks, larger digital storage spaces and affordable mobile devices, 'pervasive computing environments' (Fielding and Lee, 2008), in which we are always connected and computing, will continue to grow. Such environments have already made it possible for geographically dispersed researchers (and participants) to interact and access data across numerous sites. While mobile devices afford access and portability, the quality of the data collected must not be compromised. Writing on a tablet computer or a mobile phone for a prolonged period of time, for example, may prove unwieldy and ineffective (see Vignette 5.1). Similarly, the quality of audio and video recordings captured by specialized equipment is likely to be better than that captured by mobile phones. Given the attention to data archiving and sharing for secondary analysis (as discussed below), data quality will continue to be important and may require more sophisticated digital tool choices.

As computing environments become pervasive, so should the ability to collaborate on data analysis. Currently, software that supports real-time collaboration among research team members is still limited. Transana has been a leader in this arena, with NVivo joining more recently. Yet even these programs require access to a server and a level of technical support that may not be available to everyone. We hope to soon see more seamless and accessible server or cloud-based options across all packages that allow research teams to engage in real-time data analysis.

Pervasive computing environments will no doubt push ethical boundaries, in particular as portable and wearable embedded computing devices become prevalent. Google Glass, eyeglasses that navigate and display websites through voice recognition software, take wearable computing to a new level and may well have implications for research study designs, as predicted by Murthy (2011). Less radical are the mobile phones that many of us already carry. Eagle (2011) noted that, in essence, 'the majority of humans today already have the habit of keeping a charged behavioural sensor with them at all times' (p. 493) – in the form of a mobile phone. He suggested that the vast amounts of mobile phone data remain mostly untapped but could, for example, help social scientists create large-scale social network data sets for analysis of mobility patterns, disease outbreaks and the evolution of groups – all of which are relevant to fields such as urban studies. While collecting automatically logged data from mobile devices can provide longitudinal data and solve some of the problems of relying on self-report data, these approaches also challenge our notions of privacy.

As another example, Fowler, O'Neill and van Helvert (2011) and Holohan et al. (2011) described the use of digital homes as 'living laboratories' in which human behaviour can be explored in a variety of ways. Digitized, electronic usage in these homes is tracked for both researcher and participant use. Holohan et al. (2011) noted that:

> emerging technologies such as the digital home have the power to disrupt and transform existing social structures and social practices ... offer[ing] the opportunity to generate

usage data and allow people to manage and share that data via the Internet in a way that will have a transformative impact on consumption and decision-making patterns. (p. 663)

While qualitative researchers have yet to explore the possibilities of such living laboratories for understanding social life, the opportunities are there.

Visit Web Resource 10.1 for a link to the Digital Lifestyles Centre at the University of Essex.

Big Data, Citizen Researchers and Participatory Action Research

Automatically logged mobile phone data sets are just one example of 'big data'. Researchers of all kinds are exploring the possibilities of how to make sense of the massive amounts of data being automatically generated by virtual worlds and social media such as Second Life, Twitter, Facebook and other computing activities. So far, industry and private citizens, rather than academia, have been most active in putting this data to use. Non-expert, or 'citizen researchers', are increasingly engaged in their own use of this data to help solve pressing problems in their daily lives by, for example, making informed choices about different communities or schools. Fielding (2012) defined citizen researchers as 'people who have no social science qualifications or experience and who want to do research for purposes other than adding to academic knowledge' (paragraph 4), such as tackling environmental problems, understanding patterns of neighbourhood crime or engaging in political activism.

Visit Web Resource 10.2 for a link to e-democracy.org, a wiki compiled to gather candidate information for the 2010 UK elections.

As Fielding points out, emergent technologies, from free trial versions of CAQDAS to georeferencing tools to free online surveys, are making it possible for citizen researchers to engage in methods that were previously controlled by social scientists. Mobile devices and pervasive computing environments may enable more participatory action research approaches. Fielding (2012) suggested that qualitative researchers could choose to play an integral role in working alongside citizen researchers as they use digital tools to meet their needs. Public patient initiatives are becoming an important part of the research landscape and are often required by funding bodies. For example, the National Institute for Health Research in the UK actively promotes initiatives through INVOLVE, a national advisory group. Further, the James Lind Alliance has developed a method for bringing patients and clinicians together to pick research areas that are of mutual benefit. The public are being encouraged to be involved in all stages of research, from being recruited to deciding the direction of future research to providing information and support to researchers, even helping with data collection and final dissemination.

Visit Web Resource 10.3 for a link to public patient initiative resources.

Crowdsourcing and Crowdfunding

Crowdsourcing is one means of locating the resources for analysing these stores of publicly available data. Crowdsourcing is the practice of acquiring resources, ideas or even data from a large group of people, usually the online community. For instance, data visualization tools such as Many Eyes are designed specifically for 'crowdsourcing' data analysis. The website describes itself as 'set up to allow the entire Internet community to upload data, visualize it, and talk about their discoveries with other people'. Traditionally, it has been problematic to invite members of the public to access University facilities for ad hoc research projects. The availability of publicly available or indeed publicly generated data makes institutional access less of an issue. Further, the rise of mobile technologies means it is easier to manage large, spread-out groups with relative ease and the facilities for conducting research are much more localized for individuals. Using websites with embedded software allows great flexibility.

Visit Web Resource 10.4 for more information about Many Eyes, a crowdsourced data analysis tool.

Researchers can even raise money for their work through crowdsourcing, which is often referred to as 'crowdfunding'. By using the Internet and various social media sites, such as Kickstarter, a researcher might announce their research project and invite the public to contribute funds to support it. As research funding ebbs and flows with the global economy, crowdfunding may be one means by which researchers can generate support for their research in public and novel ways. Further, this is one tool by which citizen researchers might also elicit support for their personal research endeavours. It may be of concern, though, that while the most exciting and novel research is apt to be supported, other quite important but less exciting topics may stagnate. Innovation may be replaced by gimmickry in order to satiate the desire for novelty (Wiles, Crow and Pain, 2011).

Visit Web Resource 10.5 to listen to a story about a scientist who generated funds through crowdfunding.

New Innovations to Support Multi-Modal Research

We now turn to our wish list of innovations to support new trends in social research, particularly in the use of audiovisual data, which has often been neglected as a viable data source, in part because of limited abilities to process it. Digital tools may provide some solutions to the qualitative bottleneck described by Blank (2008); that is, where the quantity of data exceeds the resources available to do something with it. High-speed Internet networks make real-time analysis of digital audio and video possible, making it more feasible for participants to engage in interpretation of data alongside researchers. What are needed, still, are the analysis tools to support this, including tools that allow better integration of data sources and transfer of data and analysis between CAQDAS packages.

We hope that advances in voice recognition technology, both for collecting and transcribing data, continue, as discussed in Chapters 5 and 6. The accuracy of many voice recognition systems is still in flux, unable to recognize more than a single trained voice. With improved accuracy these tools could be used in more ways. Imagine being able to fully control your computer through speech, eliminating the need for a keyboard or mouse. This would radically alter the way we use computers and conduct research. Although at this time still a distant possibility, when it comes it would be a shift on a par with the earliest recording devices. More immediate possibilities include voice-command-based digital recorders (and mobile smart phones) that support generating and storing data more easily. For example, commanding a device to 'put this memo in the coding folder' would result in the file being transcribed and stored in the proper folder. When synchronized with a computer, voice memos could be automatically converted to text. We envision the day when this process is seamless and without errors requiring correction or attention by the researcher.

Some researchers have been early adopters of touch screen technology, as described in Case Study 8.2. Windows 8, for example, is designed with touch screen devices in mind. Currently, touch screen tablets and other devices allow researchers to conduct more dynamic interviews. For example, you might use photo-elicitation methods that will allow people to point to areas of screen that are meaningful to them. With the right tools, conversations about and interactions with images could be more easily recorded for later analysis. Over time, there will likely be more touch-based input systems that integrate with CAQDAS packages, allowing researchers to manage and code data in more fluid ways.

Advances in smart pens (discussed in Chapter 5 and by Murthy, 2011) with wireless Internet connections could allow researchers to immediately capture participant-generated data. This will greatly improve mobile research and fieldwork. Imagine being able to share a screencast of your notes immediately with your supervisor/research team after a fieldwork episode (even without the need for a laptop). You could retain the hard copy, but they would have a recording of your notes complete with audio commentary. This will open up the possibility of using paper as a new interactive device, changing how we disseminate information.

Both touch screens and digital pen developments may be especially useful for visual researchers: supporting, generating and coding hand-drawn or other images through touch screens in CAQDAS programs. Analysis packages could also make it possible to manipulate images in ways similar to programs such as Adobe Photoshop. For example, it should be possible for the program to semi-automate analysis through comparing pixels and making educated guesses about which portion of the image you want to attend to next. The same technology could be applied to video recordings and allow you to extract segments of video and play these clips simultaneously with others. Imagine being able to focus on just a portion of a complex video (such as the speaker's head) and this could be played in real time next to other selected clips. New facial recognition software could even automatically blur faces to protect participant identities. It would be useful if the software could automatically recognize and record facial emotion, eventually being able to select particular faces or emotional states for further analysis.

Increased use of video data will require a radical rethinking of how we consider ethical permissions and protect participants. This in turn will result in increased dialogue and debate within academia and with ethics committees as we start to grapple with the implications of its widespread use. There is certainly a role for researchers to educate and disseminate best practice. As we move to more secondary analysis of data, participant consent forms may need to reflect how digital data sources can be reused and for what purposes.

Data Archiving, Sharing and Secondary Analysis

Archiving, storing and encouraging qualitative data reuse (such as the UK Data Archive) has been an ongoing conversation in the research community, particularly in Europe, for some time now.

Visit Web Resource 10.6 for a link to the UK Data Archive.

Visit Web Resource 10.7 for a link to the Open Data Foundation and the Open Data Handbook.

Data archiving will likely become a more important part of research in the future as the cost of storage drops, archives become more sophisticated and descriptive standards become more uniform. However, some challenges remain, such as the lack of an 'open descriptive standard that will enable description and interpretation of data for the longer term in data archives and to which proprietary software, such as all CAQDAS packages, can import and export' (Corti and Gregory, 2011, p. 1). Often, researchers find themselves locked into a proprietary system with no clear way to transport data from one package to another. As new versions of the software are released, they are often not backwards compatible, causing problems when collaborating with researchers using different software versions. We strongly urge software companies to find more ways to allow data sets to be imported and exported seamlessly across platforms, versions and programs.

Advances in Qualitative Data Analysis Software

Across the board, creating more open software platforms could allow niche products to develop. For example, a researcher may want to use the video analysis tools of Transana to add time codes and create video clips, but then move to NVivo to analyse the transcripts and undertake complex searches of the text, before sharing the results with colleagues who use ATLAS.ti to create network views. This approach would allow researchers to draw upon the strengths of various software packages to support their analysis.

MAXQDA now offers a free version of its software (MAXReader) that allows researchers to browse and search, but not code data. Free 'lite' versions of software packages (see for example QDA Miner) may become more common, with the ability to purchase additional modular components as needed. This means, for example, that if you do not conduct video- or audio-based research, you could buy a less expensive version of the software without these components. By opening up the architecture of the software, researchers could have more say in the design of features that are important to them.

Free or inexpensive tools such as social bookmarking (Speller, 2007; Trant, 2009), cloud tag generators (Cidell, 2010; McNaught and Lam, 2010) and open access analysis tools offer more accessible approaches to organizing and analysing data and are likely to continue to be used by those without access to high-end proprietary CAQDAS programs such as those described in Chapter 7. While these tools are affordable and accessible alternatives, free tools can quickly change – being bought out by larger companies or abandoned when the developers move on to other projects. There may be limited to no user support. We are beginning to see new business models being used by software developers, including providing software and support for a set monthly fee (e.g. Dedoose).

Visit Web Resource 10.8 for a link to a review of word and tag cloud generators.

In the future, we hope to see data analysis software packages draw upon smart 'anticipatory' technologies to learn from the user as analysis proceeds, possibly predicting coding decisions based on past decisions. Better integration between text, video and/or voice recordings and screen capture data will be needed. Providing reports that are more graphically based and customizable through wizards would also be beneficial.

The challenges in capturing the 'big data' of online interactions are matched by the difficulties in analysing it. NVivo is the first major CAQDAS package to offer a tool (NCapture) specifically for the analysis of online interactional data (see Vignette 7.2). With it, researchers can retrieve and sort social networking interactions in Twitter, Facebook, YouTube and LinkedIn. However, there is still no way to do the same for other online interaction data, such as blog conversations or online discussion forums. We hope that this need is met in future versions of the CAQDAS tools. Turn now to Reflexive Practice 10.2

REFLEXIVE PRACTICE 10.2

Explore the links in Web Resource 10.9. Which ones look most promising as avenues to stay up to date on technologies to add to your digital toolkit?

Visit Web Resource 10.9 for a link to several blogs dedicated to technology developments in qualitative research.

Sharing Findings Through Digital Repositories

We also look forward to developments such as open access journals and digital repositories that can change the current publication models. A commissioned report in the UK recommended that researchers pay for publication as a way to create open access (Finch, 2012). There is a difference between fee-based open access journals (often provided by publishers adapting to recommendations from the Finch report) and digital repositories which are not peer reviewed but provide access to information.

Visit Web Resource 10.10 for a link to the Finch report and other open access materials.

A digital repository is 'an online open access archive for collecting, preserving, and disseminating intellectual outputs, usually scientific research articles and documents' (Gherab-Martin, 2011, p. 233). Gherab-Martin described digital repositories as 'trading zones, which are places in which interdisciplinary contact and exchange of ideas take place' (p. 231). He discussed how classifying data through collaborative social tagging, known as folksonomies, can 'create a personal catalogue of bookmarks and their associated tags to facilitate their subsequent retrieval' (p. 236). He noted that open access advocates recommend that scholars and institutions archive their work in such repositories in order to make research more visible and accessible to the public. Ideally, these digital repositories could then be tagged and explored by many users, supporting the evolution of knowledge management in new ways. He noted that, 'blogs, wikis, folksonomies … are slowly but inexorably transforming the traditional ways of communicating and exchanging knowledge as well as the way sources are located and cited' (p. 248).

Visit Web Resource 10.11 for a link to an article about folksonomies and the mutualization of knowledge.

Turn to Reflexive Practice 10.3.

REFLEXIVE PRACTICE 10.3

Now that you have become familiar with many new digital tools, what is your 'wish list' for inventions to support your qualitative research studies?

Final Thoughts

Fielding and Lee (2008) noted that 'the new digital technologies come with strings attached in the form of research policies, institutional expectations, and shifting boundaries around customary norms of what is and is not legitimate in qualitative research' (p. 491). Certainly, as digital tools continue to change at an ever-increasing speed, how we engage in the qualitative research process will continue to unfold. We are likely to encounter new debates about trustworthiness and ethics of new methods as noted in Chapter 2 (see Table 2.1). It will be critical for qualitative researchers to remain reflexive as they encounter potentially unfamiliar dilemmas. What is clear is that we are already in the midst of these changes as our worlds are saturated with digital data, technological innovations and evolving cultural norms. It is up to us to decide how to make sense of it.

Chapter Discussion Questions

1. What devices will you include in your own 'digital toolkit'?
2. Are there current conversations in your field around big data, data archiving and/or digital repositories? In related fields?
3. What digital tools are you familiar with that have not been discussed in this text, but that could be useful for qualitative research?
4. What are some strategies you will use to stay up to date on new digital tools and their implications for qualitative research?

Suggestions for Further Reading

For a broad overview of trends in technologies and their impact on social science research, we recommend Hesse-Biber (2011). Miller and Horst (2012) is a comprehensive text that provides insights into methodological approaches that integrate the use of digital tools. Fielding's (2012) discussion of emergent forms of qualitative research influenced by big data and citizen researchers provides an insightful vision of the future.

References

Blank, G. (2008) 'Online Research Methods and Social Theory', in N. Fielding, R.M. Lee and G. Blank (eds) *The SAGE Handbook of Online Research Methods*. Thousand Oaks, CA: SAGE, pp. 537–49.

Castells, M. (2000) *The Rise of the Network Society, the Information Age: Economy, Society and Culture* (2nd edition, vol. 1). Oxford, UK: Blackwell.

Cidell, J. (2010) 'Content clouds as exploratory qualitative data analysis'. *Area*, 42(4), 514–23.

Corti, L and Gregory, A. (2011) 'CAQDAS comparability. What about CAQDAS data exchange?' *Forum: Qualitative Social Research*, 12(1). Available at: http://www. qualitative-research.net/index.php/fqs/article/view/1634/3154 (last accessed 5 August 2013).

Eagle, N. (2011) 'Mobile Phones as Sensors for Social Research', in S.N. Hesse-Biber (ed.) *The Handbook of Emergent Technologies in Social Research*. New York, NY: Oxford University Press, pp. 492–521.

Fielding, N. (2012) 'The diverse worlds and research practices of qualitative software'. *FORUM: Qualitative Social Research*, 13(2).

Fielding, N. and Lee R.M. (2008) 'Qualitative E-Social Science/Cyber-Research', in N. Fielding, R.M. Lee and G. Blank (eds) *The SAGE Handbook of Online Research Methods*. Thousand Oaks, CA: SAGE, pp. 491–506.

Finch, J. (2012) *Accessibility, Sustainability, Excellence: How to Expand Access to Research Publications*. Report of the Working Group on Expanding Access to Published Research Findings.

Fischer, M., Lyon, S. and Zeitlyn, D. (2008) 'The Internet and the Future of Social Science Research', in N. Fielding, R.M. Lee and G. Blank (eds) *The SAGE Handbook of Online Research Methods*. Thousand Oaks, CA: SAGE, pp. 519–36.

Fowler, C., O'Neill, L. and van Helvert, J. (2011) 'Living Laboratories: Social Research Applications and Evaluation', in S.N. Hesse-Biber (ed.) *The Handbook of Emergent Technologies in Social Research*. New York, NY: Oxford University Press, pp. 625–46.

Gherab-Martin, K. (2011) 'Digital Repositories, Folksonomies and Interdisciplinary Research: New Social Epistemology Tools', in S.N. Hesse-Biber (ed.) *The Handbook of Emergent Technologies in Social Research*. New York, NY: Oxford University Press, pp. 231–56.

Hesse-Biber, S.N. (2011) *The Handbook of Emergent Technologies in Social Research*. New York, NY: Oxford University Press.

Holohan, A., Chin, J., Callaghan, V. and Muhlau, P. (2011) 'The Digital Home: A New Locus of Social Science Research', in S.N. Hesse-Biber (ed.) *The Handbook of Emergent Technologies in Social Research*. New York, NY: Oxford University Press, pp. 647–66.

McNaught, C. and Lam, P. (2010) 'Using Wordle as a supplementary research tool'. *The Qualitative Report*, 15(3), 630–43.

Miller, D. and Horst, H.A. (2012) *Digital Anthropology*. London, UK: Bloomsbury Academic.

Murthy, D. (2011) 'Emergent Digital Ethnographic Methods for Qualitative Research', in S.N. Hesse-Biber (ed.) *The Handbook of Emergent Technologies in Social Research*. New York, NY: Oxford University Press, pp. 158–79.

Speller, E. (2007) 'Collaborative tagging, folksonomies, distributed classification or ethnoclassification: A literature review'. *Library Student Journal*, 2.

Trant, J. (2009) 'Studying social tagging and folksonomy: A review and framework'. *Journal of Digital Information*, 10(1).

Wiles, R., Crow, G. and Pain, H. (2011) 'Innovation in qualitative research methods: A narrative review'. *Qualitative Research*, 11(5), 587–604.

Index

Page references to Figures or Tables will be in *italics*